Raroia and Takume are coral atolls, two of the
seventy-eight islands in the Tuamotu Archipelago.
They lie 465 miles from Tahiti and 1,100 miles
south of the Equator; about 4,000 miles from San
Francisco and 4,250 miles from Sydney, Australia.
(See inset map.)

Raroia

Raroia

Happy Island of the South Seas

By BENGT DANIELSSON

Translated from the Swedish
by F. H. LYON

RAND McNALLY & COMPANY

Chicago • New York • San Francisco

Copyright 1952 by Bengt Danielsson

American edition edited and published by
Rand McNally & Company
Copyright 1953 by Bengt Danielsson

Library of Congress Catalog Card Number: 53-7231

First Printing, September, 1953

Translated from *Den lyckliga ön,* Forum, Stockholm, 1951:
    Den lykkeliga öya, Gyldendal, Oslo, 1951
    Den lyckliga ön, Helsinki, 1951
    Kon-Tiki Eiland, Scheltens & Giltay, Amsterdam, 1951
    The Happy Island, George Allen & Unwin, Ltd., London, 1952
    Den lykkelige ö, Thorkild Beck, Copenhagen, 1952
    Rückkehr zur glücklichen Insel, Ullstein, Vienna, 1953
    L'ile du Kon-Tiki, Albin Michel, Paris, 1953
    Isola di Kon Tiki, Bompiani, Milano, 1953
    Isla de Kon-Tiki, Editorial Juventud, Barcelona, 1953
    Kon-Tiki Island, Tehnicka Knijga, Belgrade, 1953

PRINTED IN THE UNITED STATES OF AMERICA BY RAND MCNALLY & COMPANY

Contents

List of Photographs

Raroia

64–65
(*Cont.*) Here there are no troubles or worries! The tiny tots splash about in the cove near the village . . . .

. . . . and the young folks and adults ride their fine, shiny bicycles up and down the village street.

About once a month a schooner comes to get copra in exchange for *popaa* goods.

The Raroians hurry to exchange their copra for canned goods, tobacco, and smuggled liquor.

Almost every day Marie-Thérèse dressed leg boils and cuts from coral.

Another chronic complaint is toothache.

The finest piece of furniture in every house is an iron bed or divan.

160–61 Old Te Iho, the last sage on the island.

I went down to the landing place on the bay and sat upon the chief's seat at the stone-built *marae*.

The girls often work more than the women. The young girl astride the stool is grating coconut . . . .

Two younger girls are fetching water . . . .

An older girl is doing the family wash.

The women plait a palm-leaf mat.

Marie-Thérèse, in native costume, splits a palm leaf.

Polynesian women have a reputation for attractiveness, and many are astonishingly comely.

Back to the old times when weapons were made of wood —a spear sharpened at both ends and a heavy club!

176–77 The women practiced long and hard in order to perfect a special dance for the governor's visit.

BETWEEN PAGES

272–73   In outrigger canoes we sailed from Raroia to Takume.

The eternal trade wind gently sways the palms.

Maono brings up from the depths of the Takume lagoon a pearl mussel.

Tehei showed us how to open a pearl mussel.

Marie-Thérèse leisurely strokes our cat . . . .

I found a whale vertebra.

A youngster is given a ride on a palm-leaf sled.

Little girls munch pandanus nuts.

A boy engages in his favorite pastime, playing with a spin made from a palm frond.

Raroia

Back to the South Seas

ONE day there came a letter from French Oceania which, in rough translation, ran something like this:

Penetito Tane and Vahine. We greet you. Amen.

We send this short letter to ask why you do not come. We have waited and waited. Everything is ready for you. Come here, and we will fish on the reef at night and with a harpoon in the lagoon every morning. There are plenty of turtles this year too. Bring your box for making pictures. Mairangi has had a baby and Teua is dead. But she was no longer good for much anyway. There are plenty of coconut palms and breadfruit trees for you. Maruake planted a lemon tree for you too, but it died. Everyone will be glad when you come, and we will dance the kori haka *and the other dances. Send a letter and say when you are coming. We can now say* Couttemoro [*good morning*] *and* Couttenat [*good night*]. *Amen.*

The letter was from the chief on Raroia, an insignificant

little coral atoll in the Tuamotu Islands, which I had never heard of till I happened, with my five Norwegian comrades of the *Kon-Tiki* raft, to be cast ashore there, one day at the beginning of August, 1947. This had been my first meeting with the South Seas—an overwhelming experience! The brilliant colors of the corals, the eternal roar of the surf, the play of the sun in the palm tops, but above all the great silence and peace, made an indelible impression upon me. For a fortnight we wandered about on the sun-steeped sands, fished and dived in the crystal-clear water of the lagoon, and danced and sang with merry, friendly Polynesians, who seemed without a trouble in the world save the thought that we must leave them all too soon. We shared this trouble, but pressing duties awaited us somewhere on the other side of the globe, and with sorrow in our hearts we were at last compelled to hurry off.

During the months that followed, when city life became unbearable, and the damp and cold penetrated one's very soul, I often wished myself back on the sunny island of Raroia, where the natives were so happy and life so simple. But every time these radiant memories sprang up and made me dream of another and a better world, my reason cautioned me that not even in the South Seas could life be so carefree and simple as it had seemed during our short stay.

I knew foreigners seldom visited Raroia, and the wreck of a raft on the island was certainly an even more uncommon event. Yes, I would say to myself, we had seen our Raroia in a festal mood. To base a description of the South Seas on our fleeting impressions would be about the same as to judge the United States by a Fourth of July parade or a Christmas celebration. Others, with many years' experience of life on the South Sea islands, told depressing stories of the natives' treachery and assured me that life there was monotonous, hard, and dangerous. Yet, the dream of the South Seas would not be banished from my mind, and when, about two years later, I was given a chance of undertaking a new research expedition to French Oceania, I did not hesitate for a moment.

About the same time the letter from Chief Teka came, and I recalled a long-forgotten promise. At a moment during the farewell party for us *Kon-Tiki* men on Raroia, when the music was at its most languishing and the scent from the flowers about my neck was especially powerful and intoxicating, Chief Teka had asked me if I would come back; and at such a moment, of course, it is not surprising that I had immediately and unhesitatingly assured him that I should return, and as quickly as I could. The chief apparently had accepted the promise as a solemn pledge, and after two years of waiting he was clearly no longer able to restrain his impatience.

Soon another letter came, in which he wondered why I had not built a new raft and was not already en route for the South Seas with my *vahine* [wife]. In a special P.S. he advised us to take the Panama Canal route even if it were to cost more, as the route round Cape Horn would take too long. But however much I wrestled with the problem, it seemed to me impossible to return to Raroia. My new expedition imposed tasks and objectives which made it necessary to be continually on the move, and such a program did not allow for even a glimpse of the atoll.

While the preparations for the expedition went slowly forward, the letters from Raroia continued to pour in, and my thoughts turned more and more often to the island and its merry inhabitants. To console myself, from time to time, cyclones. One "authority" crystallized all the objections in a crushing manner by saying, with ill-concealed repulsion: "Tuamotu?—but, my dear sir, they eat dogs there and ordinary drinking water costs twenty-five francs a bottle."

We soon found out that he had never set foot on any of the Tuamotu Islands, and it was the same with most of those who most emphatically advised us not to go there. The inhabitants of Tahiti are incredibly attached to their home, and there are many who have never visited the neighboring island Moorea, which lies a mere nine miles to the west.

One administrator asked uneasily if we were nearsighted! Just after the end of the war a young Frenchman had tried to live an idyllic life on an atoll in the Tuamotu group. But as his vision was poor and he could neither use a harpoon nor distinguish the inedible coconuts from the good ones, he was compelled to abandon the experiment after a few months and return to Papeete. Without fish and coconuts paradise is not possible on a Tuamotu island—nor with them either, to be quite honest. We assured our friend, the administrator, that we did not intend to follow this example and, by way of corroboration, showed him our American army-surplus equipment and our canned food.

Unfortunately, we had not brought with us all that we needed, as we had hoped to be able to complete our equipment in Papeete. This was theoretically possible, but in practice our problems were infinitely complicated by the curious sales system practiced by the Chinese in Papeete— most of the merchants being Chinese. No business is specialized; all of them sell anything that their own inclinations or the turn of affairs dictate. It is not unusual to see such diverse goods as refrigerators, hats, cheese, razor blades, phonograph records, liquor, padlocks, and nursing-bottle nipples all mixed up in the dirty, disorderly Chinese shops. In every shop we entered there was, of course, everything but what we wanted; so we ran about the town every day for several weeks, till our heads were awhirl with Chinese names like Wing, Sang, Man, Lung, Nam, Han, Ping, Pang, Pong. Eventually we collected almost everything we needed.

But the lack of ready supplies was not our major difficulty. Rather it was the 450 miles which still separated us from Raroia, and the feat of finding a boat which called at that particular island. A dozen schooners, none over 150 tons, visit the seventy-eight islands of the Tuamotu group to buy copra and mother-of-pearl and sell in exchange flour, gym shoes, hair oil, canned goods, colored and printed cloth, smuggled liquor, and other necessities of life.

Because the output of copra is small, competition is great, and owners are therefore unwilling to disclose the exact routes or sailing times (if any) of their schooners for fear that some competitor might snap the copra up from under their noses. The authorities have many times tried to regulate matters somewhat by ordering that announcements of all voyages should be displayed at the post office in Papeete. The announcements certainly appear, but the correct routes and sailing times are hardly ever given. To obtain more reliable information, we went down to the harbor, and after a little search succeeded in finding in a tavern a captain who declared that he was almost ready to sail on a fresh trip to the Tuamotu Islands.

"Do you call at Raroia?" I asked hopefully.

"Raroia—let me see—well that depends on whether I get a full cargo of copra elsewhere in the Tuamotus or not."

"But if you've passengers for Raroia on board?"

"Well, if I do go to Raroia, of course I land them there.

If not, they have to come all the way back to Papeete."

"Hm! How long does it take to get to Raroia—if you do call there?"

"That depends on which islands I call at first. Sometimes one gets there quickly, let's say in five or six days; sometimes it takes longer, perhaps a fortnight, perhaps more—and sometimes, as I said, we don't get there at all."

The schooners were evidently not intended for passenger traffic.

Somebody told us that the *Vaiete* usually called at Raroia. We hurried back to the harbor, but soon discovered that, first the *Vaiete* usually visited a quite different part of the Tuamotu group, and secondly that the schooner had run onto a reef on Moorea a long time before, and that some mysterious "spring tide" was awaited which would get her off. Of course the "spring tide" never came.

We continued our searching with the willing help of the harbor master, Louis Carlsson, and thanks to his exertions we at last succeeded in getting a promise from the *Denise's* owner that we should be landed on Raroia, whether the schooner was to fetch copra from there or not.

In the meantime the *Denise* was still cruising about among the Tuamotu Islands, and days soon became weeks without anything being heard of the schooner. Then one day the news went round that she had sprung a leak and sunk out in the open sea. Unfortunately the rumor proved to be only too true!

More searching and long discussions about various schooners followed. Then one day the Frenchman de Bishop sailed into the Papeete harbor on board his Chinese junk *Chen Ho*. De Bishop is an adventurer of international rank who has sailed on all the seas, been a chief of police in China, been shipwrecked innumerable times, been a prisoner in Japanese hands, and had countless other unusual experiences. But he is best known for his daring voyage from Hawaii to France in 1935—round the Cape of Good Hope!—in his Polynesian double canoe *Kaimiloa*.

De Bishop's new craft, however, was in many respects more curious than his double canoe. It was a Chinese luxury junk, originally built for the Archibold Expedition, which carried on scientific research work in the South Seas just before the Second World War. After serving as a private residence, then an officers' mess, it had lately arrived in French Oceania, where de Bishop intended to use it for carrying copra.

Convinced that there must be plenty of copra on Raroia, as the island was so rarely visited, de Bishop kindly offered to call there on his proposed cruise among the Tuamotu Islands. We were eager to sail with de Bishop, for we should have to search for a long time to find a better boat than the *Chen Ho*. There was, however, a little "but." The junk was being converted into a cargo vessel, and despite daily promises that she would be ready "next week," our departure remained as indefinite and remote as ever. As we wanted to leave Papeete before the hurricane season began in November, we at last began to look around for another vessel.

The *Teretai* was our eventual salvation. It was no different from the other schooners except in one respect—she had cargo on board for Raroia! We stowed away our luggage and our two kittens (we had been told that there were plenty of rats in the Tuamotu Islands) in a cabin, which for some unfathomable reason was called the saloon, and when we were ready, it was so full that there was no room for ourselves. Everyone who had had any experience with schooners in general, and with the *Teretai* in particular, assured us that we should be glad that this was so; for in the "saloon" the smell of rancid copra, gasoline, and rotten flour would surely bring on a raging headache. We had no objection, therefore, to taking up our quarters on deck among some natives from the Marquesas Islands, who immediately offered to show us a sleeping arrangement designed to prevent a tumble overboard during the night and generously gave us a share of a mysterious green pudding from an old rusty bowl.

We rushed about saying good-by to our friends, though they all looked curiously skeptical when we told them that at last everything was ready for the start. We soon understood why. The schooner was scheduled to sail "at 5:00 P.M. at the latest." At six o'clock, however, the skipper declared, without explanation, that our sailing was postponed till nine. When we returned at nine, after having again taken leave of our friends who this time looked if possible even more dubious, not a soul was to be seen on board.

"Strike," explained an old Tahitian, who was sitting on one of the old guns which serve as bollards on the quay—surely one of the most sensible uses to which guns have ever been put.

"Strike?" we burst out in astonishment.

"Yes," said the old man. "Sailors away long from Papeete. Will have fun when they are in port. Captain goes into bar and says, 'We'll go now.' Sailors shout, 'Clear out. We're having a good time here.' Many so drunk they can't answer at all. Sometimes it's captain who strikes, sometimes engineer, or someone else."

The "strike" lasted for another three days. After that there was a film with Tino Rossi in it, which all on board wanted to see, and that meant a further day's delay. We sensibly remained ashore in order not to get tired of the schooner before she had left Papeete, but every morning we went down to the harbor with our kittens under our arms to ask if and when the ship would sail. We were always met with the same regretful gestures and vigorous head-shakings.

We had almost given up hope when, by pure chance on the morning of the fifth day of waiting, we saw the sailors casting off the *Teretai's* mooring ropes. Still with our kittens under our arms we hurried down to the quay, where the crew seemed all of a sudden to be in a great hurry (they had all evidently run through their money), and we hardly got on board before the motors began to hum. An hour later we were already rocking out on the open sea on our way toward the Tuamotus' coral islands and reefs.

We looked around us and found that in the last twenty-four hours the schooner had been turned into a regular Noah's Ark. Ten pigs were crowded together in the bow, here and there cocks and hens peered out from under tarpaulins and cargo, and on the main deck two goats ran about at their will, playfully butting all who happened to come near them. The passengers consisted of our friends from the Marquesas Islands, who ceaselessly chewed their mysterious pudding, two Tahitians who were going to search for a pirate's treasure on an uninhabited island, and a missionary in a light-blue cloak.

At the start, the treasure hunters were a trifle taciturn and secretive, which was not surprising; but the missionary was correspondingly cheerful and talkative and entertained us with accordion music and good stories. Indeed, the only thing which seemed to burden the good man's mind was how he was to make the believers in his district abandon the—in his view—barbaric custom of greeting and taking leave by kissing each other on the stomach! And he often returned to this gloomy topic. In spite of our somewhat different interests we soon became good friends with everybody, and it was not long before we were all rolling to and fro along the deck like brothers, eagerly discussing the secrets of the Tuamotu Islands, the immortality of the soul, and the fluctuations in the price of copra, while the *Teretai* slowly but surely plowed her way through the rough seas and Tahiti sank into the ocean astern.

Ever since the Portuguese mystic and explorer Quiros sighted the first Tuamotu Islands some time at the beginning of 1606, the waters round these islands have rightly been considered among the most dangerous and difficult in the world. Characteristically enough, it has been impossible to establish with certainty which islands Quiros discovered—not only because the navigational methods of the seventeenth century were somewhat unreliable and Quiros often left it to the heavenly powers to fix his course, but also due to the difficult geographical conditions. The Tuamotu Islands, which bear a similarity akin to peas, are in reality nothing but coral reefs rising a scant five to ten feet above sea level, almost impossible to discover until one is practically on top of them.

Even more troublesome from the navigational point of view, many of these reefs never reach the surface, and thus form dangerous shoals. These hazards, added to the strong and treacherous ocean currents among the islands and frequent hurricanes during the stormy season from November to March, have earned for the Tuamotus two suitable nicknames—the "Dangerous Islands" and the "Labyrinth." (The official name Tuamotu may mean "far-away islands," or "the islands behind the back" [of the Tahitians], depending on how the syllabication is formed. Another Polynesian name frequently used among the natives is *Paumotu,* which means "the conquered [or finished] islands.")

According to a popular joke in Tahiti, navigation among the Tuamotu Islands is conducted as follows:

The captain says to the helmsman: "You see that cloud on the horizon. Steer on that."

Then he goes into his cabin and lies down and does not come on deck again till several hours later, when he says to the helmsman:

"The birds are flying south-southeast. That means that there's land somewhere there. Follow them as well as you can."

Gradually land appears on the horizon as expected, and the skipper comes out after another forty winks and says:

"Let me see—there's an entrance with two rocks in the middle. That must be Tahanea."

Or he says: "No palms on the south side. That must be Toau."

And if by any chance he does not recognize the island, he simply goes ashore and asks where he is!

Fortunately it *does* really happen almost like this. I say fortunately, because if anyone tried to use a sextant and steer a course by the chart, he would soon come up against insuperable difficulties and dangers. The latest chart—if so formal a term as chart can be used for a badly drawn map bearing some haphazard deep-sea soundings—dates from 1839 and is unreliable, to say the least. A number of alterations and additions have naturally been made during the last hundred years, but they do not increase its usefulness. Most of the charts bear notations which read like the following, with variations only as regards dates and distances:

This island was reported in 1862 to lie five miles further east than the position stated. In 1911 it was reported to lie considerably further north, longitude uncertain.

The little information contained in the navigational handbooks is also most often erroneous or misleading. The well-known handbook *Sailing Directions* for a long time contained a paragraph to this effect on one of the islands in the Tuamotu group:

Tepoto. The coasts are abrupt and overhang the sea. From the coasts the land slopes downward toward a central depression, probably the crater of an extinct volcano, the center of which is occupied by a vast rainwater pond which may sometimes be evaporated by the heat of the sun. The soil is composed of a very thick, rich bed of humus, and is remarkably fertile. About a third of the surface is cultivated, but with primitive methods, and thus yields a small return. Of all the Tuamotu Islands Tepoto is perhaps the only one possessing an outer anchorage which affords to cutters and schooners a sure shelter from southerly and easterly gales.

Not till 1938 was this note altered! The gist of the corrected information was then as follows:

Tepoto. An island of coral origin, strewn with large blocks of coral deposited in the sea by the cyclone of 1906. The island is 13 to 16 feet in height and is covered with coconut trees which reach a height of about 60 feet above the sea. The population of the island is about fifty. Fish and turtle form the principal food of the natives, and although there are two wells of brackish water, the natives drink only the milk of the coconut. There is no anchorage around the island, but local craft can find poorly sheltered anchorage about 325 yards off the western side of the island by mooring stern to shore.

It is not surprising, therefore, that most of the Tuamotu skippers regard sextants, logs, chronometers, and handbooks with a certain mistrust and prefer to rely on the large collections of unwritten but exact observations which sea voyagers of previous generations have left to posterity. This traditional knowledge and their personal experiences over many years tell them, for example, between which islands there are ocean currents and in what direction they go; how deep the entrances are at the different islands; when it is high tide and low tide; how the wind changes with the seasons; and a thousand other things which are not in any books and the knowledge of which is much more important than any ingenious instruments and tables.

The captain of the *Teretai* was comparatively young, but he had already mastered most of the subtleties of Tuamotu navigation and showed himself supremely confident when on the first night in pitch-darkness he ran between two islands, divided by a strait which was only two or three miles wide.

"It's a simple matter to hear from the roar of the surf how far one is from land," he explained. "When the noise is equally loud from both sides, naturally I am in the middle of the strait, and if one listens properly, there's no difficulty in keeping a course."

I listened long and attentively, and at last it seemed to

me that we were completely surrounded by huge breakers.

"So we are, nearly," said the captain, smiling. "Just at the moment we are in a big bay. There are one or two dangerous reefs in the middle of the strait just north of us, which it is best to keep away from. But we shall soon go back to our old course. If one listens properly, there's no difficulty."

I left the bridge somewhat abashed, glad that the captain of the *Teretai* knew his business.

Next morning we steered in through the entrance to Fakarava, one of the largest islands in the Tuamotu group. On the narrow strip of beach on the eastern side of the immense lagoon, which is about fifty miles long and fifteen miles wide, we caught sight of a few red roofs among the coconut palms. This was the village of Rotoava, where the supercargo (the schooner's clerk or businessman) hoped to find a few tons of copra. When we came nearer, we were able to count about thirty houses and two churches along the shore. But not a living soul was to be seen anywhere. We went ashore; still the village was just as empty and desolate. Most of the houses seemed to be abandoned, and many were tumble-down or neglected.

At last, near the end of the one street, we found a house whose door stood open. We looked in and found an old woman and a few small children, who announced that Monsieur Homer would come in a minute. Monsieur Homer, a little man with tired eyes, proved to be the island's merchant. To our great astonishment he received us as if we had been long-awaited friends, and led us with much ceremony to a large cement house which lay a little way from the others. The house consisted of one single room with bare cement walls. In the middle of the floor stood a little round table with four stools grouped about.

"One does the best one can," said our host, and invited us to sit down.

He disappeared for a moment and returned with two bottles of American export beer.

"One does the best one can," he repeated, and opened one of the bottles of beer. It had a dubious color and also was very warm.

"One does the best one can," he said yet again, "but it isn't enough. Fakarava is done for, the Tuamotus are done for. The islands are desolate or are being abandoned. Just think that on Fakarava there are two hundred persons. Two hundred persons on an island where there is room for many thousands. But no one will stay. They all go off to Papeete. Look into the bars in Papeete. You'll find the inhabitants of Fakarava there. Sometimes, now and then, when they want money, they come here and make a little copra, but then they disappear again. How many islands are there in the Tuamotu group? Seventy-eight! How many natives are there on these seventy-eight islands? Sixty-five hundred! Of these fifteen hundred live on Rangiroa, Anaa, and Takaroa. That leaves five thousand on seventy-five islands. That makes an average of sixty-six inhabitants on each island—sixty-six inhabitants!"

He stared moodily down into his cloudy beer. We were beginning to understand him better. It looked as if he lacked customers.

"You are emigrants from Europe who think of settling on one of the islands, I understand," he continued. "Why don't you stay here? You need society, and so do I for that matter. The last time I had a visit from any *popaa* [the usual term for a white man in French Oceania] was at the beginning of the war when Admiral Byrd came in a plane from his aircraft carrier which was passing through the Tuamotu group. He had a jeep in the plane and drove right up to the house here, without so much as even looking at the other houses." (I began to understand where the beer had come from.) "But he left the next day. There was a French woman journalist here too—in 1930 I think it was—who was going to write a book about Robert Louis Stevenson. The last visitor before her was Stevenson himself, but that was in my father's time. If you stay, you can have his house. It's still standing."

Now Monsieur Homer was no longer an enigma; he not only lacked customers but was sick for human society. We were going to Raroia, however, and had no reason to stop halfway. To be quite honest, we felt a little depressed as we sat at the little table in the middle of the great bare room and looked out through the empty windows and doors at the ruined houses and the moss-grown village street. Still, to please Monsieur Homer, we praised both the cement house and the beer as well as we could. Then we said our good-bys.

"One does the best one can," our host said with true Homeric wisdom, and lapped up with surprising relish the last draught of warm beer as we were going out the door.

We were tossing on the sea again, this time with our course set for Takume, sister island to Raroia. As the wind was blowing freshly from the northeast, the captain ordered sail to be set. Like the rest of the schooners, the *Teretai* was a two-master which, with favorable wind, used her sails as a slight auxiliary to the motors' modest five knots. While the cook took over the helm, the deck hands unfurled the sails, and a couple of the passengers got hold of the sheets and pulled and hauled. There was no strict distinction between crew and passengers on board the *Teretai;* anyone who was willing to help took a turn at the helm or helped to maneuver the vessel.

Everyone regarded this quite as a matter of course, for the simple reason that all Polynesians are first-class seamen, whether they are professional sailors or not. As a matter of fact, Tuamotu skippers never take any crew with them when they go to San Francisco to fetch or buy boats. They simply make the rounds of the flophouses and shelters and collect the Polynesians they find. They can always be sure that as soon as they have found a Polynesian, they have found a seaman as well.

The only post impossible to fill in this way is that of engineer, for the Polynesians in general take very little interest in noisy complicated motors. However, one of the Tuamotu skippers found a good solution to this problem. When he last bought a boat at San Francisco, he appointed as engineer an ex-cook, on the supposition (which later proved to be quite correct) that even if his mechanical knowledge was nil, he would at least be able to bear the heat in the engine room. This experiment, according to what the *Teretai*'s captain told me, seems to have been repeated with success by many Tuamotu skippers in the island traffic also.

On Fakarava a competitor had already got in first, but on Takume the captain hoped to have better luck. Like most of the islands in the eastern part of the Tuamotu group, Takume has no entrance to the lagoon and, therefore, is considerably less attractive to the Tuamotu skippers. We soon found out what the lack of an entrance into the lagoon meant.

When we approached Takume on the morning of the fourth day after our departure, the wind was still in the northeast. Although we were still in the lee of the island, the sea was astonishingly heavy, and a huge swell was breaking in thunder against the reef, which stretched without a break as far as we could see in both directions. Nearest the land the reef was as smooth and level as a floor, and the water not more than a foot deep. On the far side, about fifty yards from the beach, it suddenly plunged steeply down toward the depths and formed a huge wall, which the waves in their ceaseless assaults had torn and mutilated. It was here that the largest and most dangerous breakers were formed. Only about ten yards outside this wall of coral the sea was already so deep that the *Teretai* could find no anchorage, and had to ride upon the swell with her engines running.

"There is the landing place," said the supercargo, pointing in toward the island.

We had expected to see a wharf or some kind of harbor, but the waves broke just as violently and the reef was just as sharp at the place the supercargo had pointed out as everywhere else along the coast. The inhabitants of Takume, however, held the same opinion as he, for they soon assembled on the beach at the so-called landing place and began to make signals that they had copra. So far all was well. But how were we going to get it on board?

This did not seem to be anything of a problem to the *Teretai's* experienced crew. The sailors calmly got into one of the ship's boats—a stout, heavy thing, just twice as long as she was broad—and took their places at the oars, while the coxswain took his place astern. Not wanting to miss any interesting experiences, Marie-Thérèse and I jumped into the boat and were soon on our way in toward the seething witches' cauldron at a good speed. We stopped a little way from the breakers and rode on the waves.

"This is just like surf-riding," the coxswain yelled at me. "We have to wait for a big wave and try to hang onto it."

One wave after another passed, but the coxswain did not seem to be satisfied with them. Then a huge wall of foaming water rose up. This was evidently the right wave.

"Now! Now!" the coxswain bellowed, and the sailors flung themselves over their oars and pulled till their backs creaked.

Suddenly we were lifted straight up in the air as swiftly as if we had been in a skyscraper's express elevator. Evidently the wave had reached us. The sailors rowed like mad, and high up on the hissing, foaming wave top we rode in toward the reef at breakneck speed. I peeped out over the boat's side. Far behind us I saw the *Teretai's* heaving deck, and right in front of and under us I saw the shining red wall of bare, jagged coral. In the next minute the wave washed over the coral reef, and we were gracefully swept in high above it toward the beach, where a few of the laughing natives stood ready and caught hold of the boat.

While the sailors were beginning to load the copra, we took a quick look around. Takume is one of the most famous mother-of-pearl islands in the Tuamotu group, and hundreds of natives from the whole of French Oceania gather there annually for a few months to dive for mother-of-pearl mussels. Our visit took place in the off-season, and the inhabitants of the island—some fifty natives—seemed to be occupied in resting for the next season. There were not more than twenty sacks of copra, and that was about what the ship's boat would hold.

As on the inward trip, to return to the schooner we had to wait for the right moment, which this time naturally came when an especially powerful wave swept back, and the water streamed out for a short time. This time, however, the difficulties were considerably greater. The boat was heavily loaded, and therefore a good deal more awkward to handle. The risk of its being caught fast on the coral bottom was ever present. Even if we succeeded in escaping this danger, we were still far from safe. The most critical stage of the maneuver was just when the outgoing stream met the first wave. Then we had not only to withstand it but also force the boat right through it.

On top of the sacks of copra Marie-Thérèse and I clung tightly while the sailors took hold of the gunwales and waded out with the boat to the extreme edge of the reef, just inside the breakers. One wave after another came and went, and when we thought an eternity had passed, the coxswain at last decided to risk a try. He hopped nimbly up into the boat; the sailors followed as quick as lightning and flung themselves at the oars. We had started. Suddenly there was a crunching noise on the bottom, and the boat stopped with a jerk! We all tumbled down in a heap, and the boat turned, broadside to the surf. Just as I crawled atop the sacks again, I saw a gigantic wave approaching swiftly from the sea outside. Before the sailors could swing the boat onto her right course, the wave was over us! We were swallowed up in foaming masses of water. When the wave drew back, we were all sitting together in a foot of water by the beach and staring at one another in bewilderment. A little farther off on the reef the ship's boat bumped against the coral bottom. Half the sacks of copra had tumbled out.

"Little accidents like this always happen," said the coxswain, laughing loudly, "but it doesn't matter. We've only to collect the sacks and try again. The boat'll stand any number of bumps, for she's got an extra layer of thick planks on her bottom, which we change every time we are at Papeete."

The sailors, laughing and joking, got the boat ready again, and we had another try. This time we made it.

About half the Tuamotu Islands have no entrance, and all loading and unloading on them, therefore, is done in this way. Whether all goes well depends more than anything on the coxswain's judgment and skill, and therefore a coxswain in a Tuamotu schooner has great prestige and is always well paid. But the landing always takes place on the side which, not without a certain degree of exaggeration, is called the lee side. It seems that the only vessel which has managed to effect a landing on the windward side of a Tuamotu Island without being smashed to pieces was the *Kon-Tiki* raft.

Takume is only six miles from Raroia, and the *Teretai*'s captain decided to go straight there. This meant that we should have to grope our way in through the entrance in the middle of the night. I knew from earlier experience that navigation in the entrance, only fifty yards wide, is very hazardous, principally due to a quantity of huge coral blocks which transform it into a regular labyrinth. The captain, however, had an important reason for proceeding at once.

"If I don't take my chance tonight when the sea rises and the water streams into the lagoon, I shall have to wait till the next high tide, and that means that I shall lose twelve hours," he explained. "For that matter, I've gone in at night many times before."

We arrived at Raroia about ten o'clock at night, just as we sat down on the main deck, to a table loaded with roast pork, rice, and ship's biscuits. The captain was equal to the navigation legends, for while the *Teretai* was cautiously feeling her way in through the entrance at low speed, he climbed up onto the cabin roof with his plate in hand and sat down before an empty case under the ship's light. Masticating vigorously, he calmly piloted the schooner past all the shoals and submerged reefs, so confident and unconcerned that he did not lay down his knife or fork for even a moment. As a matter of fact, they seemed to have a special duty to fulfill. A sign to the man at the wheel with the fork meant "port a little" and a sign with the knife "starboard a little."

As soon as we were through the entrance, the captain sought out a huge coral shoal which reached almost to the surface, and ordered the schooner to be moored there. It was not more than another mile or two to the village of Ngarumaoa on the western side of the island; but since the captain was not so much at home inside the lagoon as in the entrance, he preferred to keep the schooner stationary until the morning. We were tired after the day's activity and fell asleep at once. When we were awakened next morning by the sun streaming into our eyes, the engines were running already and the village was in sight. We had at last reached the goal of our dreams.

Here Is Our Country

WE HAD hardly dropped anchor off the village when a swarm of brown Polynesians in bright-colored clothes and loincloths appeared among the palms. In a matter of moments the whole population was assembled on the little quay of rough-hewn coral blocks, and from where we stood on the cabin roof we could plainly see the vice-chief and master of ceremonies, Tupuhoe, running about and giving instructions to his singers and guitar players.

Just as we were getting into the ship's boat which was to take us ashore, the little party struck up a song of welcome. It gave me a start. The tune seemed so curiously familiar. I listened again. It was a Swedish song—a song which we had sung to the islanders in 1947, when they had asked us, the raft's crew, to sing the "Kon-Tiki Song." Evidently some of the Raroian musicians had learned the melody with surprising ease and incorporated it in their repertory of old Polynesian songs and hymns.

Tupuhoe was so moved that he was compelled to wipe

his eyes again and again, and all the hundred inhabitants of the island formed a long queue to say *ia ora na* and shake hands. Most of them seemed so glad to see us that as soon as they had greeted us, they hurried back to the end of the queue and repeated the whole ceremony. When the "official" reception was over, our friends divided all the luggage among them and formed a long caravan which wound away from the quay along the village street. Tupuhoe, Chief Teka, and we followed. The whole party disappeared into a large wooden house with a newly painted, galvanized-iron roof.

"Your house," said Teka. "The only house with a firm cement foundation. The other houses are easily blown away when there is a hurricane. You are not accustomed to that. Best for you to take this one."

"Whose house is it?" I asked.

"Whose is it? Why, it belongs to your father-by-adoption!"

I had most certainly been adopted by Rauri and Taupua during my first visit, but I had taken it only as a mark of politeness, as a survival of an old Polynesian custom without any obligations or implications. However, my parents-by-adoption saw the matter in quite a different light. In their view both Marie-Thérèse and I were as firmly attached to the family as all the other children—who, by the way, were also adopted! And Rauri regarded it as a matter of course that we should take over his finest house, the one which he had built in his youth when, as a successful mother-of-pearl diver, he wanted thoroughly to impress the rest of the inhabitants of Raroia. The house was of the best American pine and had both glass-paned doors and windows, and it was one of the two houses on Raroia which had a ceiling, which thus kept out the worst of the blistering heat.

We directed the carriers to place our luggage in one of

the rooms and then invited them to make themselves comfortable in the other. The rest of the population sat down on the veranda, with the exception of a few children, who climbed into a tree to have a better view of what we were doing.

While we were still undecidedly contemplating the huge pile of luggage with the two mewing kittens atop it, and answering to the best of our power questions as to the use of all the queer things we had with us, Taupua came and announced that dinner was ready. She had prepared in our honor a European dish, or rather what she thought was a European dish. In the middle of the great long table in front of our "parents'" house stood a large bowl of tomato soup. So far so good; but to improve the taste Taupua had evidently made a clean sweep of the larder, and on stirring it a little we found not only small sausages, potatoes, and mushrooms, but also pieces of a carelessly cut-up fowl and a whole fish which looked as if it had accidentally fallen into the soup.

While Rauri ladled out the soup, Teka asked how our King [of Sweden] was. We replied in detail, for we knew that his interest was genuine and keen. He then proceeded to inquire politely, as became a good Polynesian, about the health of all the princes and princesses and finally went over to district chiefs, minor potentates, and relations! We replied as best we could, and asked in our turn similar questions about all the Raroian dignitaries. Then Tupuhoe wanted to hear about the conditions in *popaa* land—the white men's country, generally signifying both Europe and America—in great detail, and we naturally tried to give as truthful and comprehensible an account as possible. What they heard seemed to confirm their worst suspicions, for

Rauri summed up the impression we had given as follows:

"But it's just as it is in Tahiti. Many pay just to live in a house; and they actually *sell* fish in the market there." There was general laughter among the audience at these degenerate customs. "Many look at the clock to see when they shall work, and others perhaps have no work at all. You were sensible to come here. Here there is always food for all, and one works only if one wants to!"

When we returned to our fine wooden house, we found almost the entire population assembled outside the door. Practically all had with them some kind of gift, which they presented with many smiles and handshakes. Although most of the gifts were surprisingly modern and consisted, for example, of a loaf of bread, a can of peaches, or a bottle of beer, the actual Polynesian custom of giving presents is of great antiquity. Courtesy demands that one shall repay the kindness later on, when some suitable opportunity arises; or, if one receives great quantities of gifts, that one shall at once distribute them among all present. We, therefore, immediately shuffled the pile of gifts and dealt them out again, naturally taking good care that the person who had given us the bottle of beer got a loaf of bread, he who had given a loaf, a can of peaches, and so on. They all seemed noticeably pleased with our good manners and gladly spent the rest of the afternoon helping us put the house in order.

Before the sun had set, a remarkable concert began. Someone struck up a song far away on the outskirts of the village; others joined in; and soon the whole village resounded with singing and music. In a short time we heard the singing and music moving farther off and the voices gradually blending into one great choir. The sound now came from a certain point some way off along the lagoon. Intrigued,

Marie-Thérèse and I decided to track down the choir. In front of the assembly house, the largest building in the village, we found almost the whole population grouped. Round a great kerosene lamp on the veranda sat about ten young boys with guitars on their knees, and a little way off sat a group of women, singing. These were the best guitar players and female singers in the village. The rest of the Raroians sat below the veranda in the darkness. We quietly took our places among them.

The music had for a long time been sad and languishing, but quite unexpectedly it changed and became fiery and sensual. A shadow detached itself from the great dark mass of spectators and Tehei stood in the middle of the dance floor. To the audible delight of all he began to whirl in a solo dance, obviously improvised for the occasion. Some of the spectators came to the veranda to join Tehei, then more became visible in the light from the kerosene lamp. Soon all had overcome their shyness. This vehement, unrestrained dance went on for a good half-hour. After a short rest the "orchestra" continued, but this time the music sounded strangely uncertain and fumbling.

"This is *popaa* music in your honor," one of our neighbors explained. The music became even more dragging and plaintive, and the more it lost of its Polynesian character the less at home the dancers seemed. None of them could dance any modern dance properly, but all did their best to imitate the people they had seen in the Papeete dance halls. By degrees many of them succeeded in looking just as bored as their European prototypes, even if the steps were rather confusing. The dancer who showed the greatest ability was Kainui, but that was presumably because he was the only one who wore shoes. While the bare feet of the others often moved a great deal quicker than the music, Kainui's solid twelves helped him to keep time.

To the relief of everyone, the dance program was only an introduction to a far more interesting entertainment— Polynesian community singing. This performance was most remarkable in at least two respects: most of the songs were hundreds of years old; and all the singers knew the words by heart. The musicians laid their guitars aside and joined the choir, whose mighty voice rose and fell as rhythmically as the waves which washed the shore of the lagoon. We listened, fascinated, to ancient religious hymns, the meaning of which had long been lost; to many languishing *teki* or "love songs"; to war songs and triumphal songs.

Near the end of the evening, when we asked our friends to sing a song about Raroia, the choice seemed to be simple and unanimous. While the shadows in the moonlight grew longer and longer and the night ever cooler and more delicious, the Raroians struck up, as a final selection, a song which may have been the same that their forefathers sang hundreds of years before, when they first saw the island rise out of the sea:

> "Followed by white terns
> Steers the canoe
> Through the rainbow's gate
> Toward the land.
>
> Raroia is found,
> This is Raroia,
> The land of the cool winds.
>
> The song of joy mingles
> With the noise of the breakers.
> Here is our country."

We could hardly have wished for a more beautiful and cordial "home-coming" reception!

Next morning we were wakened by a curious whistling noise. The wind blowing through the cracks in the wall, no doubt, we thought, and dropped off to sleep again. A little later we were wakened again by the same sound, and this time it seemed to come from the porch. Marie-Thérèse whispered, "There's someone on the veranda."

Before we could decide to investigate the mystery further, the door was thrown open and Rauri's round plump figure stood out against the light background of the galvanized-iron door, which glittered and shone in the morning sun. He announced with a friendly smile that coffee was ready!

After breakfast Teka came and wondered if we would not go for a walk with him. Naturally, we were amenable. Evidently there was something special he wanted to show us, for we had hardly turned off the "main street" of the village—an avenue three hundred yards long bordered by coconut palms—than he set off at such a pace it was all we could do to keep up with him. The long trail of children which had clung to us faithfully on the main thoroughfare was left far behind. Suddenly he stopped in front of the fine assembly house and pointed with pride to a coconut palm not more than three feet high. Then I remembered it was here we had planted one of the Peruvian coconuts we had brought across the sea on board the *Kon-Tiki* raft.

"At first it seemed to have difficulty in taking root," said Teka. "But then I put up a fence and began to water it, and that did good at once. Perhaps you'll be able to pick coconuts from it before you go."

"How long will that be?"

"Oh, six or seven years perhaps, but that doesn't matter. You can stay as long as you like. My grandfather came from Tahiti as a passenger on board a schooner. He was going to the Marquesas Islands to manage a copra plantation, but he liked Raroia so much that he got off here. He stayed for thirty-seven years. Temake's father was put ashore by a Chilean ship for some reason, and he stayed for good. Neither of them had any money to begin with, but when they died they had big copra plantations. You may do still better, for you've got a palm to start with."

"Do you get many visits from *popaa?*" I asked Teka, as we trudged back at a leisurely pace along the shore of the lagoon.

"No. Before you came on the raft I can only remember three pleasure yachts, and since you only the *Starling* has been here."

We had heard a lot of talk about the *Starling* at Papeete, but it was not till then, with Teka's help, we were able to re-construct the whole tragic story—which testified clearly that I was not the only person who had been seduced by Raroia's charm. The owner of this pleasure yacht was an American weary of civilization, who, in his distress at not finding in Tahiti the paradise he was seeking, tried to commit suicide on board his yacht in the Papeete harbor by taking too strong a dose of sleeping pills. A zealous customs officer who was making an extra inspection of the yacht found him, and after he had been treated with a stomach pump at the hospital, the authorities hastily canceled his *permit de séjour* in order to get rid of him. With the idea that he might be able to execute his plan better in peace and quiet somewhere among the Tuamotu Islands, he steered east, and chance brought him to Raroia.

The result, however, was quite different from what he

had intended. A short stay among the merry Raroians restored to him his joy in living, and after a few weeks more, when he found that they were living just the life he had hoped to find at Tahiti, he decided to stay on the island for good. As he was not prepared for such a turn of affairs nor equipped for a settler's life, he decided to go back to America to get timber, cement, domestic utensils, tools, and everything else that was needed in order to live on a coral island. Before he reached America, however, his ship was caught in a gale and wrecked.

Teka added sadly that a ship's captain had found his body some time afterward. In one of the pockets there was a sketch of his new house and a list of the equipment he had meant to buy.

The same whistling noise, which we had discovered came from Rauri's kerosene stove, announced that coffee was ready and that our third day on Raroia was commencing. We had vowed we would get up a little earlier this day so as to get in ahead of Rauri, but he had been too clever for us.

While we continued our unpacking, we were besieged by a large party of children, extremely inquisitive and thirsty for knowledge. A little girl who had stayed with us ever since we landed evidently considered herself already a *popaa* specialist, for she acted as guide to the others and made professional comments as she exhibited us and the other interesting features of the house. By giving her a slab of chocolate, however, we won her over to our side; and when she exchanged roles and began instead to exhibit her friends to us, telling us their nicknames, the crowd scattered quickly. Some of the older people, who had never seen a white woman at close quarters before, also arrived. But they all asked me politely for permission before they began their inspection of Marie-Thérèse.

Temake had a long and eloquent argument with Rauri as to who should invite us to dinner, and at last he won the privilege. To our great joy Temake and his wife Tehetu had no ambition to serve queer foreign dishes, but invited us to a genuine Polynesian meal. The first course consisted of raw fish, dipped in lemon juice and coconut sauce. This was followed by pork roasted in the oven, grilled pork, boiled pork, and pork cut up into small pieces and fried. Further, for the sake of variety, anyone who wished could have a little bacon in between. Roasted breadfruit and sweet potatoes were served with the meat.

Then came the fish dishes. Of course there were roast fish and boiled fish, big fish and small fish, lagoon fish and sea fish, and all were extraordinarily good eating. Temake filled his mouth full and spat the cleaned bones onto his plate one by one very neatly. We did our best to imitate him, but had difficulty in attaining the same sureness of aim. After the last fish we all felt rather gorged, so Tehetu gave us each a coconut to wash down the many dishes before we were to attack the sweet course, which was *poe*. This is one of the greatest delicacies on the Polynesian bill of fare; real *poe* is made of fruit and starch, which is kneaded together and boiled. The *poe* which Temake set on the table was made according to all the rules and therefore, like all real *poe,* was, to say the least, filling.

The rest of that day we spent on our backs in a state of semiconsciousness. Toward evening Temake came round, fit and cheerful, and invited us to help finish up the leftovers of the dinner, but we were obliged to refuse, for we could scarcely move.

Next morning Rauri again won the race for the kerosene stove and had coffee ready when we woke.

Immediately afterward Varoa, the former chief of the village, came to call on us, dressed up in a sun helmet and a red tie. According to all the people in the village he is the oldest man on Raroia, but no one knows exactly how old he is, for he was born long before the white men began to write down in a big book such—from the Polynesian point of view—quite unimportant things as the day and year of a man's birth. He pressed my hands with astonishing strength, looked straight into my eyes, and said quite unexpectedly in English:

"My name is Isidor, one, two, three!"

He then greeted Marie-Thérèse in the same way, pressed our hands again, and slowly withdrew, followed by admiring glances from the Raroians.

I suspected that Varoa-Isidor could seldom put his linguistic knowledge—acquired at Papeete some time in the seventies—to any practical use; but it was enough, anyway, to give him the envied position of the only English-speaking person in the village. Of the other Raroians, Tufaka, who was at school in Papeete for four years, spoke French quite fluently; Chief Teka had a pretty good knowledge of the language, though he often confused *l* and *r*, like most Polynesians; and there were two other men who knew a few single words. That was all. The rest talked a mixture of Tuamotuan and Tahitian, which are kindred dialects of the great Polynesian mother tongue.

The Tuamotu dialect was originally about as different from Tahitian as French from Spanish, but the numerous trips to Papeete and regular contact with businessmen, missionaries, and the crews of schooners—who all spoke Tahitian—left their mark on the Raroians' language and leveled out the differences. Nowadays, at any rate, all those under fifty speak a mixture of Tahitian and Tuamotuan, and there is only a handful of old people who speak something like a pure Tuamotu dialect. Teka even told us that the difference between the youngest and oldest generations had already become so great that boys and girls often find it hard to understand their grandparents!

It did not, therefore, matter much to us that there was no grammar or dictionary of the Tuamotu dialect. We got on well with the vocabulary we had acquired during our six months in Tahiti and with the schoolbooks in Tahitian which we had obtained with great difficulty. These schoolbooks consisted of a complicated grammar, abounding in such phrases as "Homer wrote the Iliad," and a lexicon, half the words in which were medical or poetical terms, so that its utility was unfortunately rather limited.

To fill this gap we began to draw up a supplementary list of words, and the good people of Raroia were so interested in this work that they assembled round us in large crowds as soon as we appeared with our books. Most of them were so eager to tell us the names for everything that they interrupted one another all the time, and we experienced only one difficulty—getting them to stop. To be sure of making as quick progress as possible we engaged Tufaka as teacher and interpreter.

By getting up at five o'clock one morning we at last managed to be ahead of Rauri, and when he came creeping in to arrange our breakfast, we were able instead to invite him to sit down to a fully laid table. Despite his ardent protests that it was only his duty, as a good father-by-adoption,

Marie-Thérèse and I aboard the *Teretai* in the Papeete harbor.
Soon we would leave Tahiti, bound for the coral atoll, Raroia.

The letters from kindly Chief Teka (*above*) brought me back to the island paradise we *Kon-Tiki* men had discovered in 1947, and he and the vice-chief, Tupuhoe (*below, left*), were on the quay with all the others to say *ia ora na* [may you live] when we arrived. A few days later Varoa (*below, right*), the former chief and oldest islander, came to greet us.

The long, narrow belt of coral atoll, which is Raroia, encloses a vast lagoon. Although one cannot see either the northern or southern tips from the village of Ngarumaoa, the eastern side is clearly visible as a green band on the horizon.

A little Polynesian girl came with me this time when I visited the three-foot coconut palm protected by a fence. Teka grew this tiny tree from one of the Peruvian coconuts which crossed the Pacific aboard the *Kon-Tiki* raft.

Raroians faithfully observe Mass in a church built of coral cement in 1875 (*above*). The natives dress carefully each Sunday, and some even put on shoes, surely a sign of genuine penitence (*below*).

to prepare our breakfast every morning, we at last succeeded in persuading him that there must be a limit even to kindness and helpfulness. As he would not leave us without making himself useful in some way, for the rest of that day he helped us put the house in order. He was so thoughtful that he even nailed up pieces of galvanized iron everywhere he thought there might be a draft; and as there were plenty of holes and cracks, he left behind a rather complicated but not positively ugly iron mosaic.

People of the village were greatly astonished at Marie-Thérèse cooking and doing housework. The popular view among the Raroians is that white women never work. In the evening a big man of about thirty, named Maono, who had been for a long time on one of the small islands on the other side of the lagoon and only had come to the village that very day, looked in to obtain confirmation of the strange rumor.

"Are there many women in *popaa* land?" he asked with interest.

We assured him that there were many more than on all the islands in French Oceania put together. This made a great impression on him!

"It's a pity that I'm a Tuamotu man," he said, "for if I wasn't, I should be able to marry a *popaa* woman."

"But what's wrong with the Raroian girls?" I wondered.

"There's nothing wrong with them except that they don't stay on Raroia. They go to Tahiti and marry some Tahitian or other. It's the same on all the islands round here. All the prettiest girls go to Papeete. If they don't get married, they sit about in the bars. Some sailor with plenty of money always comes along. There are five of us here on Raroia who can't find wives."

"But if there are so many women in Papeete, why don't you go there and get one? There must be many who have got tired of life in Papeete."

"No, they never get tired of it. They can dance, drink, and amuse themselves forever. To be able to marry nowadays, one must live in Papeete and have dollars, plenty of dollars."

Clearly some of the Raroians' problems are surprisingly modern and familiar.

On our first Sunday on the island the church bells summoned us to Mass at 7:00 A.M. With some few exceptions, the Raroians are Roman Catholics, and several days in advance most of them reminded us delicately of the Sunday service and the importance of not missing it. Marie-Thérèse and I decided to be among the first, but when we arrived at the church at the second bell, it appeared that instead we were the last. The whole population was assembled outside the entrance. We learned afterward that it was good form to be at the church while the first bell was being rung!

All the natives were dressed in their best clothes, properly starched and pressed in every possible and impossible place. Many had even put on shoes, surely a sign of genuine penitence, for Raroians always go barefoot on weekdays and suffer great pain whenever they have to force their feet into a pair of leather cases. As soon as the ringer caught sight of us, he began to sound the bell afresh with great force. The whole crowd immediately thronged into the church, which the thick walls of coral cement kept pleasantly cool. Everyone had his fixed place, the women on the right and the men on the left—the children in front, and the old people at the back.

Since no priest lives on the island, the service, therefore, consisted entirely of hymns and prayers, in Latin and Tahitian alternately. There was a happy, friendly atmosphere about this service, as there is about everything the Polynesians do, and both hymns and prayers carried a noticeable undertone of rejoicing. After three-quarters of an hour the service ended as suddenly as it had begun, and all trooped out in good order: first the old men, then the other grown men, followed by the boys; and last the women and girls, likewise in order of age.

The rest of the day was quietly spent in doing absolutely nothing. At the islanders' general request we got out our portable phonograph and entertained them with a short program. Our records of genuine Tahitian and Hawaiian music were, of course, by far the most popular; then came cowboy songs, which is quite understandable since the instruments and rhythm are roughly the same as in the Raroians' own music. The South American rumba and samba records went over all right; on the other hand, Armstrong, Ellington, Goodman, and the other jazz kings simply bored the listeners. And the classical music we tried—including Grieg, Chopin, Ravel, and a few symphonies—had an even worse reception. Some laughed and many went away!

Our new friend Maono and his comrade Tehei came early one morning and asked if we would accompany them on a trip over to the other side of the lagoon. Of course, nothing could please us more. We flung some canned food into a knapsack and put on our dark spectacles.

"Leave the sack at home," said Tehei. "We're providing the food today. It'll be real Raroian food too."

Tehei's sailing canoe lay in readiness down on the beach.

It was twenty-five feet long, three feet wide and, like all Polynesian craft, had a large outrigger which was fastened to the hull by a strong crossbeam forward and a branch of solid but supple wood aft.

Due to the lack of proper timber on the Tuamotu Islands, in old times the canoes were made of a number of small wooden planks, many not more than a foot or so wide; holes were laboriously bored in these, and sennit ropes were laced through the holes, connecting all the planks, to make large hulls. These "sewn" canoes, as they were called, disappeared long ago, and nowadays imported pine planks are used. The sails, which in pre-European times were made of plaited pandanus leaves, are also of modern cut and material.

While Marie-Thérèse and I stretched ourselves out on the narrow deck, Tehei and Maono took hold of the canoe, waded out a short way into the lagoon till the sails filled with wind, and then jumped on board. The canoe shot away at once. The pressure of the wind against the sails became so strong that the outrigger was lifted up out of the water dangerously. But Tehei knew what to do in this emergency. He ordered us all over to the windward side, and he crawled far out onto the outrigger to press it down with his weight. This put things right, and the canoe ran on safely and steadily, while the hull and outrigger drew on the ruffled surface of the lagoon two broad lines, as parallel as railway tracks.

Raroia is long, narrow, and oval in shape, with its axis running from northeast to southwest, and like all the other Tuamotu Islands it consists solely of a narrow belt of coral, from 200 to 550 yards wide, enclosing a vast lagoon; thus, an atoll. Here and there on this coral reef, sand and crushed corals have become piled up in such quantities that a little island has been formed. Altogether there are hundreds of small islands and islets on the Raroia reef: most of them are only a few hundred yards long, and only three can boast the imposing length of two-and-a-half miles.

No one knows the exact size of the atoll, for it has never been surveyed, but most people estimate it at about twenty-six miles long and six miles wide. This must be about right, for from the village one can see neither the northern nor the southern tip of the oval ring, but the eastern side is quite clearly visible as a narrow green band along the horizon. The greatest depth of the lagoon is 160 feet, but in many places huge coral blocks rise right to the surface and are a considerable hindrance to navigation.

The morning sun shone right in our eyes as we skimmed over the waves, so Tehei stationed himself at the farthest end of the outrigger and kept a sharp lookout for the coral shoals, all the time shouting orders to Maono, who sat at the tiller. We soon discovered that they had different names for the shoals according to their size and depth. A shoal which did not reach the surface and which the canoe, therefore, passed over with ease was called *marahi*. For the shoals which reached the surface there were two different names. If they were not more than about fifteen feet in diameter, they were called *puteu,* but if they were larger, they were called *karena*.

Thanks to a language which had been adapted to the islanders' special needs, Tehei could issue terse navigational directions much more quickly and more precisely than would have been possible in English or any other European language, and Maono was not slow in acting upon his instructions.

After an hour's cruising against the east wind we reached Tetou, the largest island on the eastern side of the lagoon.

Here there was once a flourishing village, but the great cyclone of 1878 destroyed it so completely that nowadays only scattered coral blocks and shattered foundations of houses witness that between three hundred and four hundred persons once lived on the island. Those who survived the catastrophe, comprehensibly enough, preferred to settle in the village of Ngarumaoa, on the opposite side of the lagoon.

The island was replanted just before the First World War, and now long straight rows of coconut palms sway in the breeze. Otherwise the vegetation is as scanty as on all the other islands on the Raroia reef. The only trees of any size besides the coconut palms are a few pandanus palms—graceful, pretty trees with long aerial roots—and two species of deciduous trees. There are, in all, about twenty kinds of plants and bushes.

Raroian traditions tell of yet another dramatic event which once happened at Tetou. One dark and stormy night in the 1860's the inhabitants of the village of Tetou were suddenly awakened by a tremendous noise from the outside of the reef. On hurrying across they saw to their amazement a large vessel high up on the reef. Lights were still burning in the cabins, but not a living creature could be descried on board. Before they had recovered from their astonishment at the uncanny sight, the ship quite unexpectedly slid back into the sea and then was immediately flung by the breakers back again at the reef with such violence that she was at once transformed into a shapeless wreck, which slowly sank.

During the weeks that followed pieces of the ship and her fittings washed up onto the beach every day, and there they still lie. Many of the iron plates are of huge dimensions, and according to the story handed down the vessel was at least as large as the foreign ships which now call at Papeete

—which means that she must have been four to five thousand tons.

Where the ship came from and what happened to the crew are two questions which the Raroians have never been able to answer. But somewhere in some old shipping register there must be a note of a vessel having been lost in some manner unknown between Valparaiso and Papeete, which would fill in the missing links in this tragedy.

A little farther north lay the little round island paradise on which the *Kon-Tiki* raft stranded. We waded across to the island and strolled round it along the beach. The promenade took just two minutes. A few rusty tin cans, and a screw top which had belonged to I could not remember what, were the only reminders of our visit two years earlier.

"The *Kon-Tiki* canned food was the best I've eaten," said Tehei, poking his big toe cautiously into one of the rusty cans. "The whole village thought so too, for when you had gone, everyone stayed at home and ate canned food morning, noon, and night. No one did any work, no one fished, no one did anything but eat canned food. Some people mixed the contents of all the different kinds of cans, others ate only pineapple or meat. We finished them in a week."

This was certainly good testimony to the excellence of the canned food and to the Raroians' appetites, for we had left behind about fifteen hundred cans!

"But when there are no rafts," Tehei added, gazing sadly out over the empty sea, "we have to get along with Raroia's own supply. Wait a minute and you'll see what they look like."

He took two spears out of the sailing canoe, gave one to Maono, and waded with his companion out into one of the many channels a few feet deep which joined the sea to the lagoon. Tehei raised his spear and struck. The next moment he drew his arm back and flung a big fish onto the beach. It resembled an eelpout more than anything and was about eighteen inches long! Immediately afterward Maono harpooned a fish, and in less than ten minutes four fish of about the same size were heaped upon the beach.

While Maono disappeared among the palms, Tehei collected a mound of coconut fiber, lighted it, and laid the fish on the fire unscaled and uncleaned.

"As in old times," said Tehei. "There were no frying pans in those days and no cooking fat either. The coconut fiber was the frying pan and the guts were the cooking fat."

Maono returned with some tender palm shoots and a couple of fresh coconuts—our salad and dessert. After a time Tehei decided that the fish were grilled enough and raked them out of the fire with the branch of a tree. They were charred and did not look particularly appetizing. Then he threw them far out into the lagoon with a graceful gesture and waded after them. Retrieving them one by one, he slit them and cleaned away all the fins, guts, and charred parts.

"In the old times there was no salt on Raroia, and so they used to dip fish into the sea," he explained when he returned to the shore and laid the fish in rows on the green leaves which Maono had spread out on the ground.

"Now when we are in the village we eat fish fried in a pan," he continued, "but when we go over to the small islands to make copra, we often cook the fish as it used to be done. I think it's better like this."

After the first mouthful we thoroughly agreed with Tehei. The fish cooked on the embers and salted in the sea was indeed a real delicacy. We finished the meal with a foot or two of palm shoots and a few coconuts each.

"Now we'll go and sleep," Maono announced. "When one has had a good meal, one must sleep. It is good for the stomach."

Soon we were all snoring in the shade of the palms, full and happy. When at last we woke, it was late in the afternoon and we didn't reach the village until the twilight was fading into darkness.

"Tomorrow we can eat other Raroian dishes and sleep on another island if you like," said Tehei when we parted. "There are always fish in the lagoon, and there are so many islands that no one has been able to count them."

Time passed quickly and we adapted ourselves gradually to the new conditions and acquired continually more and more friends. One of the funniest was Rehua. I remember especially one occasion when he suddenly appeared and asked if it was really true that I had a machine with which one could write the letters of the alphabet. When I replied that I had one, he wondered if it was also possible to write Tahitian with it. I assured him that it could be done perfectly well, which seemed to please him very much. He took out a paper and asked politely if I would be so kind as to help him to write a letter on my machine. I nodded my head yes, and put the sheet of paper into the typewriter. Then he dictated the following curious document:

Ia ora na Jack *with the blessing of Jesus Christ and Maria Immaculata. Amen.*

It is I who have your boy, whom you gave to me in Tahiti. Do you remember? I look after him well and feed him every day. When he grows big I shall send him to school in Papeete, so that he shall learn French and all that a popaa *can. I will pay for this. Then when he grows still bigger perhaps you will send him to America. Then you will pay for this. If you agree with me, write to me. When he grows big he will inherit half of all that I have.*

Written by Rehua a Tuamea

Rehua read the letter through twice with delight.

Then he said, "Can you put it in an envelope and write the address too, so that it will look like a real letter?"

"Yes, certainly," I replied, and with unaffected delight he took out an envelope with a cellophane "window."

"To whom is it to be sent?" I asked.

"To Jack in Tahiti."

"H'm, there are sure to be many Jacks in Tahiti. Has he no surname?"

"Oh yes, but it was so strange that I have forgotten it."

"H'm, but who is Jack?"

"He gave me the child. He is from *popaa* land. Write, 'To Jack,' it'll get to him all right."

I wrote, "To Jack, Tahiti."

A great commotion interrupted us unexpectedly. A crowd of children came running and shouting, *"Inaa, inaa,"* at the tops of their voices. Some of them took us by the hands and pulled us along. They were so eager that they stumbled over the coconuts in the village street, and their enthusiasm began to infect us. Ahead of us, half the population had assembled down on the quay. Most of them had pails in their hands.

"Will you have *inaa?*" asked Tarakeha.

"What's that?"

"Little, little fish. As good as sardines."

When we looked more closely, we found that the water round the quay was swarming with little fish about a half-inch long.

"The whole bay is full of them," Tarakeha explained. "They stay quite still and we have only to scoop them up. We don't need to look for fish here on Raroia. They come to us."

He plunged his pail into the water, let the water run off, and poured a few pounds of fish out onto the sand. Then everyone began "fishing." We followed Tarakeha's recipe, mixed the fish with flour and water, and fried the whole mess over the oil stove. The dish when cooked looked like toffee but tasted like fried Baltic herring.

At twelve o'clock it was so hot that the air quivered in front of our eyes and the thermometer showed 95° in the shade. Just as we were on the point of collapse, Maono came and asked if I would not play football with them! I tottered off to the "football field" and sat down under the shadiest palm I could find, doubtful whether I should even be able to keep my eyes open. But I soon became so interested in what I saw that I forgot the heat and my weariness.

The Raroians were playing quite a new kind of soccer-football, which should properly be called "coconut football." *In addition to the living players a considerable number of coconut palms also took part in the match!* The most skillful players not only seemed able to avoid the palms but cunningly collaborated with them. The ground stretched as far as a man could run, and the goalkeepers often had to be ready for attacks both from in front and from behind. High kicks were particularly difficult, for when a player kicked the ball up into a palm top, it often happened that a coconut came down instead.

All who felt inclined took part in the game, but only for as long as they liked; and all, of course, were barefoot. The referee sat on a wooden box and blew his whistle practically without stopping, but none of the players took any notice of his whistling except when they considered that they had scored a goal. The match ended in a draw, 2-2.

"Maono's team ought to have won," I said.

"Perhaps," replied the referee, "but here all the matches end in a draw. As soon as it's 2-2 or 3-3 I blow the whistle. It's best that way. No one is annoyed and all are friends."

"But what do you do if one team is much too strong for the other?" I objected.

"That is impossible, for if one team is getting the best of the other, one player goes over to the other side. If that doesn't work, another goes over. And the result is a draw. We like that best here on Raroia."

It cannot be denied that the Raroians' original view of competitive sports has much to be said for it.

On one of our first days on the island Tarakeha began to bring us fresh fish every morning, and suddenly one morning Tapakia arrived with half a dozen of his innumerable children, each of them carrying one or two coconuts. He bored through the eye with a sharp piece of wood and handed each of us a nut.

"There is a story of how the coconut came to exist," he said, choosing a nut for himself. "Once long, long ago, there was nothing but bushes and grass here on Raroia. A woman called Hina often used to lament this, and her husband Tuna therefore began to consider how he could get some useful plant. One day he said to her: 'When I die, cut off my head and plant it.' Soon after he did die, and Hina planted his head as he had told her. Soon a green shoot appeared, which grew up into a big tree. The curious new tree was full of nuts, all shaped like Tuna's head. Hina picked a nut and took off the fiber. When she discovered the three eyes she was pleased and said: 'Look, there are Tuna's eyes and mouth. I knew he spoke the truth.' "

Tapakia emptied his nut and gazed at it reflectively.

"Some say it's only an old story, but one can never know," he added. "The eyes and mouth are there. . . . ."

Marie-Thérèse and I went for a long walk along the shore of the lagoon that afternoon, and when darkness began to fall, we were still a long way from the village. For a moment we were uncertain as to our way back, but then a familiar sound reached our ears. The young people of Ngarumaoa had begun their evening singing, and the guitar music and voices told us in which direction the village lay. We went on slowly while the stars began to peek out in the dark-blue tropical sky above us. Suddenly a familiar tune was borne to us on the cool night breeze. We stopped and listened. It was the same song our friends had sung for us the day we came to Raroia, and we crooned the words softly to ourselves as we stood motionless in the dark:

> ". . . . this is Raroia,
> The land of the cool winds.
>
> The song of joy mingles
> With the noise of the breakers.
> Here is our country."

We felt already as if Raroia was our country too.

Aita Peapea

I YAWNED, stretched, and turned over in bed. Marie-Thérèse was up, busily puttering about the kerosene stove. More than six months had passed, and although Rauri, our "father," had long since been convinced that we didn't regard it as his duty to make our breakfasts, little else had changed since that day we were received with songs and music down on the quay. Everyone was still as generous and effusively friendly as on the first days, and we could not recall a single occasion on which we were badly or coldly received. These were undeniably admirable qualities, but still more striking was the Raroians' unequaled carelessness and levity.

Although we had come to know them pretty thoroughly, and thus ought to have been accustomed to their peculiarities and special characteristics, we were often left speechless by their incalculable behavior. Nothing can depress or perturb them, and like children they have the enviable capacity of living just for the moment, oblivious of the day before and untroubled by the morrow.

The slogan of this optimistic philosophy of life is a cheerful *aita peapea:* No matter! Why worry? Who cares! The first time we heard the expression was the very day of our arrival. In the crush down on the narrow stone quay one of the singers suddenly fell into the water and thoroughly splashed the whole reception committee, who were dressed up to the ears in their best Sunday clothes. At once an *aita peapea* ran through the crowd, and everyone laughed till they could laugh no more. This was, of course, no more than could be expected in such a situation. But the frequent use which the Raroians made of their favorite expression was overwhelming.

For example, one day Tehei showed us his house, which although obviously newly built had a strange tumble-down appearance. On closer inspection we found that this was simply because hardly one wall was at right angles to the ground or its adjoining wall, and all the measurements were ludicrously out of proportion. Tehei's explanation was very simple.

"All the different measurements are such a bother, and I'm so bad at counting. The only man who can build decent houses is Ruto, but he was staying with relations on Hikueru when I wanted to build, so I had to do the job myself. Of course the house is a bit crooked, but it's none the worse for that. *Aita peapea!*"

And other astounding examples can be found. In the first week we were sometimes surprised to find wheelbarrows and bicycles abandoned in the village street or thrown down in the most unexpected places. We supposed that the good Raroians were too lazy to put them under cover, and we soon had confirmation that our suspicions were extremely well founded.

One day it suddenly occurred to our neighbor Tefau to fill up a number of holes on his piece of land, and he got out his wheelbarrow. We saw him make several trips down to the shore, where the waves had washed up the finest white garden sand imaginable. Then he suddenly disappeared. When we investigated more closely we found, as we had expected, that he had abandoned the wheelbarrow, full of sand, in the village street. Days passed, but the wheelbarrow remained in the same place. Although Tefau passed it at least twice a day, and although it was obstructing traffic, neither he nor anyone else showed an inclination to move it. About a week later Tefau quite unexpectedly took hold of it one morning and continued his work as if nothing had happened!

This was not an exceptional case; Raroians as a rule are just as capricious in everything they undertake. They abandon their work on the spur of the moment because they have seen a curious fish or some other object of interest. *Aita peapea.* Why hurry? There's always tomorrow.

Raroians will set off on long journeys unexpectedly and without any preparation. Young and old delight in seeing the world, and every call of a schooner is a strong allurement for them. As soon as anyone has reason to go to Papeete, the urge to travel spreads at once; and at least half a dozen of the Raroians suddenly find that they have important business to do there, or that their relations are desperately anxious to see them. They have relations everywhere in the Tuamotu group, and if the schooner should not be calling at the particular island they meant to visit, that does not matter, for there is always an aunt or a distant cousin on the next one. *Aita peapea.*

Like the Tuamotu natives in general, Raroians have

Poe is made by dropping red-hot stones into a mixture of fruit, starch, and water (*above*). (*Below*) the islanders have found a use for their empty beer bottles—they use them for a decorative border around their flower beds.

Here there are no troubles or worries! The tiny tots splash about in the cove near the village where the temperature of the water averages about eighty degrees . . . .

. . . . and the young folks and adults ride their fine, shiny bicycles up and down the village street which is about three hundred yards long. Bicycles on Raroia are only playthings, for there are no other streets or usable roads on the atoll. And the natives, not knowing how to repair the bicycles, discard them often for new, shinier ones.

About once a month a schooner comes to get copra in exchange for *popaa* goods (*above*). This is the Raroians' only connection with the outer world, and they hurry to exchange their copra for canned goods, tobacco, and smuggled liquor (*below*).

Almost every day Marie-Thérèse dressed leg boils and cuts from coral (*left*). Another chronic complaint is toothache (*right*), for all have decayed teeth from childhood.

The finest piece of furniture in every house is an iron bed or divan. But in spite of their well-made beds, Raroians sleep on the floor on pandanus mats, as their ancestors have done since the beginning of time.

preserved this typically Polynesian carelessness a good deal better than most of their kinsmen in other parts of French Oceania, for the Tuamotu group is still quite untouched and isolated. While most of the other native peoples have suffered severely from the processes of civilization, conditions on Raroia and the other Tuamotu Islands are in many important respects still the same as in the good old heathen days, before any copra schooners had ventured in among the treacherous coral reefs.

Of course this does not mean that the natives are still bloodthirsty cannibals who run about among the palms half-naked and live in the palm-leaf houses of Hollywood romance—as perhaps has already been gathered from all that has been said about galvanized iron, wooden houses, shoes, newly pressed clothes, canned foods, and football matches—but simply and solely that the milieu and conditions of life are in the main unchanged. Despite the outward similarities, and despite the many manufactured wares and other paraphernalia of civilization with which the islanders surround themselves, Raroia is essentially different from Tahiti and most of the other more famous South Sea islands.

First and foremost, the Raroians are still surprisingly free and independent. In pre-European times there was a native dynasty on the island, and the chiefs or hereditary kings ruled more or less arbitrarily. When the French extended their power over the Tuamotu Islands in the middle of the nineteenth century, they put an end to this system and installed a chief nominated by the authorities at Papeete. But in other respects they left the natives to themselves.

The chief is now elected by the Raroians themselves—a step forward which naturally has been greeted with unmixed pleasure—but otherwise the changes are small. The officials are few, and their rule is mild, to say the least. The chief's most important tasks are to supervise the sale of copra, to keep a record of births and deaths, to marry couples, and to direct all common work; but these duties can hardly be said to weigh very heavily either on him or on the population. Certainly Teka has several times complained of the amount of work he has each time a schooner arrives, for he has to sign all business documents. But as there is at the most a schooner a month and he never reads the papers through, it is hard to take him seriously.

From the inhabitants, characteristically enough, no complaints are ever heard, but if anyone should be dissatisfied with anything, he has ample opportunities both of saying so and of getting any abuse rectified. Now and then the chief calls a meeting of the village council: this consists officially of five elected members, but anyone who likes can take part in it and express his views.

Besides the chief there is only one other civil official, the so-called *mutoi,* who is nominated by the authorities at Papeete. In theory the *mutoi* is postman, policeman, and assistant to the chief, but in reality he has no duties of any kind. The Raroians never write or receive letters, crime is unknown, and the chief never requires any help. The office, however, is keenly sought after, for the holder has the right to wear a uniform with red stripes and braid!

In addition to the civil officials there are church officials —two catechists. Their tasks are to conduct the services and otherwise deputize as best they can for the priest, who only comes on a visit once a year. The duty the catechists prize most highly is ringing the church bell, and only in an emergency will they hand it over to anyone else. Even when the greater part of the population goes off to the islands in the lagoon to make copra, the catechist who is on duty remains in the village and rings the bell for a handful of old women and children—or simply for himself.

So long as this simple and democratic system works— and it has worked now for several generations—the central authorities at Papeete do not interfere in any way. Once a year the administrator of the Tuamotu Islands comes to listen to complaints. His visit usually takes a few hours, or at the most one day. On rare occasions a higher official pays a lightning visit. That is all.

It should perhaps be added that the Raroians, like all the other natives in French Oceania, are French citizens and have exactly the same rights as all other Frenchmen in the mother country or in the colonies. At the same time their obligations are considerably more restricted; for example, the Raroians are not liable to conscription, do no war service, and pay no taxes except the dog tax. Even the latter tax is illusory. Ratters are exempt from this regulation, and consequently all the dogs on Raroia, irrespective of breed or size, are ratters.

The Raroians have not only been able to keep their right of self-determination to a very great extent, but they have also managed to keep their land, which is at least as important. The isolation and insignificance of the island are largely to be thanked for this fortunate circumstance, but the understanding attitude of the authorities has also played a considerable part.

At the beginning, isolation was the most important protection against intrusive foreigners. The hordes of ruthless adventurers, arms smugglers, dealers in liquor, and robbers from every corner of the globe who invaded the South Seas in the nineteenth century preferred, naturally enough, to seek their fortune on rich, fertile, mountainous islands like Tahiti, Samoa, and Hawaii. They regarded with contempt the miserable little atolls of the Tuamotu group. At the most, the boldest of them paid a short visit to the best known of the pearl islands in the hope of being able to make a dishonest fortune quickly; but no one ever dreamed of settling in the Tuamotu group. While other Polynesian peoples succumbed to diseases, war, and drink, and to a great extent lost their freedom and their land, the Tuamotu Islands were left almost completely in peace.

When, later, France brought the islands under her sway, her main policy was still, as far as possible, to prevent the natives from being exploited and from losing their lands. So successful has the colonial policy been that there are only half-a-dozen white plantation owners in the whole group, and all the inhabitants without exception have their own land. Certainly some have more and some have less, but no one on Raroia is so poor that he has not a site of his own on which to build a house and a piece of land with enough coconuts to supply his wants.

The exceptional characteristics of the Tuamotu natives are still more striking on the spiritual plane. Having been left to themselves to so great an extent, far off the shipping routes and the beaten tracks of civilization, they have succeeded in preserving their original unity. While we so-called moderns in the West are split up among ourselves into a thousand different groups—parties, professions, and nations —the Raroians are still united and harmonious. For them there is only one way of doing a task and only one way of looking at existence; no religious doubts have yet appeared, and they seldom come into contact with other peoples and races. All are equally good fishermen, copra workers, and craftsmen—there is no specialization of labor, there are no classes. And a uniform system of social conventions and prohibitions determines what they shall or shall not do. In other words, they are whole and believing whereas we are divided and skeptical. They have succeeded in preserving the homogeneity which is so characteristic of most so-called primitive peoples.

Significantly, nervous diseases are quite unknown among the Raroians. When I described in detail one of the commonest neuroses of civilization—schizophrenia—to the oldest and most intelligent natives, they listened mistrustfully and then declared with one voice that they had never seen or heard of any such queer disease on their island.

The weather has also helped preserve the basically Polynesian life: it is summer all year round on Raroia. The balmy climate simplifies existence and considerably limits requirements. Everyone solves his housing problem by putting together a house of palm leaves, galvanized iron, fir wood, or lids of cases, according to his taste and means. There is plenty of water for washing in the lagoon, and drinking water falls from the clouds free of charge or can be plucked from the trees in the form of coconuts.

Fuel consists almost invariably of coconut husks, which Mother Nature strews about generously everywhere. In a quarter of an hour one can collect a week's supply of fuel. The lagoon teems with hundreds of fish of different kinds, and a short fishing trip of a morning is bound to give splendid results. The necessity for clothing is reduced to a minimum. One pair of shorts yearly, with a loincloth by way of change, are quite enough. Generally speaking, of course, the Raroians do not live in quite such simple style, but more important, they *can* do it at a pinch.

To these four important factors—independence, security of tenure, spiritual wholeness, and simplicity of life—which now as in the past are the basis of the Raroians' safe and untroubled existence and certainly the basis of their merry, carefree character, at least one new gain can be added. The last seventy-five years of French rule have not only preserved what was best in the old social order but have definitely put an end to the wars and hostilities between the islands—often cruel and bloody in pre-European times.

Since then their remote location has effectively kept the Tuamotu natives out of recent world wars and is, of course, still their best protection. They are, therefore, in a torn and suffering world, one of the few peoples who have really attained what so many humans long for—freedom from hardship and fear. Can one then be surprised that they are so carefree and always laughing and singing?

And further, as a result of the last seventy-five or one hundred years of contact with Western civilization, the Raroians have begun to dive for mother-of-pearl and to make copra, both of which bring them in regular and surprisingly large incomes.

An American, well aware of his need for money and lots of it, might be tempted to attach great significance to these big incomes, or even consider them the most important reason for the Raroians' carefree, happy outlook on life. Curiously enough, money does not play the same decisive role among them as among us Westerners. The whole money system is a loan from the outside world which the Raroians do not yet fully understand, and they are happy in spite of their money rather than because of it. We have to go only a short way back in their history to find that money has been almost forced upon the Raroians.

In pre-European times mother-of-pearl was valuable only as a material for fishhooks and tools, and no one troubled to grow more coconut palms than he needed for his own private economy. In the middle of the nineteenth century, however, schooners from Tahiti began to appear among the Tuamotu Islands, and to the amazement of the natives the queer strangers who were on board gave cloth, knives, and other articles of value in exchange for pearls and mussels! The natives were delighted; there were great quantities of mussels in the lagoons and anyone could fish them up without any great trouble.

Soon they found that the schooners were glad to take coconut oil also in exchange, but in spite of the relatively good payment in the form of goods this trade never developed to any great extent, for the Tuamotu natives found it far too much trouble and too hard work to make oil in the quantities the schooners wanted. The only method of production then known was to chop the nuts in half, take out the flesh of the coconut, smash it, and then stand the whole mass in large wooden dishes in the sun, which in a few days turned it into a thick oil. The buyers were just as dissatisfied with this method as the natives, for it was both wasteful and unpractical (only about half the oil content of the kernels was obtained).

In another few decades the method of drying coconuts in the sun spread to French Occania. The advantage of this new method was that whole nuts could be sent to margarine and soap factories, where they were utilized 100 per cent. The natives on their side also appreciated this change, as it meant considerably less work for them; all they had to do was to chop the nuts in half, let them dry in the sun, and take out the kernels. Many, of course, still rejected with con-

71

tempt the idea of working and sweating in the sun for a few scraps of cloth or knives, but the number of natives who now and then condescended to cut up a few nuts increased steadily.

Trade in mother-of-pearl mussels advanced along with the copra industry, and many natives became professional divers. Diving for mussels was not so dull as making copra, and there was always the possibility of finding a large shining pearl, which could be exchanged for undreamed-of quantities of liquor and bolts of cloth aboard a schooner!

Soon some skipper found it simpler to introduce money, and as everywhere in French Oceania before the Panama Canal had been opened and when Valparaiso was still the most important transit port, the first coins were the Chilean dollars. These were large silver coins with an eagle on the face, and therefore the natives called them "bird money." Many of the Raroians and their kinsmen were so fascinated by these shining coins that they collected them in heaps, and even today there are still plenty of them in hidden chests and boxes.

Others found that these coins were both practical and convenient as a medium of exchange for things they wanted, and the most enterprising accompanied the schooners to Tahiti and returned with envied riches in the shape of canned foods, meat mincers, furniture, ball dresses, Bibles, iron bars, and a thousand other assorted things which, in most cases, they did not know how to use. As a memento of those times the Raroians and Tuamotu natives reckon all prices in *tara,* the Polynesian form of the word "dollar," although the only coins used nowadays are French francs. A *tara* means five francs because in the good old times the rate of exchange was five francs for one Chilean dollar; and force of habit is so great that a Raroian will say that copra costs two *tara,* rather than that it costs ten francs.

This first contact with Papeete and the wonders of civilization, of course, created a number of new and artificial needs. To satisfy them, more and more of the natives began to make copra or dive for mother-of-pearl mussels. Production increased and trade flourished, to the great satisfaction of the buyers and skippers. All the schooners went both to and from Papeete with full cargoes, and the Tuamotu Islands were flooded with worthless rubbish which was sold at shameless prices.

By and large, the situation is still the same. The worthy Raroians' annual earnings are astoundingly high, but the money is quickly wasted on senseless or useless things. Exactly how much each man earns is rather difficult to determine, for of course no one troubles to keep accounts; but the figures which the copra buyers have given are fairly eloquent. (There has been no diving for mother-of-pearl mussels on Raroia for some years.) According to these men Raroia's annual output of copra is about 250 tons. The price in the last two years has been about 10 Tahiti francs per kilo (2.2 pounds) which means that the Raroians together earn not less than 2,500,000 Tahiti francs or about $40,000 a year. The population consists of rather more than a hundred persons divided into twenty-five households. The average yearly income of each household is therefore about $1,600.

This money is paid cash down on delivery on board the copra schooners. Income tax is as unknown as capital tax. No one puts any money into the bank for the simple reason that there is no bank. Except for a few old people who laid the foundation of their saving habits when money was solid silver coinage—a joy to collect and count—nobody hoards. On the contrary, it is unusual to find anyone who has any money left if he has to meet any unexpected demand. Where does the money go?

About one-third goes to the two merchants on Raroia, one of whom is Chinese. Everyone buys on credit from one or both and pays as much as suits him every time he sells some copra. Only in very rare cases do the people know whether they are in debt to the shopkeeper or have a credit with him. What they buy and how much only the tradesmen know. One of the tradesmen gave me the following expenditure for a month, which can be regarded as typical of most Raroian families. The household consists of husband, wife, mother-in-law, and two boys, aged ten and twelve years.

In the following table the quantities purchased are given in the metric system—that used in France and her colonies—but the conversions to American standards immediately follow in parentheses. The actual cost is quoted in Tahiti francs and centimes, followed by the dollar equivalent. Tahiti francs have an exchange rate of .016 per franc in United States dollars.

		Tfr.	c.	Dollars U.S.
Jan. 1	1 kilo biscuits (*2.2 pounds*)	46	20	$ .74
	1 can beef	22		.35
	½ kilo candy (*1.1 pounds*)	105		1.68
	2 packs American cigarettes	40		.64
	10 kilos flour (*22 pounds*)	153		2.45
Jan. 2	1 carton American cigarettes	375		6.00
Jan. 3	10 kilos sugar (*22 pounds*)	130	20	2.08
	2 cans beef	45		.72
	1 liter kerosene (*1.056 quarts*)	10		.16

Jan. 5	2 kilos coffee (*4.4 pounds*)	160		2.56
Jan. 6	1 can beef	26		.42
	1 can pears	45	50	.73
	2 mirrors	244		3.90
Jan. 8	1 kilo rice (*2.2 pounds*)	29	50	.47
	1 liter kerosene (*1.056 quarts*)	10		.16
	3 packs French cigarettes	45		.72
Jan. 9	1 bottle perfume	90		1.44
Jan. 11	1 pack American cigarettes	20		.32
	1 box macaroni	26	60	.43
	½ kilo candy (*1.1 pounds*)	105		1.68
Jan. 13	1 kilo rice (*2.2 pounds*)	29	50	.47
	11 kilos flour (*24.2 pounds*)	168	30	2.69
	1 pack American cigarettes	20		.32
Jan. 14	2 kilos coffee (*4.4 pounds*)	160		2.56
	2 packs American cigarettes	40		.64
	2 cans beef	45		.72
Jan. 16	1 kilo biscuits (*2.2 pounds*)	48		.77
	10 yards cloth	518		8.29
	1 pack American cigarettes	20		.32
Jan. 18	4 packs French cigarettes	60		.96
Jan. 19	2 kilos rice (*4.4 pounds*)	60		.96
	1 liter kerosene (*1.056 quarts*)	10		.16
	5 bottles lemonade	60		.96
Jan. 20	1 can tomato sauce	9	60	.15
Jan. 21	1 pack American cigarettes	20		.32
Jan. 23	2 cans beef	45		.72
	2 packs American cigarettes	40		.64
	2 kilos coffee (*4.4 pounds*)	160		2.56
Jan. 25	1 kilo onions (*2.2 pounds*)	25	50	.41
	2 packs American cigarettes	40		.64

Jan. 26	1 kilo biscuits (2.2 *pounds*)	46	20	.74
	3 packs French cigarettes	45		.72
Jan. 29	2 cans beef	45		.72
	TOTAL	3,448	10	$55.09

This is the total expenditure for a month on so-called necessities, and yet an American housewife would certainly have a somewhat different opinion regarding the necessity of at least half of them! And note the exorbitant prices! They are due more than anything to the high freight charges and the roundabout selling procedure. Most goods have an abnormally long way to travel before they reach the customer.

The first middleman is one of the general agents at Papeete. After having paid customs duty (often as much as 30 per cent of the value) and added his commission, he sells the goods to one of the shipowners who sends them off to Raroia. On the way the price rises by 30 per cent, which is the percentage of profit allowed by law. On their arrival one of the merchants receives the goods, and after he has added a further 10 per cent, they at last appear in the shop, ready to be taken away by the customer. The price is now double the original price.

Of course the Raroians could save large sums by ordering the goods directly from the importer at Papeete instead of buying them from the tradesmen, and they have considered the matter, but hitherto they have always come to the conclusion that it would be too much trouble. They have a decided repugnance to letter writing and are weak in all the four simple rules of arithmetic. But if there is one thing the Raroians are not, it is stupid, and they understand very well that the goods they buy are much too dear, but what does that matter? Have they not always plenty of money? *Aita peapea*. And they like to have a shop full of brightly colored canned food and gaudy trash, where they can get what they want whenever they like.

The Raroians spend the rest of their income on quite senseless and useless things—useless from our rational standpoint. In the first place they have objects of snob value. Most of the Raroian people have been in Tahiti and have seen how their more advanced relations live, and they do their best to imitate their "urban" relatives. For example, during the past several decades every self-respecting Raroian family has had to have a house in the European style. Wooden houses of genuine deal planks are naturally considered the smartest. Next come houses of galvanized iron, then wooden huts built of old boxes. Lowest in the scale come the palm-leaf houses in the old Polynesian style.

One thing, however, struck my eye one day as I was walking round the village with Teka. Practically all the wooden or galvanized-iron houses were flanked by small houses of plaited palm leaves. I asked him what they were used for, and his answer was undeniably illuminating.

"You understand, it's hot in the middle of the day in a wooden or galvanized-iron house. It's good to have a palm house to be in then."

Clearly the classical best-room system on a magnified scale.

But the lunacy does not end with the buildings themselves. The fine European-type houses must also be furnished, and the standard furniture, for some inexplicable reason, consists of a few chairs, an iron bedstead, and a chest of drawers with a glass mirror. This sounds comparatively reasonable, but in reality is not. With the possible exception of the mirror, none of these fashionable objects serve any practical purpose and are obtained simply for the sake of prestige. Like their forefathers from time immemorial, all Raroians always prefer to sit and lie on the floor, and the few belongings they want to lock up they keep in large wooden boxes. As an experiment we often offered chairs when they came to visit us, but they invariably sat down on the floor *between* them!

We were at first a little more doubtful about the large iron beds with embroidered bedspreads and bolsters, which were to be found in every house, but we discovered that these too were only decorations. The Raroians sleep on pandanus mats on the floor beside their well-made beds! The most important thing is to *have* a bed, not to use it.

It is the same with the bicycles. There are at least twenty-five bicycles on Raroia, and all of them are new and shining. As soon as a bicycle loses its shine or gets broken, it is condemned and the owner buys a new one—for the simple reason that no one knows how to enamel or repair it. But even more ludicrous than this trivial inconvenience—there are no roads on Raroia! The only way of making use of these smart bicycles is, therefore, to ride up and down the village street, which is just over three hundred yards long. A trifle monotonous, perhaps, but more than enough for Raroians, who would find it wearisome to cycle for any longer distance. And in any case the most important thing is to show what a fine bicycle one has. Sunday is the chief parade day, and in the hours after Mass the village street is usually full of cyclists, pedaling to and fro in a leisurely and dignified manner, punctiliously ringing their bells.

By far the most stupendous example of this prestige

competition and unreasoning worship of the marvels of civilization is Tutepo's motor. On a visit to Papeete he was so fascinated by a boat motor that he would not rest till he had collected enough money to buy one. (His determination in saving methodically for nearly a year is still admired as a performance unexcelled on Raroia.)

The motor he had originally seen was a 5 H.P. outboard motor, which would certainly have been well suited to his canoe, but of course he was not content with that, and bought the largest he could get for his money—a 15 H.P. inboard motor. Of course there was no boat on Raroia for which it was suited, but that did not trouble Tutepo particularly. The motor was his, and he was the only person on the island who had a motor. After various misadventures he at last succeeded in starting it, and since that happy moment hardly a week passed without his taking it out and running it, basking in his friends' undisguised envy and admiration.

Buying furniture, bicycles, machines, and other similar things achieves at least a certain prestige. Many, however, throw away as much money on some chance caprice or fixed idea. The Raroians are impulsive and incalculable, and as they live for the moment only, it often happens that they start upon undertakings which cannot possibly be carried out, as a rule not discovering this until it is too late. A typical example is house-building. Everywhere in the village one sees cement foundations of giant size; many of them are mossy and weather-beaten. At first we thought that they were the remains of houses which had been pulled down or destroyed by hurricanes, and we were briefly choked up at the thought of all the Raroians who had perished.

But we deceived ourselves greatly. With one or two exceptions these houses are uncompleted masterpieces and shattered dreams. They have all been built by some villager, who in his delight at an especially good deal has hastened at once to lay the foundations of a new house; and this project, on account of its huge dimensions, lack of material, inability to save systematically, general weariness of the whole business, and a number of similar causes, he has never been able to complete. We have counted more than ten of these monuments to the Raroians' optimism and impulsiveness, and only in one case have we been able to discover that the building has served any reasonable purpose. Tatehau uses his imposing foundations, three feet high, as a pigsty!

Cement, however, is useful not merely for laying the foundations of houses, but can, as is known, be employed for countless other purposes, which the Raroians unfortunately have discovered. Most of them, in fact, suffer from an unlucky love of cement. Once, I found Rauri digging a ditch across his piece of land. This was undeniably a curious occupation for a Polynesian, and I questioned him closely as to what he meant to do.

"It's not to be a ditch," my foster father explained, "but a wall."

"A wall? But you've no neighbors."

"No, that's right, but this is to be a wall to keep the weeds out."

"To keep the weeds out?"

"Yes, there are so many weeds outside, and they're always getting into the garden," Rauri replied emphatically and went on digging till his back creaked.

I felt a little anxious for Rauri's sanity and asked his son-in-law what he thought of his plans.

"Pooh!" he replied. "It's just that he's got hold of a few bags of cement. He's built so many houses and foundations that he had to think of something else. He's like so many others here. He acts first and thinks afterward. When the wall is finished, he'll laugh at the whole thing. *Aita peapea!*"

The wall never was finished, but Rauri laughed at it none the less for that.

Another important item of expenditure is liquor and merrymaking. Out of consideration for the natives, the authorities long ago forbade all selling of alcoholic beverages in the Tuamotu Islands, but as liquor is sold freely in Tahiti, it is naturally impossible to secure respect for the prohibition. The Tuamotuans not only learn to drink during their visits to Papeete but get all their smuggled liquor from that place. The customs men do search the schooners when they sail from Papeete, and the fines are as high as 1,000 Tahiti francs (about $16) for every liter (about one quart) that is confiscated, but there are many hiding places on board a schooner; and since the schooner can always take liquor on board after leaving Tahiti, the traffic flourishes pretty well unhindered. That the Raroians have to pay dearly for this smuggling is a matter of course, and the price of a liter of rum—the most popular drink—usually varies between 600 and 1,000 Tahiti francs, or from $9 to $16. (The price at Papeete is $2.80.) Characteristically enough, the Raroians are less indignant over the price than over the rum sometimes being mixed with water or tea.

Some reformers, anxious for the natives' pocketbooks and health, put forward a proposal that beer should be admitted in the Tuamotu Islands. The authorities decided to make an experiment, and it would certainly have turned out well if they had introduced a rationing system at the same time.

They failed to do this, and the result was that the islands were flooded with beer. The good people of Raroia could hardly believe their eyes when they saw cases of beer in great piles on board the schooners, and when they heard that each case contained forty-eight bottles and yet cost so absurdly little as 1,200 Tahiti francs (about $19), they immediately bought ten cases each.

For several months they ignored flour, biscuits, cloth, and cement and put all their money into beer in the not unwarranted fear that such a happy state of things could not last long. The festivities at last assumed such proportions that the authorities canceled the permission to import beer. As a memento of these times there are still thousands of beer bottles in the village, which have been put to good use. The Raroians use them as borders to their flower beds, and even these bottles play a certain part in the social prestige system. If the bottles had contained only cheap beer, the labels are turned round to face inward, but if they had contained first-class, expensive beer, the labels are left facing outward.

If by some chance any money remains after all the thoughtless purchases and merrymaking, the Raroians do not hesitate a moment as to how they will use it. Papeete is only a few days' journey from Raroia, and at Papeete there are always unbounded possibilities of obtaining still more attractive things and continuing the junketing. The shops are full of trash from all quarters of the globe, the bars are open from morning till night, the taxicabs are always ready to drive those who have money, and there is a fresh program at the two movie houses almost every evening. They stay at Papeete as long as they have a franc left, and almost always have to travel home on credit.

The Raroians' charming way of doing business with one another shows, even more clearly than all this careless spending, how happily and fundamentally ignorant they are of our modern money system and ideas of competition. Tara, a man of thirty-five, had returned to the island after more than ten years in Tahiti. As he had been foolish enough to dispose of all his land when he left Raroia, he wanted to buy a new piece of land with enough coconut palms to supply his needs.

The only person who was willing to sell was Tekura, and Tara gladly paid him 50,000 francs ($800) for a piece of land which he had never seen and the exact size of which Tekura did not know. Of course no contract was drawn up. After a time Tara found that his newly acquired piece of land was too small, and that the income from copra was sufficient only for drink and feasting but not for food and other secondary expenditures. He complained to Tekura, who was much distressed, as he had absolutely no idea of cheating Tara.

As Tekura had no more land to spare, and naturally had drunk up all the purchase money, he did not quite know at first what he should do to help his unlucky buyer, but after thorough reflection he hit on an excellent solution. Tekura had so many friends who ate at his house that he could use a cook. Would Tara not be his cook? This would solve his food problem, and he would be able to use his copra money for other and more important things. Tara was willing, and since that day neither party has had anything to complain of.

Not even those who claim to be businessmen have succeeded in becoming particularly shrewd—luckily. On one of the first occasions when we went over to Temake to do business, he said: "Haven't you anything better to eat than canned food? Take this fish instead. It's fresh, for I've just caught it."

We thought this was a gesture of welcome, but that can hardly have been the case, for this act was repeated even though each time he lost a sale.

However, Temake is a regular calculating businessman compared with Tukaoko and Rehua. Tukaoko's story is the saddest. Last year he had the idea of opening a shop. The stores kept by Temake and the Chinese certainly provided amply for the Raroians' needs, and there did not seem to be any great prospect of another one paying its way, but such petty considerations counted for nothing with Tukaoko. He built with much trouble and expense a shining new galvanized-iron house, which he painted blue and yellow outside and green inside. He placed along the walls shelves of the finest wood from Tahiti, and on the door a board with his name in large black letters. All this cost a lot of money, and when Tukaoko at last reached the point of laying in a stock of goods, he found to his great distress that he had not a franc left.

Tukaoko easily consoled himself, however, with the thought that as soon as he had made a few tons of copra he would get going in earnest. He scraped together by degrees a fairly imposing sum and went to Tahiti. Evidently he quite forgot the object of his journey, for positively the only thing he brought back to Raroia was the memory of a splendid time with many parties, motor trips, and visits to bars. This happened a few years ago. His shop is still as shining and colorful as ever, and although Tukaoko still talks at great length of the wonderful stocks he is going to lay in next time he goes to Tahiti, it looks as if his friends were right when they said compassionately: "Tukaoko was a fool to spend so much money on his shop. He'd have done better to drink it."

Rehua's story is a little different and according to Raroian standards not nearly so sad. Rehua also suddenly wanted to open a shop. But, rendered wise by Tukaoko's misadventure, he did not build a new shop but simply moved his old grandmother to a relation's household and established himself in her wooden house, which had a good position for a shop. As he had just come back from one of the small islands with a good load of copra, he was able to make large purchases from one of the schooners; and soon canned goods, gym shoes, soap, and biscuits were arranged neatly and in good order on shelves newly cut from packing-box lids. Despite this good start, however, things went no better for Rehua than for Tukaoko. One of his neighbors told us why:

"To keep a shop one must be able to count and write well, but Rehua both counts and writes badly. He bought a whole lot of goods at once, and so he could not remember how much he had paid for the different things. And when he set himself to work out how much each thing cost, he worked it out wrong. He sold beef for eighteen francs a tin although he had paid twenty francs for it himself on board the schooner. But he had forgotten that. It was the same with many other things. His relations always got everything free. Rehua has many relations. Each month he took in less and less money. At last he had not many goods left and no money to buy fresh things with. Then he did not want to be a merchant any longer, but gave a great party for us all. In two days we ate up all there was left in the shop."

All things considered, Rehua, Tukaoko, Temake, Tutepo,

and all their relations are lucky not because they have so much money to throw away recklessly, but because if necessary they can do without it altogether—even do without it joyfully. For example, the great depression at the beginning of the 1930's had repercussions even in the South Seas and for several years the Raroians had no income. In other parts of the world unemployment was a great and tragic problem. But it afflicted none of the Raroians. When they no longer had any flour, coffee, biscuits, or beef, they returned to their ancestors' simple way of life and ate fish, sea birds, eggs, roots, and coconuts. Instead of suffering, they were all the healthier for it.

Indeed, they could not buy any furniture, bicycles, machines, or other fine manufactured wares, but on the other hand they were free of all the tedious work of copra-making and had more time for singing and dancing! The way in which the Raroians met this world crisis is the most positive indication that money has very little effect on the happiness of this enviable island. It is good to have money, but if it suddenly disappears it does not matter much. *Aita peapea!*

The Doctor Can't Come

WE HAD not been on Raroia for more than a few weeks when a loud report, which sounded more like an explosion than anything, reverberated throughout the village. Probably someone fishing with dynamite, we thought, and went out to look at the spectacle. But we had not gone far before we discovered that, whatever it was, it was not fishing with dynamite.

There was not a living soul on the beach; all the villagers seemed to have assembled at Tutepo's house a little way off. The women were waving large palm leaves, the men were all talking at once, the children were running to and fro shrieking; even the dogs seemed to have been infected with the general excitement, for they were leaping and howling like mad creatures. Marie-Thérèse and I started to run, for the natives' peculiar behavior indicated an unusual turn of events. When we came nearer, we saw Tutepo stretched out on the ground, apparently lifeless.

"What has happened?" we asked Tchetu, who seemed

to be the only one with any degree of self-possession.

"Tutepo was filling his engine with gasoline, and all of a sudden it went bang!"

"Was it going?"

"Yes, it was going very well, but then all of a sudden, when he began to pour in gasoline, it went bang, and he began to burn."

Tutepo had severe burns on both legs, his chest, and one arm. A couple of the men were rubbing the burns with their dirty fingers, while his wife and daughters were fanning him with palm leaves. We stopped this maltreatment, and while I was rolling him up in what clothes and copra sacks I could get hold of, Marie-Thérèse ran to fetch our handbook on first aid, which, we felt, ought to contain something about the treatment of burns.

We searched in the chapter on burns and frostbite and read: "Take off clothes. If they have stuck to the wound, clip round them and leave the material. Cover the wounds with vaseline or oil. *Call a doctor immediately.*"

I could not help smiling a little when I read the last piece of advice. The nearest doctor lived at Papeete, four hundred miles away, and there was no sailing boat at Raroia which could make such a long voyage.

"The best thing is to try several different medicines and treatments," said Tehetu, "for then one often finds out at last which is the right one."

Her advice was a good deal wiser than it sounded, but as it happened we did not think we needed to experiment on Tutepo. We greased him with vaseline from top to toe, and to the horror of the spectators, wrapped him up in the household's best bedspread. Next day he was in great pain and had such enormous blisters that he resembled a balloon more than anything. We saw that he drank extra quantities of nonalcoholic liquids and kept him well vaselined for days. A few weeks later we pronounced him cured. But the happy result was probably due as much to his own constitution as to our vaseline.

After this successful cure patients began to flock to us as if we were licensed doctors, or better still, famous faith healers. Our medical knowledge was naturally rather hazy, but at all events we could read what was in our medical books, and we did have some ideas of anatomy and hygiene, which was hardly the case with the Raroians. To be able to deal with the rush, we fixed visiting hours and installed our medicine chest on the veranda, sending, as we did so, a grateful thought to Dr. Carson in San Francisco.

It was due, in fact, to Dr. Carson and good luck that our medicine chest was so well filled. Some days before our departure from San Francisco an employee in the shipping office suddenly discovered that we lacked certain certificates of vaccination, without which we should not be able to land at Papeete. We had indeed, during the past year, been inoculated at least twice in each case against typhus, paratyphus, diphtheria, smallpox, and a host of other unpronounceable diseases, but we had no certificates to show this, and, we were assured, the certificates were the most important matter, not the actual vaccination.

We therefore trudged off to a skyscraper twenty-six floors high, all of whose twenty-six floors seemed to be occupied by doctors and dentists. The doctors had odd and the dentists even numbers. A staff of operators, directed by a nurse, was in continual contact with all the reception rooms and distributed the patients so that they got to the right specialist and the time of waiting was made as short as possible. The nurse listened to us in a friendly manner and announced rapidly and with machinelike precision: "Vaccination against tropical diseases, Room 1735, Floor 17, Dr. Carson is waiting."

Half a minute later we were there and Dr. Carson was receiving us at the door. He greeted us as cordially as if we had been friends from childhood, produced a file, and said:

"Let me see, French Oceania. You will be vaccinated against smallpox and diphtheria."

While he was preparing his syringes, he changed the subject of our conversation easily and gracefully, and we were soon in the middle of a detailed account of the weather on the West Coast, the miserable climate of the eastern states, the construction of the Golden Gate Bridge, and the growth of San Francisco since the earthquake in 1906. There followed a thorough discussion of Marshall Aid and the postwar economic problems in Europe while, smilingly and almost casually, he pushed the syringes into us with precision and skill. Then he began to relate his experiences during the war, in the Pacific, and to describe the best methods of protecting ourselves against the dysentery and amoebae of the tropics. Just as we were leaving, he stopped us, opened a large wall cupboard, and took out an armful of sample medicines.

"Look here," he said, "I know what it's like in the South Seas. You can never get enough medicine."

Dr. Carson was perfectly right, and his sample medicines —like those from an equally friendly Seattle dentist—immediately supplied a great and long-felt need on the island. The only remedies known to the Raroians when we arrived were aspirin and iodine, and they had few boxes or bottles of these. Temake did have a small store of medicines, but all were of doubtful value. We inspected it one day at Temake's request, and as the pillboxes and bottles were stowed away all over the house in crates and under beds, the whole family joined in the search for them.

"Look, here's my cough mixture," Tehetu cried, holding up a dusty bottle. "I'll take a dose now."

"No, stop," Temake protested at once, "that's not your cough mixture, it's my lotion. Will you rub my back?"

Tehetu shook the dust off the label and said triumphantly: "You see I was right. It's *penikire.*"

"Yes, of course," said Temake and handed the bottle back to Tehetu, who took a good dose.

"Let me see," I said, taking hold of the bottle. Right across the label was clearly printed: *"Painkiller.* For external use only."

Terava found some pills which she thought were for stomach-ache, or perhaps for fever. She offered to try them on one of the invalids. Similar confusion existed with all Temake's medicines. No one really knew what they should be used for, and the labels were either missing or were illegible. We confiscated the whole store. Dr. Carson's sample medicines were more reliable.

Investigation soon proved that all the Raroians' home remedies were as barbaric as those they had employed when Tutepo burned himself. If anyone had fever and was hot, he ought, according to their naïve thoughts, to cool himself in the lagoon; if anyone had a stomach-ache, he should tie a rope around the waist to prevent the pains from spreading to other parts of the body; and if anyone had attacks of vomiting, the remedy was to stuff into him as much food as possible—and as quickly as possible—to replace the lost nourishment. Surprisingly enough, for a people who lived so close to the sea, they did not even seem to know how a drowning man should be treated. To the best of their recollection, it had only once happened that anyone had been in danger of drowning. This was a Tahitian who, ignorant of local conditions, had tumbled off the outer reef.

"What did you do then?" I asked.

"We laid him on his stomach across a barrel and rolled it backward and forward."

"Did that do any good?"

"No, but then we tied him on tight and rolled the barrel right around once. That did good."

Much has been said and written of the natives' remedies, and even many Europeans are convinced of their healing value (although they naturally prefer to go to a hospital if they are *seriously* ill). This native healing art, in pre-European times, flourished most in Tahiti, where the flora is far richer and more varied than on the barren Tuamotu Islands. But even on Raroia many different recipes were known for the preparation of the few herbs that existed.

I will not deny that many of the herbal medicines which were made in old times had therapeutic value and were relatively effective. But, in the twentieth century, still to prefer these native remedies to the products of modern science is, of course, as out of date and stupid as making fire by rubbing sticks together instead of using matches. As a rule it can be said that in every case—and there are few—in which one can point to an effective native remedy, there are at least half a dozen better ones at the drugstore.

Another thing which must not be forgotten in this connection is that the great majority of the diseases which ravage French Oceania in our days are *new* diseases imported by the white man. For these the Tahitians and the other

Polynesians had, of course, no medicines at all—and still have none. In spite of this the natives almost always prefer, even in these cases, to make a mixture of a few herbs rather than buy *popaa* medicines, and this has even more catastrophic results.

A typical example is seen in the repeated attempts which our friends on Raroia made to cure an ordinary periodic headache. Almost everyone had a different recipe—and everyone claimed, without exception, his was old, authentic, and reliable. But the method was always the same. They boiled their herbs in a large saucepan, strained them, and wrapped them up in a cloth which they bound tightly around their heads. During our long stay we saw innumerable poor wretches, all of whom regularly submitted to this treatment with a sincere belief in its efficacy. The reason why there had so far been no improvement, they assured us, was that it was a long and difficult cure. The real reason, of course, is that they suffer from hereditary syphilis.

But it was even more absurd when they began to mix other substances than herbs. Eggs, for example, enjoy great popularity for their healing powers, and the great majority of the inhabitants of French Oceania firmly and fully believe that all diseases from measles to lunacy can be cured by drinking a raw egg. If, however, one has sharp pains in the chest (pneumonia) the yolk of an egg should, of course, be smeared on the body externally!

The most laughable example of blind confidence in the wonderful effect of their queer remedies was in connection with a case of serious infection, which an anxious relative wanted to cure with "real *raau* Tahiti" instead of penicillin, as we proposed. Curious to see what concoction he had brewed, we told the self-appointed wonder-worker to fetch his *"raau* Tahiti." Beaming with delight, he returned and showed us some soup in a bowl.

"How did you make that medicine?" I asked.

He looked round, as if afraid to betray his miraculous recipe, but at last managed to utter the words:

"If you want to know, it's lemon, condensed milk, and *rakau kurakura* in equal amounts."

The lemon tree was introduced by Cook; condensed milk obviously did not exist before the arrival of the Europeans; and *rakau kurakura* is an ornamental plant which an American botanist imported into French Oceania about twenty years ago. This, then, was what the Raroians called *"raau* Tahiti," a genuine Tahitian medicine which would stop an infection.

The remedies described certainly have the common attribute of being completely harmless, which unfortunately cannot be said of all the mysterious decoctions and treatments which certain native "doctors" prescribe. Unhappily enough there are still here and there in French Oceania charlatans who practice for or without payment, and most of these criminal individuals (who are always shielded by their patients) have a good many lives on their consciences.

One of the most distressing cases I heard of was that of a "magician" who on one occasion tried to cure a baby "who was possessed by the devil" with a decoction of liquor, ashes, crushed shells, and various other ingredients! The outcome was, of course, that the devil survived, but the child died.

On Raroia we were fortunately free from professional healers, and the general level of medical knowledge can in spite of everything be described as above the average, thanks to the wise, devoted work of one or two missionaries.

Another difficulty with which both the missionaries and we had to contend was that even if the patients could be convinced of the superiority of a treatment, they drew back as soon as it was painful. They wanted to be cured, but not if the cure gave them pain or trouble. They then preferred to keep the illness. One of our first patients was a little girl of five who had thorns about three-quarters of an inch long in her neck. The wounds were open and purulent.

"She jumped into a hedge with long thorns in it," her father explained.

"Did it happen a long time ago?" I asked.

"Perhaps two months, perhaps three, I don't know exactly. . . . ."

"But haven't you tried to take them out?"

"Yes, but she screams every time, so I daren't."

We let her scream and took out the thorns.

After this incident we decided to make a tour of the village to see if there were not some invalids who were keeping out of sight. The result was overwhelming. Almost all the villagers had either stomach trouble, toothache, or open infected wounds; many had bad chills and half a dozen had asthma. We also found a woman who had sprained her foot and one case of paralysis.

On a walk to the outskirts of the village, we stopped at old Varoa's house. Sitting in the garden, weeding, was a strange woman—at least we had never seen her before. She introduced herself as Mahia and continued to weed. Marie-Thérèse and I immediately sensed something amiss, for she showed no sign of wanting to invite us into the house. Everywhere else people exhibited with pride their houses, their children, their gardens, and all the other "sights." Mahia energetically declared that unfortunately she had so much weeding to do that she had no time to receive us. This finally convinced us—something was wrong. A Polynesian woman who had no time for a chat because of her work must be abnormal in some way.

We hurried across to Tehei's house and asked the meaning of the woman's mysterious behavior. Tehei hesitated a little, but at last revealed Mahia's secret to us:

"Mahia has trouble in her legs. She can't walk. Once when she was a little girl, she climbed up into a coconut palm. As she was not used to climbing palms, she tumbled down. When she tried to get up she found that her legs were paralyzed. She couldn't walk home, and she was so far from home that no one heard her calling. Next day her papa found her. Since then she has crawled about like a child. Not in the daytime of course. Then she sits in the garden and weeds. But at night she crawls over to some other house to talk, or to the assembly house to watch the others dancing."

"But has she never been sent to the hospital at Papeete?"

"Yes, but not till several years after the accident, and then it was too late."

"But why did she wait so long?"

"Because she was afraid the doctor would cut her legs off. She didn't want that. But perhaps someone could work a miracle."

Miracles were not in our province, but we did propose that someone in the village should make her a pair of crutches, and with the help of a drawing Tehei made a pair which would have perfectly fulfilled their purpose. But no one ever saw Mahia use them.

We were hardly more successful in our attempt to cure Kuraingo, who had sprained her foot. When we found her she was sitting on the extreme edge of the veranda dangling her badly swollen foot.

"How long have you had a bad foot?" I asked.

Kuraingo counted on her fingers. "Ten days."

We put the foot in splints as well as we could, established Kuraingo in a corner with her leg in the air, and told her to keep still till further notice. Next day, when we came back to look at her, to our consternation we found her in the kitchen with no splints or bandage on.

"Why have you taken off the splints?" I asked.

"I couldn't walk with them on."

"But you were to lie still."

"Yes, but it's so boring to lie still."

Marie-Thérèse and I withdrew, helpless in the face of Raroian philosophy. This was not the last time that the natives' carelessness and levity aggravated an illness or made it impossible to cure one.

Most distressing of all were not these isolated accidents, but the "national illnesses"—stomach trouble, toothache, and chills. All the old people assured me that stomach disorders and toothache were unknown in their youth, when the inhabitants still lived in the primitive Polynesian manner. In those days their nourishment consisted exclusively of fish, which was often eaten raw; sea birds, which were baked in earth ovens, as cooking pots and frying pans were unknown; turtles; raw mussels; coconuts; pandanus fruits; taro; and pokea—*Portulacca johnii,* a kind of purslane. The only beverages were rain water and coconut juice. Day after day, month after month, year after year, people always ate the same food and thrived on it.

In the last seventy-five years conditions have changed radically. Taro and pokea are no longer grown, raw fish is seldom eaten, and raw mussels hardly at all. The copra schooners have introduced a quantity of new foodstuffs and canned goods, and the Raroians' menu is sadly barbaric. Naturally they still eat a great deal of fish, but it could be said with as much justification that canned corned beef and dumplings are now the favorite dishes. The chief reason for the popularity of these dishes is that they are easy to pre-pare—the meat only needs to be heated up a little and the dumplings consist of a piece of dough which requires only brief cooking. The consumption of coffee and sugar is also alarmingly high. A "normal family" of five persons con-sumes four pounds of coffee a week, and as it is always roasted immediately before use, it is excessively strong.

A typical weekly menu, therefore, with extremely small modifications, consists of the following fare:

MONDAY

Morning meal (8 A.M.) Coffee and biscuits. Coconuts.
Midday meal (3 P.M.) Corned beef, dumplings, and rice. Sauce made of coconut milk and sea water.

TUESDAY

Morning meal Corned beef and dumplings. Coffee.
Midday meal Fish, canned sardines, and coco-nuts. Coffee.

WEDNESDAY

Morning meal Fish, bread, and coconuts. Coffee.
Midday meal Corned beef and rice.

THURSDAY

Morning meal Fish, dumplings, and coconuts. Coffee.

Midday meal	Fish. Sauce made of coconut milk and sea water. Coffee.

FRIDAY

Morning meal	Coffee and biscuits. Coconuts.
Midday meal	Corned beef and dumplings. Coffee.

SATURDAY

Morning meal	Fish with coconut sauce.
Midday meal	Fish, bread, and rice. Coffee.

SUNDAY

Morning meal	Fish, dumplings, and bread. Coffee.
Midday meal	Fish, corned beef, dumplings, and canned peaches. Coffee.

No wonder they have stomach trouble; such important foodstuffs as milk, cheese, butter, and green vegetables are entirely lacking!

To bad diet habits should be added the fact that men, women, and young people of both sexes—all without exception—are chain smokers, and that many have acquired an unquenchable thirst in Papeete bars. When they have no smuggled spirits, they use well-known surrogates, and one of the most popular drinks is hair tonic. Most people seem to be so hardened that they can drink the stuff without any unpleasant consequences. This immunity, unfortunately, does not transfer to all the other peculiar surrogates which the Raroians cheerfully test. One day a little girl came and asked if I would do something for Heiao, who was ill.

"What's the matter with you?" I asked, slightly surprised to find him sitting on the steps of his house, well and in good spirits, chatting with his friends.

"I get drunk whenever I drink water!"

"What kind of water do you drink?"

"Ordinary rain water. Other people who drink it don't get drunk."

"That's queer. Have you drunk anything else?"

Heiao turned and twisted a little and cast down his eyes.

"No—yes—that is, I did drink a little methylated spirit [denatured alcohol] yesterday. I daresay it was stupid, but it was so hard not to. I was getting out a bottle of hair tonic, and I suddenly caught sight of a bottle of methylated spirit. I never put methylated spirit next to hair tonic; it was my wife who did it. As the methylated spirit was there, it occurred to me that it might be better and stronger than hair tonic, so I poured out a glass, mixed it with a little water, and drank it. It was good. But today I get drunk as soon as I drink ordinary water."

The situation was tragicomic and I could not help saying: "But that's a cheap way of getting drunk. I think I'll try a little methylated spirit myself. . . . ."

"No, don't do that," Heiao said in alarm. "Don't do that! I shall never drink anything but hair tonic after this."

To Heiao's disgust I prescribed hot milk.

The result of all the starchy food and the abuse of the hair-tonic bottle, of course, can only be the ruin of stomachs and teeth. The Raroians, I am sure, see where the trouble lies, but find it hard to give up their habits. A grotesque example of this was furnished by Teua, a middle-aged woman who one day came to "consult" us.

"I've got a pain in my chest," she declared.

"Point to where the pain is," I said, knowing from dearly bought experience how vague is the Raroians' knowledge of anatomy.

She pointed to her stomach.

"But that's your stomach, not your chest," I said.

"Perhaps, but that's where the pain is."

"Have you been drinking rum lately?"

"She was drunk all yesterday," her twelve-year-old daughter, who stood by, informed us.

"Have you pain often?"

"Always, but more when I drink rum."

"Stop drinking rum. What do you eat?"

"Beef and dumplings."

"That's why you have a pain in your stomach. Drink hot milk in the mornings, eat fish, macaroni, and canned green vegetables in the middle of the day, and a few coconuts for supper."

"Can't I eat chocolate and canned peaches? I don't like milk, and I shall only get worse if I eat macaroni."

"Have you ever tried macaroni?"

"No, but other people have, and they have been ill."

"Perhaps that was because they were ill before. Take this list and eat nothing but what I have written on it."

Teua took the list and looked at it gloomily. Clearly it was not what she had expected.

"Ugh, a diet," she said. "I've a diet list already which they gave me at the hospital in Papeete. Haven't you any medicine which can cure me right away, so that I can eat what I like?"

Teua was not alone in seeking a miraculous medicine which could cure all illnesses in a moment. The Raroians have seen how the missionaries have cured infections and fevers with sulfas, and they have drawn the somewhat hasty conclusion that such remedies exist for all diseases. That one must practice hygiene and ordinary precautions, they will not understand.

This absence of common health-sense was particularly irritating where illnesses caused by colds were concerned. Strangely enough, the natives of a South Sea island are subject to the common cold just as any American is during a wet, slushy spring. As in so many other cases, the main causes of colds were carelessness and neglect.

The day temperature was usually between 86° and 95° in the shade, and the night temperature between 68° and 77°. This difference was very noticeable, and we found it necessary to use woolen blankets at night. Raroians, on the contrary, used only one thin cotton covering and most often slept on the floor in their drafty houses. Further, during violent rain and squalls the temperature fell swiftly and the wind became unpleasantly cold. Raincoats were unknown and, what was worse, the Raroians often went about in the wind in wet clothes for a whole day without troubling to change. Hardly a day passed without our hearing somebody with a hacking cough, and on several occasions the whole village was chilled and feverish.

Another common illness which may also be due to neglect is asthma. We did out best to convince sufferers that they should stay in bed and put on warm clothes. But as soon as our backs were turned the patients were running about. To stay in bed for as much as a day, or even a few hours, is more than any Raroian will stand.

The missionary who introduced the use of cups as a remedy for colds was more successful. Cups are small glass vessels which are fixed tight to the skin by dropping in a scrap of burning cotton, whereby a vacuum is created. The natives took great delight in seeing the wisps of cotton burn and the skin swell up; the cups achieved tremendous popularity!

Unfortunately, the thoughtful missionary who taught the Raroians to use cups against colds at the same time introduced enemas as an offensive against gastric disorders. But this was too much medical knowledge at one time for the good islanders. Most of them confused the two treatments or drew the rather hasty conclusion that one was as good as the other. Often we found a sick person using a cup for a stomach-ache and just as often a poor wretch with a cold trying to cure himself with an enema.

Although this interchange did not make anyone better, it made no one worse; and the missionary had much better luck with his enemas and cups than the doctor who tried to teach the natives the use of such simple remedies as iodine and cotton. The doctor explained in clear language that iodine was meant for the cleansing of wounds and even described in detail the manner in which the wisp of cotton should be dipped into the solution of iodine and rubbed against the wound. Raroians all declared that the whole thing was childishly simple and wondered why no one had taught them to use iodine earlier.

To start with, all went well. Wounds were cleansed as never before, and iodine flowed in rivers. Then someone got eczema and had the idea that iodine might be good for eczema too. It proved to be excellent for this purpose, and soon they began to use iodine for warts, sunburn, muscular pains, sprains, and various other troubles. Obviously, the Raroians said to themselves, this was the panacea. Why had no one said that it was good for so many different pains?

Then one day the chief (this happened long before Teka's time) got a fearful stomach-ache. It was evidently some new and peculiar illness, for neither enemas, cups, nor aspirin had any effect. At last he became so weak and ill that he was obliged to go to bed. As he was chief, he had charge of the village's big bottle of iodine, and one night when the pains were attacking him worse than ever, he thought of the new panacea. It had been good for cleansing wounds and curing all external pains, why should it not relieve his stomach pains? He emptied the bottle at a single draught. A few days later he was dead.

"His stomach was burned up and he had terrible pain," added Tehei, who told us the story.

Since this calamity all the islanders have developed a decided repugnance to iodine. Many have even become so frightened of it that if they are given any, they secretly throw it away. This was particularly distressing since almost everyone on Raroia always had open wounds, which often became infected as the result of neglect.

Most frequently of all, the men cut themselves on the coral when fishing on the reef, where the breakers are so violent it is hard to get a footing. These coral wounds were the most difficult to heal, and it was often weeks before we could get the better of them. But they also took long to cure because the Raroians could not refrain from scratching the wounds with their dirty fingers. Some who had heard vaguely that it was not a good thing to touch open wounds with dirty fingers used another and more elaborate technique. They scratched themselves with a comb!

One malady—*kota*—we were never able to conquer. This unpleasant illness begins with an insignificant boil, no bigger than a pea. After a day or two the boil swells up and forms a regular miniature crater as large as a half dollar. If it opens at this stage one is lucky, for then one gets off with only a week or two of severe pain. Often, however, the boil continues to expand, and then sometimes several weeks can pass before it finally opens and the slow process of healing can begin. The pain is so great that it is difficult to move. Marie-Thérèse and I both had boils of this kind several times, and there were periods in which many Raroians were severely afflicted. The cause of these boils is presumably a lack of vitamins, for the natives of Tahiti suffer from them a good deal less.

The lack of medicine and medical care can be ascribed to the same basic conditions which make Raroia so happy and idyllic—the isolation and primitiveness. In other words, the diseases are the reverse side of the coin, the price which the Raroians have to pay for their free and careless existence. But they do not take their illnesses and other afflictions particularly hard; they rather regard them as a necessary evil, which they accept with dignified calm. There is so much to make them happy that occasional sufferings that now and again come their way are mere trifles to be forgotten. They do not seem to be able to take even chronic ailments seriously, as Taipuhia's case shows.

I noticed that he often rubbed his feet with something, and at last asked him what was the matter.

"I've always had an itching in my feet," he said. "Ever since I was a small boy. When I can't stand it any longer, I rub them hard with a stone."

"You'd better take care not to wear out your feet," I advised him, trying not to smile.

"My feet are all right," said Taipuhia. "But I've worn out several stones!"

The bystanders grinned as broadly as Taipuhia.

We gave him vitamin capsules, but they had little effect. Of course, this may have been because he never took them.

Temake's case was a good deal more comic, but also sad. He stopped me one day as I was passing the canvas chair in which, more or less compulsorily, he spent his time.

"Penetito [Bengt], I've got a pain in my back."

"H'm. Perhaps you've been carrying too much copra. Have you had the pain long?"

"Since 1920. My back's hurt me ever since then."

"That's a long time. Have you never been to a doctor when you've been in Papeete?"

"Oh, yes, often."

"Well, what do they say?"

"That it shouldn't hurt me."

"Don't you rub yourself with lotion or something of the kind?"

"No, but my wife irons me every evening."

"Irons you! What do you mean by that?"

"I put on a wet shirt, and then she irons it with a hot iron right on my back."

"Does that do any good?"

"No, and sometimes she burns me."

"But if that's so you'd better stop the treatment."

"Perhaps, but someone at Papeete said it was good for rheumatism."

We tried lotion and coconut oil, but his case was clearly hopeless. The most unhappy part of the story is that he had come through the whole of the First World War and was injured only after his return to Raroia, when a coconut fell on him from a great height. Temake was one of the volunteers from French Oceania who took part in the war, and he had the good luck to return with a whole skin.

According to his own account he had first been somewhere on the Western Front—the names were too queer for him to remember—and afterward "between Greece and Turkey." He returned at the very end of the war, covered with medals for bravery but without having learned a word of French or having been particularly impressed by so-called Western civilization, which is quite understandable. On the same day on which he returned to Raroia he went and lay down to sleep under a coconut palm and a large nut weighing over ten pounds fell on his back.

"I was so unaccustomed to its being dangerous to lie down and sleep on the ground," Temake explained. "During the war we could always sleep on the ground without being afraid of coconuts."

We soon became so used to the light, unconcerned way in which the Raroians took their diseases and ailments generally that we were quite astonished to hear one Sunday loud weeping and a tremendous hubbub at the farther end of the village. What we had long feared had happened— a serious accident.

As always, it was the children who reached our house first but they were so agitated that they could not utter a single sensible word. But immediately after them Tehetu came running and shouting breathlessly:

"There has been a dreadful accident."

It really was dreadful in several respects. Marau, a little girl of four, had begged her uncle to let her sit on the back of his bicycle when he was having a ride down the "main street," and as there was no carrier on the bicycle, she naturally slid back down the fender and caught her foot in the hub. Before her uncle could stop, the big toe had been crushed. But worse, the foot became more mutilated when, in his frenzy, he pried it loose instead of lifting off the chain.

When he came along carrying her in his arms, the blood was pouring from the shapeless mass of flesh full of broken-off pieces of bone that had once been a big toe. We cleansed and cut with the courage of desperation, while the little girl uttered piercing screams. Of course we could not save the toe, but we did succeed in stopping the flow of blood and cleansing the wound fairly well.

After bandaging the tiny foot, we carried the sobbing child to her home. We thought that this distressing event would at least make her parents and relations for a time less frivolous than usual, but we deceived ourselves mightily, and even this tragic accident ended in sheer comedy. The parents had been so desperate and agonized when we were attending the child that we ourselves had tears in our eyes and were obliged to send them away. But when we called to see our patient a few hours later, they were sitting there chatting with almost the whole population round them.

"Really her losing her big toe doesn't matter so much," said her father philosophically. "One can walk quite well without a big toe, and girls never play football."

We were not so optimistic. A large piece of bone was sticking out of the wound, which had to be cut away before the wound could heal. The only place where the child could be properly treated was Papeete. We explained this to the parents, Rakenui and Titi, who declared with suspicious eagerness that they would go anywhere for the child's sake. They agreed to go on the next schooner.

On one point Rakenui had slight misgivings. He had, of course, already dissipated all the money he had received for selling his copra on board the last schooner a week or two before. But he found what, in his opinion, was an excellent solution to the problem. He had recently covered his house with shining galvanized iron. If he went to Papeete now, he reasoned, he would naturally not need the house during the time he was away; and as he did not need the house, he might as well sell the galvanized iron to one of the merchants. When he came back, he could always make copra and buy new iron.

"But you've got your brother and his family in the house too," we objected, when he described his plan to us. "What do you think he'll say if you pull off the galvanized iron?"

"Oh, he can come to Papeete too."

Rakenui asked his brother, and it appeared that neither he nor his family had anything against such a solution to the problem. Soon the whole family was busy taking the house to pieces and carrying the bits over to the merchant. Pulling away the galvanized iron was all right, for it made such a funny noise when it hit the ground; but to carry it the three hundred yards to the shop was a task which went a good deal slower.

Then Rakenui's brother found that if he held a sheet of the metal in front of him, it acted as a sail. This discovery stimulated them all, and soon they were having "sailing races" among the palms, amid laughter and shouting. The wind, however, was unsteady, and all of a sudden Rakenui's ten-year-old boy tumbled down with a crash and cut his foot on one of the iron sheets. We were not absolutely unprepared for such an accident and dashed out like lightning to bandage him.

"He'll be good company for Marau," cried Rakenui. "She's beginning to be tired of being alone."

I carried the boy into the house and laid him beside his sister, and Marie-Thérèse brought a prop to hold his leg high in the air. The sight of the two invalids, in the same positions, was too much for the Raroians. They all laughed till they nearly choked.

Apart from the fact that the house became so drafty that nearly all the residents caught colds, all went well and at last the schooner came. When we went down to the shore to say good-by to Marau and Rakenui, to our astonishment, we found the ship's boat full of Raroians. Besides Rakenui and his brother and family of five children, there were a brother-in-law and a distant cousin and his wife. All these were evidently going to accompany Marau to Papeete.

Since this was a trip undertaken for medical reasons, we decided to send another invalid who had long caused us anxiety. Tiapara, a youth of twenty, had had a curious swelling over one eye for a month. At times the swelling disappeared, but every time it returned it was larger and the headaches more severe. According to Tiapara himself he had contracted the illness from a hat.

We had searched vainly in our medical books to find some more rational explanation of the mysterious swelling, and had used up half our medical chest in experiments without any visible results. It was, therefore, obviously a case for the hospital at Papeete. Tiapara was more than willing to go, and so that he might not feel utterly lonely and abandoned in the big town, two sisters and an aunt immediately volunteered to accompany him. When at last the schooner sailed amid hymn-singing and guitar-playing, there was a decided majority of Raroians among the passengers.

Six weeks later Tiapara and his relatives came back. But none of the other Raroians could be discovered on board the schooner. Of course, the whole village was down on the quay to receive the travelers, and these had hardly got ashore before a hail of questions began to descend upon them.

What was it like at Papeete? Had they met uncle this or cousin that? What movies had they seen? Had they seen the mail airplane? Were there any big ships in the harbor? How often had Rakenui been drunk? Had they brought back any rum? Curiosity was unbounded.

Tiapara replied eloquently to all questions and related his adventures in the big town with sweeping gestures. After a time he ran out of glowing phrases and I had an opportunity of asking how he was.

"I'm all right," said Tiapara with a smile.

"What did the doctor say your trouble was?"

"I don't know. I haven't been to the doctor."

"You haven't!" Marie-Thérèse and I exclaimed in unison.

"No, when I got to Papeete the swelling had disappeared, so I didn't think there was any sense in throwing away money on expensive doctoring. But it's begun to hurt a bit again . . . ."

"H'm. And how's Marau?"

"All right. They cut off the bone at the hospital and sewed up the wound. It had almost healed when we left."

"Excellent. But why haven't Rakenui and his relations come back with her?"

"Why, you understand, there's so much to see in Papeete, and they haven't seen it all yet. Rakenui came down to the schooner when we left and said they meant to stay at least till the Fourteenth of July to see all the celebrations."

It was February then!

Sons of Cannibals

DURING their time of greatness, before any European ship had yet found the way to their islands, the Polynesians possessed a uniquely rich and comprehensive oral literature. It was based on the collective secular and religious experiences of countless generations, and large parts of it would in our day be classified as theology, philosophy, history, geography, or astronomy, while the remainder consisted either of prayers, poems, love songs, or heroic verse.

A special class of scholars and priests watched closely to see that not a word was changed, and acted as living books of reference and teachers. In this way the Polynesians successfully performed the feat of preserving and passing on the whole of their vast oral literature, which if it had been put on paper would certainly fill a small-town library.

Only a small part of this literary treasure, which in many cases had been inherited by generation after generation for more than a thousand years, survived the chaos and destruction which were the immediate result of the Polynesians' first contact with Western culture. Most priests and scholars, like chiefs and other political and military leaders, succumbed in the furious wars and epidemics following the violent break between old and new; and those who survived soon found that new leaders had taken their place.

Overpowered by the white men's superior material culture, the Polynesians quickly abandoned not only their stone tools and bark clothes, but also their old gods and their old faith. All that was new and strange became good and admirable, while all that was Polynesian came to be regarded only as something primitive, barbaric, and inferior. The new generation, which strove to be civilized and Christian, took no interest in its fathers' culture and traditions, and most of the old men, therefore, took their knowledge with them to their graves. Some few conscientious and understanding men—generally missionaries and explorers—tried to record the Polynesian traditions before they fell into oblivion, but what they were able to save was only a fraction.

This rapid transformation of Polynesian society took place on most of the islands as long ago as the end of the eighteenth or the beginning of the nineteenth century, and if, for example, one asks a present-day Polynesian in Tahiti or Hawaii about the past, he generally knows no more than the American man in the street knows about early colonial history. Rather less.

But in this respect, as in others, the Tuamotu group is an exception. While on practically all the other groups of islands in Polynesia the good old heathen era lies 100 to 150 years back in time, it is only 60 or 70 years since it slowly began to disappear in the Tuamotu Islands. Consequently, scattered here and there over the atolls of this group of islands, a few sages are still to be found who not only know all the traditions of their nation but have even seen its native culture with their own eyes. There are certainly not more than a dozen of these old men in the whole group, and significantly enough they are found only in the eastern half of the group—that part which lies farthest away from Tahiti and civilization. Most of them are the last of the old ruling or learned class, and they themselves were either chiefs or priests before the old social system collapsed.

As the younger generations take no interest whatever in the old literature and the old traditions, it is only a question of time before even this first-hand knowledge of a Polynesian people as it used to be is lost. And as far as it can be judged, this period is not more than about ten years distant.

In the 1930's the Bernice P. Bishop Museum at Honolulu, which houses the world's largest collection of Polynesian ethnographic objects and documents, was quick to sense the impending loss and sent out two expeditions which succeeded in preserving a vast number of traditions, genealogies, and songs. After the thorough work done by the Bishop Museum's expeditions, and knowing how swiftly all memories of old times disappear, we naturally did not expect to find any ethnographic material of great value on Raroia. Our intention was to do research work of another type. But to be on the safe side, we made a tour of the village immediately after our arrival.

Someone had told us before we started from Tahiti that there was a *tahunga,* or learned man, named Tei-hote-pangi on the island, but all our inquiries were met with head-shakings. All the Raroians declared emphatically that they could not remember anyone of that name, and tried instead to interest us in questions of the day. The old heathen times must have been something awful, they thought, with no flour, no bicycles, no proper clothes—and if by any chance anyone knew anything about them, we would surely be bored by his tale. But if, in spite of their admonitions, we still wanted to hear about these awful times, we ought to apply to Temorere, who had a number of books full of traditions and genealogies and was a mighty learned man.

We sought out Temorere at once, and he declared himself willing to answer all our questions. His books, however, containing genealogies and traditions written down by his father some time in the 1870's, he would on no account show us. This did not surprise us much, for the Polynesians generally regard their family books as private documents, which no outside person should see. This attitude survives from pre-European times when genealogies were a family secret and served as a kind of title to possession: by correctly reciting the family's genealogy a man showed that he was the legitimate heir to the family titles and lands, and to betray it to some other person amounted to giving away these privileges. All land is now protected by a legal system similar to Western methods, but the attitude regarding genealogies still persists.

We made the best of the situation and paid regular visits to Temorere to try to extract from him, bit by bit, the information we wanted. Each time we called on him, he would receive us with great ceremony; and when we asked a question he would put on his homemade spectacles of window glass, withdraw to a little side room, take out his books, and mumble to himself for a long time; then he would finally reappear with the answer. The songs he gave us tallied quite well with what we had had from other

Raroians, but the rest of his information about the old culture was both confusing and contradictory. We gradually became more and more suspicious, but of course it was impossible for us to compare his statements with the original text, for, despite all our flattery and attempts at persuasion, he refused to show us his books.

After some months Temorere was obliged to make a journey to Tahiti. He left the house in his nephew's charge, and as the nephew and I were particularly good friends, a time came when I could not resist the temptation to persuade him to show me Temorere's books. (In science, as in many other things, the end justifies the means.) The nephew was surprisingly easy to handle and soon came creeping round to us one evening with the ardently desired books.

Eagerly I opened one of them. The first page was blank —so was the next, likewise the third, fourth, and *all* the rest! I opened the next book. It too was empty, but for one genealogy and a few songs. It was the same with all the books. *Temorere was simply a fraud!*

The next person we tried was old Varoa, the former chief of the village, who was considered to be the oldest inhabitant of the island. Not to miss any important detail because of language difficulties, we asked Tufaka to come with us as interpreter. Varoa had very vague ideas of our method of calculating time, but by cross-examining him about all the cyclones he remembered and comparing what he told us with the official reports published by the meteorological station in Tahiti, we found that when the cyclone of 1878 swept over Raroia he was already married.

This meant that he was at any rate over ninety and ought therefore to be able to tell us about the old conditions. He also assured us that he had often taken part in heathen religious ceremonies and even showed us the place where the principal *marae,* or cult site, on Raroia had been. But the worthy Varoa could not supply either direct answers or a connected description of bygone days. His memory was weak, and he was often at a loss for words. Furthermore, he muttered to himself continually. At last he said:

"Come again early tomorrow morning when it's still cool. It's the sun that makes me muddle-headed."

But sunrise the next day found Varoa just as confused. He again lost the thread of his narrative time after time. In his more lucid moments he had many interesting things to relate, but in between he sat for long periods immersed in his own thoughts or held endless monologues. We had just given up hope of getting any real information out of him when all of a sudden he woke up and said:

"But why don't you ask Te Iho?"

"Who is Te Iho?" I asked.

"He's the last *tahunga,* the last learned man. He knows everything."

"Strange," I said, "but I cannot remember having met anyone of that name."

"That's probably because Te Iho never goes out," said Tufaka. "He sits at home thinking all day."

Names kept whirring about in my mind. Te Iho had a curiously familiar ring.

"What is his full name?" I asked.

"Te-Iho-a-te-pange," chanted Varoa.

Of course, that was it—the correct name for Tei-hote-pangi, the *tahunga* whom we had heard about in Tahiti and had given up as dead after questioning the Raroians.

Led by Tufaka we hurried across the village, and soon stood outside Tapakia's foster son's house, where, we were told, Te Iho lived. "Where is Te Iho?" Tufaka and I asked almost simultaneously.

Tapakia pointed to a small shed a little way off. We went over and peeped in. The walls were of unpainted galvanized iron, and the only ornament was a soiled picture of Jesus, gaudily colored like an American cigarette advertisement. In one corner stood a torn sack of kapok "cotton," the contents of which lay scattered all over the place. The floor consisted of rough unplaned boards which evidently had never been worn smooth by a scrub brush. In the middle of the floor an old man lay asleep with an empty tin can as pillow!

We called to him, and he scrambled up and came out into the sunshine. In the half-light of the shed I had not been able to distinguish his features properly, and when I now saw him in the full light of day, I was so astonished that I almost burst out: "But it's a white man!"

His complexion was no darker than that of a southern European; his hair and beard were grayish-white, and his features were not too foreign for him to have played Santa Claus in any American home.

He greeted us amiably with the usual *ia ora na,* and sat down quietly in the doorway waiting for us to explain our errand. We went straight to the point and asked him if he would tell us something about old times. Te Iho leaned forward as if he had not heard, or had not understood our request, looked at us long and curiously and, quite unexpectedly, began to laugh. Then he grew serious again and said:

"Forgive me, but I can't help laughing when you *popaa* ask me about the old times; nobody else on the island ever does."

He sat for a moment or two in silence, and then continued:

"Look at my hair. It has been white now since Tapakia was a little boy sailing toy boats made of the halves of coconuts. He's grown up now and himself has children playing on the shore of the lagoon. When my hair first began to grow white I thought: I am an old man now and I feel tired. I have seen Raroia in the old times, when the people still worshiped the old gods and the old customs were still good. I am the last who has the old knowledge. When I die, the old times will die with me. I shall collect the young people round me and tell them all that I have seen and heard, so that they and their children shall not be ignorant of where they came from and what their forefathers achieved and how they lived.

"After I had taught the young people all the old songs and dances I could—and they had liked them—I asked them to listen to what their forefathers had thought and experienced. But they just laughed and said: 'Pooh, your boring old stories are not true. We'd rather hear stories about motorcars and airplanes and ships.' As my sight was bad even then, I told Tapakia to write down all that I narrated in a big book, but after a few days he got tired, and no one else wanted to, or had time. Then I thought: Perhaps it is God's will that the old times shall die with me.

"But one day there came a boat with three *popaa* on board. They came straight to my house and asked if I would tell them all that I knew. Then I realized that God had not forgotten me and that he had sent the three *popaa* to write down the old knowledge, so that all should understand that it was as important as all that is in the Bible. I therefore replied that I would gladly tell all that I remembered. They were very pleased and promised to come back soon.

"When they had gone, all the young people came and said that as three *popaa* had come especially to write down accounts of the old times, these accounts were certainly worth money. They begged me to teach them what I knew so that they too might become rich, and for several weeks I taught them just as Moses taught his people the law on the stone tablets. Tapakia actually wrote a whole book full of my teaching, but of course that was still only a small part of all the old knowledge. He gave up before he had finished, and many more of them soon began to grow tired. In a few months all had abandoned me and forgotten what I had said. For a long time I waited eagerly for the three *popaa,* but they never came back."

Te Iho smiled sadly and produced an old tin can from an invisible hiding place. He felt about inside it for a long time and at last fished out the stump of a cigarette, which he lighted carefully. Then he gazed reflectively in front of him and continued:

"Since that time fifteen years have passed, or perhaps twenty or twenty-five. How can I tell? No one has asked me about the old times until today—and again it is a *popaa* who asks. Perhaps there is some hidden meaning in this. I will gladly tell you all you want to know."

We asked him to tell us everything that he had once meant to teach the youth of the village.

"It is a long story," said the old man, blinking his eyes, "for it begins with the creation."

We assured him that we had nothing against this. After many moments' hesitation, Te Iho at last began to speak. He began to recite an old *fangu,* or religious song. Naturally, when translated into English prose, most of its beauty is lost, but its contents ran roughly thus:

"In the beginning there was only void. Neither darkness nor light, neither land nor sea, neither sun nor sky, yet existed. All was one great, silent, motionless void. Countless ages passed. But then the void began to move. It seethed and grew and at last was transformed into Po, the great night without limit and shape. All was darkness, a deep impenetrable darkness.

"Again countless ages passed, and then Po also began to change. Strange new forces were active, the night was transformed into sea, and in the depths of the sea a new substance was formed. To begin with it was only sand, but the sand became firm soil which grew upward. At last Fakahotu, the earth mother, revealed herself. Fakahotu spread herself out and became a great land, the first which ever existed. Over Fakahotu, the earth mother, rested Atea, the sky father.

"New ages passed and then from the union of the earth and sky, two sons were born—Tane and Tangaroa. They looked round them and found that there was neither light nor space. 'Let us separate Atea from Fakahotu,' said Tane to Tangaroa. They tried to lift up Atea but could not move him. Soon, however, the Ru brothers were born, and with their help the attempt was more successful.

"The Ru brothers with Tane and Tangaroa formed a living pyramid by standing on each others' shoulders. Slowly they lifted up Atea, who at last arched himself as a sky high above the earth. In this way the three spheres were formed —Rangi-po, or the region beneath the surface of the earth and sea; Rangi-marama, the world we live in; and Rangi-reva, the sky above us. Tangaroa became ruler of the sea, while Tane fixed the stars, the sun, and moon in the sky and became their ruler.

"Gods, earth, sky, and sea were created. In the sea plants, animals, small creatures, and fish began to increase. The only thing lacking was man. Then Tangaroa created Tiki, who thus was our ancestor. After a time Tiki wished no longer to be alone, and then Tangaroa created a woman from a heap of sand and gave her to Tiki. Her name was therefore Hina-ahu-one, 'Hina made of sand.'

"From Tiki and Hina all mankind is descended. Time passed and generation followed generation. At last was born Maui, who was the greatest of our forefathers. Maui found that the days were too short and therefore caught the sun with a kind of lasso. He did not let it go again till it had promised to move more slowly. Maui also created the first dog and gave fire to men, but his greatest deed was done when he fished up new land from the depths of the sea. With a large hook fastened to a long line he drew up Raroia and all the other Tuamotu Islands. In this way Maui completed the creation."

We thanked Te Iho and came back next day curious to hear the continuation of the story. Te Iho had promised to tell us the history of the whole island and people right down to our days. To get him to continue where he had stopped the day before I asked him:

"But if it was Maui who fished up Raroia and all the other islands round about here, where did the creation of man take place?"

Te Iho looked at me with his humorous friendly eyes and said, laughing quietly:

"Don't you know that? The *popaa* usually know that it took place in Paradise."

Then he grew serious and continued:

"But I often wonder if your Garden of Eden is not the scene of our creation too. All things considered, may not Tiki and Hina be only the other names for Adam and Eve? However that may be, at any rate we Polynesians know the name of our homeland, and you *popaa* do not. Come nearer, and you shall hear the truth about our origin, as my father taught it to me word for word."

Te Iho shut his eyes to collect his thoughts for the impending test of memory, muttered quietly to himself for a few moments and then began to recite in a clear ringing voice:

> *"Havaiki-te-a-runga*
> *Havaiki-te-a-raro,*
> *Havaiki-tautau-mai,*
> *Havaiki-tautau-atu,*
> *Havaiki-ka-apri-i-te-tua-o-Atea,*
> *Haviki-nui-a-naea . . ."*

We understood only a word here and there, but we were so fascinated by the rhythm and melody that we did not want to interrupt Te Iho for explanations. In the same singsong monotone, the old man continued to recite with inspiration the legend of the lost homeland Havaiki, where his fathers had lived long ago in the morning of time. His thin voice came to us as a voice from the past and disclosed the primeval lore which once was so sacred that no one but the initiated priests knew it.

Suddenly Te Iho checked himself and was again absorbed in his thoughts. I looked at my watch. He had recited for more than half an hour without a break. After a little while he tried to continue, but his memory failed him and he could not find the words. At last he gave up and brought out the old tin can where he stored his cigarette stumps. He had difficulty in finding them and, annoyed, poured out the whole contents of the pot. These consisted, besides cigarette stumps, of two matchboxes, an onion, and a plastic belt! We were definitely back in modern times.

Te Iho recited for us regularly, and gradually the main features of Raroia's strange history began to grow clear to us. It was undeniably a little difficult for him to piece together the mythical stories of Hawaii and the long sea voyages into a connected account. But from the moment when a Polynesian exploring expedition first came to Raroia, Te Iho seemed able to give a quite plausible and detailed narrative of his people's destinies. One day he counted up his whole family tree, which began with the first inhabitant of the island. There were thirty generations! Counting each generation as eighteen years, this would mean that the island had been inhabited since the beginning of the fifteenth century.

The first man who found Raroia—and at the same time the neighboring island Takume—was a certain Taneariki, who came from the Marquesas Islands. His grandson Varoa became the first chief or king, and during the following three hundred years his descendants ruled over the islands. Some time at the beginning of the eighteenth century this reigning family was deposed—according to tradition because the king had brought his queen from another island and that a hostile one. After that coup, power lay in the hands of the minor chiefs of the different tribes or subgroups right down to modern times.

Life in the time of the first chiefs was hard and primitive. The sandy strip of land round the lagoon supported even fewer plants and animals than in our days, and to begin with there were not even coconut palms. Even the dog was unknown, and when at last it was introduced it was valued primarily as an article of food. (The Raroians still regard dog's flesh as a delicacy and gladly pay a couple of hundred francs for a fat dog.) The only clothing was a girdle of plaited pandanus leaves for the men and a leaf skirt for the women. The sleeping mats, which served as either mattresses or coverings, were of the same material, and the implements were of wood, bone, or mother-of-pearl.

The islanders gradually learned to adapt themselves and make better use of their meager resources. The most impressive evidence of their foresight and ability is the great taro plantations which they made on the neighboring island of Takume, where there was more room and a more fertile soil. The tradition which Te Iho recited to us described in detail how, at the chief Varoa Tikaroa's installation fourteen generations ago, the huge ditches in which the taro was planted were dug with mother-of-pearl spades.

Not only the inhabitants of Raroia-Takume, which then already formed a political unit, but also guests invited from every part of the Tuamotu group took part in the work, which to judge from its size must certainly have taken several years. The hundreds of ditches, no longer used, cover an area of about 1,000 by 500 yards, and many of them are more than 20 feet deep. Few works of this magnitude exist elsewhere in Polynesia.

The social and religious organization which could achieve such co-operation must indeed have been perfect and full of vitality. There were special craftsmen for all important occupations or works. Some were canoe builders, others house builders, while a third group manufactured tools. The most important, however, and those enjoying the highest prestige, were the doctors, the priests, and the scholars—the people's spiritual leaders.

Political power, on the other hand, lay in the hands of the chiefs, whose positions were most often hereditary. They were bold, proud men, who were jealous of their honor and often, like the Viking chiefs, made long voyages of discovery and warlike expeditions to other islands in their large plank ships with double hulls and pandanus sails. Alongside the chief were one or several *kaito,* or warrior chiefs; these acted as officers.

Te Iho remembered many of the old heroic songs describing these sea voyages, and chanted many of them to us. One of the longest and most beautiful told of a chief's son named Mapu-teretere [Mapu the seafarer] and his journey to Tahiti to fetch his father, who had been captivated by the charms of a fair lady there. (Tahiti clearly exercised a strange attraction even in those early times!) The songs gave a detailed account of Mapu's itinerary and described in glowing phrases all his exploits and combats—in which of course he was always victorious.

Another epic song celebrated the hero Honokura. Te Iho proudly pointed out the stone called Mitimitakura on which Honokura had stood when he made his speech of greeting to the Raroians, and he showed us the stone in the bay by the village to which the warrior hero had made fast his ship. The stone is still called Tangohe after Honokura's ship, and the captains still use it for mooring their schooners.

The Raroians' forefathers, like those of so many other Polynesian peoples, were cannibals. A stranger was always regarded as an enemy, and anyone shipwrecked on the island or driven ashore by the wind was killed and eaten immediately. Similarly, after victory in a battle, all fallen enemies were roasted and eaten at once on the spot. Cannibalism, however, was principally due not to any desire for human flesh but to a magical belief that those who ate their enemies acquired their strength and vitality.

"To eat an enemy was, moreover, the strongest mark of contempt for him," said Te Iho when, after some hesitation, I questioned him. "For this reason, too, the warriors flung the bones over their shoulders when they had eaten them clean. But if the enemy had been brave and strong, they collected the bones afterward to use them as tools. My father once gave me a drill which was made from a leg-bone of Reao's greatest warrior. I have never seen such a drill. I used it, by the way, when I made the bench you are sitting on, when I was a young man. See how neat and level the holes are."

Te Iho himself had never seen a cannibal feast, but Varoa, who was sitting by him with his great-great-grandson on his knee, told how as a child he had twice been an eyewitness of battles against foreign invaders, both of which ended in the Raroians' devouring their fallen enemies.

"I myself was too small to take part in it, but Father was one of the leading warriors and was always served next after the chief," said Varoa. "I remember that Father often used to complain that the Tuamotu warriors were too tough. The Tahitians were fatter and better."

"What barbarism!" exclaimed Tufaka, who was a good Christian.

But Varoa took no notice.

"The children were the best and tastiest of all, though," he added, laughing, and stared at his great-great-grandson so intently that Tufaka snatched the child away from him.

We thought it was time to change the subject and asked Te Iho when the first whites had come to the island.

"It was when my father was a young man," he said after a few moments' reflection. "There were two *popaa* who came in a schooner and wanted mother-of-pearl in exchange for *popaa* goods. The next time they came a warrior chief assembled all the men and asked, 'Why should we work and dive for mother-of-pearl to get all the new things there are on board the ship? If we kill all the people on board we can take what we want without giving anything in return.' Several men were angry, too, because the foreigners had seduced their women, and they supported the proposal.

"The warriors stole on board the schooner and killed the crew with their spears. The French soon learned what had happened and sent out an expedition to investigate. The officials arrived on a gunboat, landed, and asked who had led the men in the attack on the schooner. The warrior chief and two others said it was their plan, and by way of punishment the Frenchmen hanged them from a palm down by the shore.

"After a time a chief came on a visit from the eastern islands, to which the French had not come. He wanted all the Tuamotu fighting men to attack and take their revenge. My father, who was the leading *tahunga* and had great prestige, said it was better to be friends with the French, as they had many new things which it was good to get in exchange. Most people thought that my father was right, but our chief and some of the fighting men left with the men from the eastern islands when they went back. Time passed, and when at last we heard that they had all been drowned in a storm, my father became chief. So we got peace.

"As my father grew older, more and more schooners came, seeking mother-of-pearl and coconut oil in exchange for what they brought. Often there were *popaa* on board, but they were always afraid and never came ashore without firearms. But one day a *metua* [priest] came, and he was another kind of *popaa*. He was alone, and had clothes which reached down to the ground and a long beard. He was friendly and cheerful and often played to us on his *vivo* [flute] and taught us many songs. He cured sick persons and showed us how to build better canoes and houses. When the schooners came to get mother-of-pearl, he helped us, so that we got twice as many new things as before. He taught many to read and write and gave us many pictures which were pretty to look at. He talked often with our *tahungas* and told them of his god, who would prevent all wars and make all men happy.

"We had already heard of this god from the men on Anaa who had been converted to the new religion—they were called Iseraela [the original Church of Jesus Christ of the Latter Day Saints before the split] and several men on Raroia had become disciples. The *metua,* strangely enough, seemed hostile toward these converts and continued to visit the *tahungas*. A long time passed before he was able to make them listen seriously and discuss his teaching. At last the *tahungas* began to believe in the new god, and when they declared that they would no longer worship the old gods, all the rest did as they did.

" 'The *tahungas* themselves know best which are the right gods, and if they believe in the new *metua's* god, he is certainly the best for us too,' all the people said. In a week we destroyed all our altars and were converted.

"*Metua* Apereto [Albert] remained among us and helped

us to build the first church, which is the same we still use today. It took three years to build and was finished in 1875, which is written in large figures over the door. But to begin with no one would go to the church. Everyone said, 'No doubt the new religion is better, but why should we shut ourselves into a big house to worship the *popaa* god?' So they continued to go to the great stone-built *marae,* or cult site, which lay down by the landing place in the bay. One of *Metua* Apereto's successors, however, hit upon a shrewd way of changing this. He had the biggest stone of the *marae* broken loose, transported it up to the church, and used it as a step outside the entrance. After that the church was always full.

"We built a prison next door to the church, but it looked so gloomy and depressing when it was finished that we seldom used it, although the missionaries wanted it. We promised never to kill anyone any more and to treat all *popaa* well, and soon more schooners were coming than we had ever seen before. They brought many curious new things, among them rice, flour, and canned food which we saw for the first time.

"To begin with many people laid the bags of rice straight on the fire and mixed the flour with water and tried to drink it as soup, but we gradually learned how to use the new *popaa* food. Since that time no one has grown any taro."

The next time I talked to Te Iho, I asked him, "How many inhabitants were there on Raroia when you were young, before everything was changed?"

Te Iho counted on his fingers for a while and then answered:

"In the village here there were over seven hundred and in

the village on the other side of the lagoon between three and four hundred."

"That makes more than a thousand," I said. "Today there are only just over a hundred. How has it come about that the population of Raroia has been so heavily reduced in only seventy-five years?"

Te Iho reflected and answered:

"Many have gone to Tahiti and stayed there. Others have shipped on board the schooners and never come back. New diseases broke out, and as we did not know how to cure them, many, many died. Our own *tahungas* knew how to cure all the diseases that were on the island in the old times, but against the new and unknown diseases they could do nothing. A number, of course, disappeared in the hurricanes and cyclones."

At our request Te Iho told the dramatic story of the worst cyclone that ever struck Raroia. This cyclone, like most of the others which have ravaged French Oceania, originated somewhere in the neighborhood of the equator and swept southward on a semicircular track.

It began on the morning of January 14, 1903, and passed right through the Tuamotu group just west of Raroia at a speed which meteorologists estimated at between fifteen and twenty miles an hour. The vortex of the cyclone itself was 250 miles in diameter, but the huge waves it stirred up had devastating effects 600 miles away from the cyclone's center. During the twenty-four-hour period that the cyclone lasted 517 natives in the Tuamotu group lost their lives. Most of them perished in the gigantic swell the cyclone stirred up. Te Iho knew nothing of these statistics taken from official French publications, but his account was none the less dramatic for that.

As usual he lit the stump of a cigarette and meditated for a time before he began:

"The sun had already passed its highest point and gone a little way down toward the horizon in the west, and it must have been about two o'clock according to your way of calculating time, when the cyclone began. I was on my way to one of my friends and had with me some of my grandchildren, who were running and jumping in front of me. I had just turned into the main village street when I heard a rustling in the palm tops. The wind had been gusty and fitful for the past few days, so I paid no particular attention to the noise. Before I had gone ten steps, however, coconuts began to shower down on the ground round me, and when I had at last got hold of all the children, the wind was already so strong that boughs and leaves were being torn off. This is a danger sign, for it means that old weak palms can be broken clean off. I picked the children up and began to run. Just as I reached the nearest house there was a crash! A tall palm had fallen down near the spot where I had been standing. At the same moment the rain came. You know how it can rain on Raroia, but this time it was more violent than you can imagine. It was as if the breakers on the outside of the reef had flung themselves upon the houses. Soon we were all wet through to the skin.

"After a time the chief came and said that everyone was to assemble in the church, where *Metua* Amedée was. Some of my friends who were in the house carried two of the children, and Mahia there in the corner, who was not more than five, clung round my neck. When we came out into the street, the wind had become so strong that the coconuts were no longer falling straight down as they usually do, but came flying sideways, as if they had been shot from guns like those you see on board the warships in the Papeete harbor. One of my relations was hit by a coconut and fell down unconscious. We did not notice his absence till we had reached the church; then we had to go out again to find him.

"It was better inside the church, for the walls were several feet thick and the galvanized-iron roof was watertight. When we counted all the people who had assembled in the church, we found that seven were missing. Two parties of five men each went out to look for them. One party came back with four women and two children. The other party never came back. *Metua* Amedée bandaged all those who were injured and talked to us until we grew calm.

"One of the old men who was rather weak in the head cried out that the deluge had come and that we ought to build an ark. We told him that we had no time to build an ark, but he did not believe us and wanted to go out into the storm to build one himself. Then the chief said that there was no point in building an ark, for there were no animals on Raroia to fill it with. The new 'Noah' thought that was good sense and said nothing more.

"*Metua* Amedée said that gigantic waves would certainly come and wash over the island, and therefore we ought not to stay in the church, where we should be caught like rats in a trap. Some became panicky and took to their canoes. They were never seen again. Others proposed that we should climb up into the palms or onto the roof, but of course that was impossible in the high wind, so we decided instead to make for the highest ground on the island. The churchyard lay a little higher and was in addition surrounded by a thick stone wall, so we all tried to get across to it.

"The wind was now blowing so strong that no one could

walk upright, and we therefore crawled on our hands and knees. *Metua* Amedée tried to speak to us, but we could no longer hear what he said. All the houses on the west side of the island except Tepuka's had collapsed, and wooden planks and iron roofplates were whirling past.

"Tepuka, who had always been very proud of his fine wooden house, wanted to crawl over to it to see if he could save anything. We tried to stop him, but he went anyhow. He had almost reached the house when it suddenly came crashing down. The wind took hold of the galvanized-iron roof and swept it right toward Tepuka. He tried to get out of the way but could not. His fine bright metal roof, which he had worked so hard to get, cut him right in two, The last I saw his hand was clinging convulsively to a corner of the roof.

"We made two big heaps of stones in the churchyard and sought shelter under their lee. Two hours passed, perhaps three. Then we heard a roaring noise which even drowned the thundering of the wind and rain. It was the first tidal wave. It was not high and quickly washed over the island. But the sea began to rise at the same time, and soon the waterline was high up among the palms on the lower level of ground.

"Then the next wave came, and we had to sit up to keep our heads above the surface of the water. Some were seized with panic and turned back to the church, but as luck would have it they were washed out through the windows every time they tried to get in. Exhausted, they came back and clung tight to the heaps of stones as the rest of us were doing.

"For a long time the water rose slowly but relentlessly; it was as if we were in the middle of the strongest current of the Punaruu River in Tahiti. Broken-off palm trunks, gables of houses, flowers, furniture, and canoes floated past or were swallowed up by eddies which had formed here and there where the flow of the water met with resistance. All of a sudden broken wooden chests and ship's planks came floating along, and we realized that a vessel had been smashed to pieces in the midst of the cyclone. We gave thanks to God that we had ground under our feet—although we found it hard to stay on it.

"The sun had disappeared as soon as the cyclone began, and now it was almost as dark as at night. How long we lay there in the churchyard I cannot tell but when the fifth wave came—*Metua* Amedée counted them—I saw a star in a rift in the clouds and realized that evening must have come. The fifth wave reached about our waists, and we were compelled to take most of the children on our shoulders. Then we noticed, to our joy, that as the waves became more violent the wind and rain eased up; and we considered taking shelter in the palm trees.

"When the seventh wave came and washed round us up to our chests, no one but *Metua* Amedée would remain in the churchyard any longer. We let ourselves be carried by the current, clung to the first coconut palm within reach, and clambered up. Many of the women and old people were so tired that they could not climb up, but the chief found a rope and we hoisted them up into the palm tops with it and tied them fast. I myself ended up on the roof of the prison, the only building besides the church which had withstood the storm. I was so tired that I stayed there. It was positively the first time that the prison had served any reasonable purpose.

"The seventh wave washed *Metua* Amedée away, but he

made his way back to the churchyard and shouted that he would rather die there than leave his place. We all realized that the eighth wave would be the end of him, and we were sorry it should be so, for *Metua* Amedée was always helpful and kind. But the eighth wave never came! Instead the water began to fall slowly, and next morning we were all able to climb down out of the trees. All the palm trees were broken and the ground was covered with hundreds of kinds of fish. Eleven Raroians had lost their lives in this cyclone, the worst I have ever experienced."

Te Iho's story set the Raroians' imaginations working, and for several days we heard of nothing but cyclones and storms. Many people still lived who had been through the cyclone of 1903, and they related their own experiences during the catastrophe. All tales, however, had a general pattern and confirmed everything that Te Iho had said. Similarly all agreed that the next, and to date the last, cyclone—that of 1906—had passed at a much greater distance and had been much less violent and destructive.

These natural disasters brought in their train the most decisive break with the past. Before the cyclone burst over the island in 1903, there were still many houses built in the Tuamotu style, and old objects and implements were still used to a great extent. The violent tidal waves which washed over the island carried away the last remnants of the native culture. After the calamity, when the Raroians set out to replace what had been lost, they naturally found it simpler and quicker to buy what they needed on board the schooners than try to imitate the work of early craftsmen.

Even more disastrous was the disappearance of the old family books. These contained genealogies and other traditions, which the Raroians had recorded immediately after the first missionaries had taught them to write. When the books, like so much else, were lost in these natural calamities, the last link which united the Raroians with their past was broken.

According to Te Iho, all the family books without exception were lost in the first deluge of 1903, but for safety's sake we made a tour of the village to ask if, by chance, any remained. The result was only headshakings and a vigorous *aita, aita* (no, no), till we came to Tehei's house. As soon as we had explained our errand to him, he said:

"But it's not true that all the old family books were destroyed in the 1903 cyclone. My grandfather lived on Hao then and he had with him four books, which were saved. Several years later he moved back to Raroia and brought the books with him. Perhaps they are still somewhere here in the house. I don't know exactly, for I've never thought about them."

Marie-Thérèse and I eagerly helped him search the house from top to bottom, but without result. At last Tehei said:

"They may be at my grandmother's. She kept a lot of things when my grandfather died. If you like, I'll go over to her and ask."

He disappeared. In a quarter of an hour he returned.

"You should have come ten years ago," he said gloomily. "When my grandfather died, my grandmother and my aunt Teua collected the books and all the other old rubbish that was in the house and burned them. I'm sorry, but it can't be helped now."

We wanted to have this confirmed—or perhaps we still had a faint hope that the books had not gone up in smoke after all—and therefore paid a visit to Teua. However, she confirmed that she had torn up the books and then burned them.

"Are you sure you burned every scrap of them?" I tried lamely.

"Yes, certainly, but I used some of the pages as wrapping paper."

This confession naturally did not raise our hopes. Just as we were about to go Teua added amiably:

"For your sake I'd like to have the books back, but the only thing I can give you is the family tree, which I copied before I burned them."

We could hardly believe our ears! And we were still more astonished when Teua produced an account book with MADE IN U.S.A. printed in large letters on the cover. We did not need to turn over its pages for long to discover that it contained not only an imposing family tree—more than five thousand names written on more than two hundred pages—but also quantities of songs, legends, and traditions which in one way or another had some connection with the family.

Next time we called on Te Iho, we took Teua's book with us, and asked him to recite a long *fangu,* or religious song, which we knew that he had by memory. Without hesitation he chanted the whole hymn from beginning to end, which took about ten minutes. We followed with the book all the time and found that his oral version tallied *word for word* with the text we had before us. Te Iho could hardly have given us better proof that he really was a genuine *tahunga* who had piously and faithfully preserved the traditions of his people.

Life Story

THE "average American" is a statistical construction, the flesh-and-blood equivalent of which it is best not to seek for in the world of reality. No one person corresponds in all respects to the mathematical average; indeed, strictly speaking, there should be several kinds of "average American," instead of just one. The reason is evident: in a modern society we are divided into countless professions, interests, and classes—all with different conditions of life, habits, and ideals.

But it is quite different on Raroia. The uniformity is astonishing, and it is possible to describe the course of an "average" Raroian's life with much greater likelihood of the chosen example being representative of the whole population than if one sets out to describe the ways of an "average American." Let us see how such a Raroian life story takes shape.

What takes place when a new member of the happy island community comes into the world, we saw for the first time in the house of Tinorua and Hamau. They were our nearest neighbors, and we often stopped in for a chat. This day we found Tinorua alone on the pandanus mat in front of the house, which rather surprised us, as the couple were usually inseparable. Still we did not think of asking after Hamau, but began to discuss copra and fishing with Tinorua. In the middle of a lively description of shark fishing, he suddenly rose and said casually:

"Wait a minute, I'll just go in and have a look at Hamau. She's having a baby."

"Having a baby!" I almost shouted. "Then why are you here talking to us?"

"Oh," Tinorua replied, "she'll be all right. She never has any difficulties."

Of course we knew that Hamau was expecting a baby, but both she and Tinorua had just the day before declared that the happy event would not take place for some weeks. When Tinorua reappeared, we inquired anxiously about Hamau and reminded him of his previous calculations. He did not seem to share our misgivings, and replied calmly:

"Oh, it's time all right. We always lose count after a few moons."

"Is there no woman in the village who helps with deliveries?" Marie-Thérèse asked cautiously.

"No," said Tinorua, "here on Raroia every family looks after itself. But if you'll give me a hand it would be good, of course."

Neither of us had had any experience at midwifery, but naturally we did not want to let our friends down. While Marie-Thérèse remained behind to arrange everything, I hurried back to our house to fetch *The Perfect Baby-Book*, an American handbook on the care of babies which we always carried in our luggage—just in case. When I came back, I found Marie-Thérèse seriously agitated.

"Nothing is ready for the child," she declared. "There's no clean linen, no hot water, no absorbent cotton, no alcohol, no diapers, no clothes!"

We asked Tinorua how this could have happened.

"But one only needs a few bits of cloth to wrap the child in," he said in astonishment. "When the rags get dirty, we throw them away and put on new ones."

To show how simple it was, he took some old shirts from a corner and tore them into pieces. Marie-Thérèse and I exchanged glances, tacitly agreeing to give a demonstration of modern delivery-room technique and baby care.

To heighten the effect of our demonstration, we fetched our huge medicine chest. Then we sat down on it and studied *The Perfect Baby-Book*. It certainly lived up to its name, for it contained everything from diet lists for the expectant mother to psychoanalytical advice and photographs of toys suitable for different ages. We turned to the first chapter, which was, with singular appropriateness, headed "The Right Start." It began with a summary of the pros and cons of delivery in the home and in the hospital. We skipped this—there was no choice—and stopped to read a detailed description of what the expectant father should do to conquer his nervousness during his wife's labor. We looked at Tinorua, but he did not exhibit one of the symptoms described. We therefore quickly riffled the pages until we came to a list of the things required for a delivery. We decided to content ourselves with half of these, but even this was so much that we asked Tinorua to send for his mother to help with the work.

In a little while the old woman came, and she was so

overwhelmed at all our preparations that she simply had to fetch two more relations to show them what we were doing. We hailed the reinforcements with joy and set them all to work heating up water. There was not a saucepan in the village which held more than three pints, but by collecting all that the neighbors had and making each relation look after two, we hoped to get enough hot water.

We worked energetically for a time. Then Tinorua suddenly called for Marie-Thérèse, and she disappeared into the house with him. Five minutes later she put out her head and cried:

"It's over now. Bring the water!"

"The water isn't hot yet," replied a voice from the kitchen. "Can't you wait a little while I go and fetch more wood and coconut fiber?"

Marie-Thérèse gave a sigh of resignation and took out a bottle of coconut oil. That was at any rate better than cold, dirty water. The grandmother had followed the course of events with a haughty calm from her place in a corner of the room. Now, however, she could keep silent no longer! She said in annoyance:

"Why don't you do as in my young days? Then we used to wash all newborn babies in the lagoon.

"But didn't many children die?" I interjected cautiously.

"No, not at all," the old woman snorted. "It was only the weak children that died, and they wouldn't have lived anyhow."

In a short time both Hamau and her little girl lay wrapped in blankets. Both looked fit and well and, as we evidently could do nothing more, we went home and studied the next chapters of *The Perfect Baby-Book* to be able to impart to Tinorua and Hamau all the up-to-date dictates of medical science in the matter of baby care. When we returned a few hours later crammed with knowledge, Hamau was squatting in a corner talking and laughing with some relations.

"The baby's begun to eat already," she cried, on catching sight of us.

Quite true. Beside her Tinorua sat on the floor with the newborn child on his knee. In one hand he held some green blades of grass.

"Are you giving the child grass to eat?" we cried in alarm.

"Oh, no," Tinorua replied soothingly. "I'm dipping them in sugar water and letting her suck them."

We summarized briefly the main outlines of modern ideas on nutrition, exactly as we had learned them from *The Perfect Baby-Book,* but Tinorua only laughed politely and went on giving the baby sugar water. Then I noticed a smell of cigarette smoke in the room.

"Cigarette smoke is not good for newborn babies," I admonished conscientiously. "Who has been smoking?"

"Oh," said Tinorua, "it was Hamau"—and they both laughed again, this time till they nearly choked.

At last both Marie-Thérèse and I realized that we and the book were a little too advanced for Raroian conditions and discreetly withdrew.

All deliveries take place in the same painless, free and easy (not to mention careless) manner. Most women recover surprisingly quickly. Hamau was up and walking the very day after her delivery and began to work as usual on the third day. But, contrary to the grandmother's assurances, infant mortality is by no means normal, but appallingly high, mainly, of course, as a result of ignorance and negligence. Our researches showed that, in the last twenty years, of 77 babies born alive no fewer than 17 have died in their first year. In the United States, of 1,000 children born alive presently about 29 die before reaching the age of one. The corresponding figure for Raroia would be 220!

The most usual causes of death have been chills and infections, which is not surprising seeing that baby clothing in most cases consists only of a few rags or towels, and that parents often insist on taking children only a month old with them when they go to the islets across the lagoon to make copra. Some time ago, a man came in a sailing canoe from the neighboring island of Takume to report a birth to Teka, who is chief of that island also. To confirm his statement, he had brought the newborn child with him!

Another cause of the huge infant mortality is certainly the great number of premature births. In such cases the Raroians rightly consider that extraordinary measures should be taken—and they give the poor undersized babes grated coconut as soon as they can open their mouths! Few have survived this diet, but those who have done so are really first-class specimens, which can hardly be the result of the coconut diet, as the Raroians think, but must be ascribed instead to the simple fact that only the strongest survive.

If the newborn child remains alive, the next important event in its life is baptism. The important fact that the Raroians are citizens of two worlds—the Polynesian and Western—is shown in their naming. All children always have two names, one Polynesian and one French. What name or names the child is given is unimportant—the parents never give it a thought in advance. For the Polynesian name they fasten onto the first one that some relation suggests. The French name, according to European custom, ought to be that of the saint of the child's birthday; but if the parents do not like that name, they take the saint's name for one of the days immediately before or after the birth. As long as they keep to saints' names any will do, even if the names are old-fashioned.

The case of Tinorua and Hamau is typical. To begin with they wanted to call their little girl Reva Anselm. We objected quietly that although these were very pretty names, Anselm at least was a little unsuitable because it was a man's name. This made them rather crestfallen, but Tinorua turned over the leaves of the almanac for a moment or two and quickly found another name which seemed suitable.

"I think we'll call her Koratika," he said.

"But aren't you going to give her a *popaa* name too, as everyone else does?" I asked.

"Koratika is a *popaa* name," he said resentfully. "She's Benedict's sister. You ought to know that."

We looked in the almanac, and Tinorua proudly pointed out a passage where the name of Scolastique was printed in large letters—and Scolastique was certainly Koratika in Polynesian. After a little persuasion, however, he agreed to call the little girl Martine. Of course there was no particular reason for calling her Martine, but at any rate it was a name which nobody would laugh at.

The only European names in daily use are, significantly enough, those which have been rewritten according to the rules of Polynesian phonetics. Often, however, the changes are so great that it is almost impossible to recognize them. It was a long time before we discovered that Kikeria was Cecilia; that Peni was Benjamin; Titin, Christine; Ruita, Louise; Tihoni, John; and Teretia, Thérèse.

Up to the age of two or three the lives of Raroia children differ very little from those of their American and European contemporaries, except, of course, that they are not cared for nearly as well or as hygienically. At about this age a great change often takes place for many of the children: they are adopted! Adoption takes place to an extent quite unknown to us; more than a third of the children can be sure of changing their families before the age of five. Boys are more valued than girls because they always mean more copra workers, and therefore families are more apt to hand over a girl than a boy. Curiously enough it is not only childless families who adopt children; even families who have already four or five children of their own do not hesitate to increase the number by another one or two. It often happens, too, that one child is handed over at the same time that another is adopted. This custom is typically Polynesian and is so old that it is now difficult to explain how it arose. The Raroians at any rate are satisfied with the good old familiar explanation that it has always been done.

Of course, all this adoption is illegal, for according to French law, which in this as in so many other cases exists unaltered in French Oceania, no one may legally adopt anyone till he or she has reached the age of forty. But the natives pay no attention to this, or other laws which do not harmonize with their customs, and regard a verbal agreement as binding. Although parents seldom want their children back, this system has a serious disadvantage. Adopted children are in an insecure position materially, and whether they inherit anything or not depends entirely on the good will of their adoptive parents. In many instances on Raroia the adopted children have, significantly enough, inherited considerably less than the children by blood.

That adoption does not take place before the age of two

or three, or in some cases till later, is due simply and solely to the Raroians' realistic attitude. They want to see how the child is turning out before they adopt it! A modern child psychologist would probably consider it reprehensible to try to transplant a child so late, but in the conditions prevailing on Raroia this factor is certainly of no great importance.

In contrast to what is the case in our society, adoption seldom involves a sudden and definite change of environment. Instead, an adopted child slowly and gradually fits into its place in the new family, for contact with the real parents and brothers and sisters is never broken. And as the greatest possible distance between two houses is three hundred yards, the original family can keep an eye on the child after it has moved to its adoptive parents.

It often happens, too, that the child lives now with the one family and now with the other, alternately. For Raroian children there is nothing peculiar and abnormal about this as they have several papas and mammas from birth. There are indeed no special words for uncle and aunt in the Polynesian language; these relations are called father and mother and are regarded and treated in the same way as the real parents. A few parents more or less, therefore, mean nothing to a Raroian child.

Children begin to have certain duties at the age of three. The Raroians' view is that the children, like all the other members of the family, ought to make themselves useful; and they give quite small children astonishingly heavy and difficult tasks. Children of four or five are sent regularly to fetch water from the large communal tank; many of them make as many as ten trips a day with their gallon bottles. Others are set to grate coconuts, wash dishes, or do other kitchen work.

A girl of eight washes, irons, and cooks; a boy of the same age helps to make copra or is sent out fishing. At about the same age, many girls begin to look after their younger brothers and sisters, which does not mean just that they are told to keep an eye on them now and then; they have to wash, dress, and occupy them—in other words, entirely replace the parents. It is quite usual, too, for a boy or girl of eight to be left behind in the village for several weeks to keep house for a lone grandmother when the family goes to the islets across the lagoon to make copra.

Yet, the Raroians are logical. As they set children to do adults' work, they regard them, too, as grown-up. There are no secrets from them, and they learn early to take a realistic, practical view of life. Parents are seldom uneasy about their children or ask what they are doing; they take it for granted that the children can look after themselves. As soon as the children have discharged their duties—but not before—they have unrestricted freedom and can do what they like. Many parents even go so far as to let their children make decisions, even if they know that these decisions are unwise or hasty. It often happened that parents handed back our medicine with the naïve, revealing explanation that their children would not take it because it tasted nasty!

A typical case was that of Rari, a little girl of four. She had a serious attack of influenza and a high temperature, for which we had prescribed sulfathiazole. When we visited the house again, her parents declared that we must give her some other medicine, for the child could not keep the sulfathiazole down. We were searching through our medicine chest and reading our handbooks, trying to find some medicine which would suit her better, when a friend of the family told us that the little girl was simply spitting out the sulfathiazole because she did not like the taste. The parents naturally preferred telling us a lie to making the child take the medicine. Compulsion and corporal punishment are taboo in bringing up children in Polynesia.

As a result of their working and assuming responsibility at an early age, the children make rapid progress. When only ten or twelve both boys and girls have nothing more to learn—they can do everything that grownups can do. Many are also fully developed physically, while others may take a few more years to mature.

In our so-called civilized communities adolescent difficulties, which generally become apparent at this age, are most often attributed to the biological transformation from child to adult. Several anthropologists, however, have pointed out that in many primitive societies this transition is not at all a critical period of storm and confusion, but a quiet, harmonious stage of life. In other words, in modern society the causes of adolescent difficulties are not biological but rather social. The conditions on Raroia seem to confirm this, and a comparison with American conditions is really quite instructive.

For an American boy or girl adolescence is the time when adaptation to the adult world begins in earnest, a time when a career is to be chosen, a time when the family and society make demands which are often mutually conflicting. This can only create uncertainty and a spirit of rebellion. Further, economic reasons and long professional training compel most young people to wait many more years before they can start a family, and a natural result is sex problems and personal difficulties.

For a boy or girl on Raroia everything is different. They are at home from birth in the limited world which the village and island form. The choice of a profession is no problem, for specialization is unknown and a boy continues to make copra as his father and grandfather did before him; it is equally a matter of course for a girl to become a mother and housewife. There are no economic obstacles, since the island directly or indirectly gives everyone a secure livelihood, and the young people can marry as soon as they like.

Finally, sexual difficulties and repressions are quite unknown. The Raroians' attitude toward sex life is open and candid—there are absolutely no secrets about it. The whole family lives and sleeps in the same room, so the children have an opportunity of finding out all they want to know at an early age. Both young and old discuss quite openly details that we can speak of only in the greatest intimacy or at the most describe in scientific works with Latin technical terms. As is to be expected, the symptoms which we consider typical of adolescence are absent in the young people of Raroia; instead of being uncertain, split, and rebellious, they are open, merry, and sure of themselves.

This undisturbed transition from childhood to adult life was marked in old days by sensual dances and love feasts, whose motto seemed to be "One for all and all for one." Many old people have told me, with regret, of their happy youth, and if they are to be believed, they led during these years of transition a kind of Freudian dream existence, in which no one needed to seek for partners and fidelity was a breach of the rules.

On moonlit nights the young people used to assemble in some glade in the palm forest for singing, dancing, and amorous games. The boys and girls who had the most love affairs and were the most accomplished in this field had great prestige. On Raroia, as on most of the islands, there were traditional meeting-places; parents helped their children to arrange trysts, and more than one thoughtful mother helped her daughter plait soft pandanus mats which were to be spread out under the palms.

These public sex games had, above all, an important social function: they were actually a long series of brief trial marriages and helped the young people to find the right partner for life. It was therefore, despite vigorous efforts, a long time before the missionaries succeeded in putting them down; and they did not positively disappear till the population was so catastrophically reduced that there were too few young people left to be able to continue them with profit. This does not mean that the young Raroian people in our day are more restrained, but simply and solely that the outward forms of this period of trial and play have become less conspicuous and startling.

Thus, most of the young people on Raroia have their first sexual experiences as early as twelve or thirteen. As modern preventive methods are unknown, it is not long before the results of these associations begin to appear—if the girls are not already sterile. The youngest mother in memory is Hinano, who was only twelve when she had her first child. But everyone except Hinano considers this a little too early. (Hinano has since then had three more children by three different men.) But there are several mothers aged fourteen—and fifteen is regarded as a mature, respectable age.

Most expectant mothers seem, before the child arrives, to have very vague ideas as to who the father can be. But once it has been born the matter is quite simple—the young man whom the child most closely resembles is indicated as the father! The male chosen usually undertakes fatherhood without a murmur—presumably for the simple reason that it does not involve any trouble or obligations. If the parties want to come together, they are glad to have a child to start with; and if they want to continue to live a free life, there is always some relation who will adopt it with pleasure. The social problems are as nonexistent as the economic. The Raroians are so blissfully out of date that they do not understand the difference between so-called legitimate and illegitimate children.

But, someone may ask, are the Raroians not afraid of contracting venereal diseases through all these free liaisons?

In regard to syphilis the answer is very simple. They have no reason for being careful, as they have all had this disease for a long time, in most cases from birth. But they have some fear of other venereal diseases, and it is significant that the Raroian women in general avoid contact with sailors and other casual visitors. Of course a Raroian can contract a venereal disease during a visit to Papeete, but as everyone on the island hears news of this kind at once, the risks of infection are reduced.

After a period of free liaisons most young people feel ready to set up housekeeping with one of the opposite sex. But no one takes their living together seriously at this stage, and few whom we have observed have continued to live with their partners for long. Many have two or three marriages of this kind, and some seem never to get beyond this state. Any children resulting from these marriages are handed over to relations as easily and casually as before. If, however, a couple continues to live together for a long time and has several children, it is considered good form to be properly married.

In the Polynesian view the most important parts of a

wedding are the feast and the ceremony in church. On the other hand, the legal form of marriage can, according to the Raroians, be dispensed with altogether. It only complicates matters and brings with it economic problems. During our stay on Raroia there was only one wedding; but as if to make up for the lack, this was a real top-notch Polynesian wedding.

After mature consideration Poekura and Suei had decided to get married. Poekura was fifteen and a pure-blooded Polynesian girl. Suei had a good deal of Chinese blood in his veins and had no idea of his age, but was certainly about seventeen. They had lived together for more than a year and so were regarded as inseparable.

As all the inhabitants of the village had, of course, been invited, the bride's parents made a long table of old boxes, with room for fifty persons on each side. When we arrived the feast had already begun, and the guests were busy helping themselves to "cocktails" of rum, hair tonic, and coconut beer out of a large kettle.

In a little while some of the bride's relations began to prepare the earth oven. They dug a hole in the ground, about 10 feet square and 18 inches deep. They laid stones at the bottom of the hole and built a huge fire of palm logs on top of the stones. When the stones were red-hot, they swept away the ashes and spread the food on them. The most important dishes were roast pork, fish, chicken, breadfruit, and quantities of dumplings wrapped in palm leaves. But to this everyone added whatever he had been able to get hold of—pies, cakes, canned goods, and coconuts. Then the "cooks" laid big leaves over it all and covered up the hole with sand. While we were waiting for the food to cook, we all paid another visit to the cocktail pot.

Two hours passed before the hosts at last signified that it was time to open the earth oven. For this important event the bridal pair made their first appearance. Suei was dressed in white-linen trousers and a blue-silk shirt with a yellow tie; on his feet he wore highly polished, green shoes. Poekura wore a red-velvet dress, her bare feet peeping out from under the long hem-line; naturally she was perspiring heavily.

For the first half-hour after the food had been placed on the table not a sound was heard but the munching of a hundred persons, who eagerly licked their fingers clean between each course. Then their tongues were suddenly loosed and eloquence began to flow, animated and unrestrained. As Poekura's father had dipped too often and too deeply into the cocktail pot, it was her uncle who opened the long series of speeches in his stead. Then came the turn of the chief, the vice-chief, and the bridegroom's father; and then, in order of rank and dignity, all the rest who were able to stand on their legs.

An old Polynesian custom demands that a new name shall be taken on each important occasion in life. Thus in earlier times a Polynesian changed his name often—on his marriage, the birth of his first child, a particularly good catch of fish, a successful war, a serious illness, and a child's marriage. As it is rather difficult to keep track of people who change their names several times during their lives, the authorities have tried to put an end to this custom; at least they have succeeded in getting most Polynesians to use one principal name, even if it is not the right one.

The wedding guests suddenly remembered this old custom, for each speaker unfailingly ended by giving both the bride and bridegroom new names. This would have been all right if it had just been a formality; but every speaker insisted they not only forget all their old names but also that they should choose from all the new ones, the one just given by himself. After a time the verbal duels between the different christeners became so shrill that I began to fear the feast would end in a free-for-all! In the chaos of nomenclature the real names of the bridal pair had long been forgotten. I therefore rose, managed to obtain a semblance of silence, and suggested that the couple be given two names which no one had thought of—Poekura and Suei. All were so delighted at this proposal, which saved everyone's honor, that the bridal pair still have these names.

Not till a feast of this kind has been held is a couple considered to be properly married. Of course this does not mean that a marriage signed and sealed in this manner lasts for a lifetime. The process of seeking and adapting continues, and the parties often grow tired of each other and "remarry." There is, however, a certain difference of degree. While the young people, during the period of trial marriages, change partners perhaps two or three times in a year, the adult Raroians often live together for years before they break up a marriage; and the older they grow, the more settled their marital relations become.

This traditional Raroian custom of experimenting till the right partner is found has naturally been opposed by the missionaries and authorities; but the results of these attempts to convert the Raroians to Christian and Western ideals have been meager. The first missionaries to visit Raroia tried to introduce some order simply by marrying in church all the couples who were living together and persuading them also to go through a civil marriage ceremony before the chief. Most of them agreed to this, and when the missionaries at last left the island to continue their circuit tour, there was hardly a Raroian over fifteen years old who was not properly and legally married.

About a year later the missionaries paid another visit. All the natives, of course, were still married, but a closer inquiry showed that very few of the men and women who were living together were married to one another. After a few years the confusion had become so great that no one could remember any longer who was married to whom. As a Catholic marriage is indissoluble and a legal divorce means a lot of writing and juridical embarrassments, the Raroians gradually returned to the old customs and snapped their fingers at the white men's queer ideas. The missionaries, wiser by the experience, have now abandoned this marriage policy, and marry only those couples who have remained together for a long period of years and whose marriages in consequence seem durable.

Despite these precautionary measures, the situation is still in the highest degree confused and confusing. Our neighbors on the other side of the village street are the Tukaoko family. They consist of Tukaoko, a man of about fifty, his wife Hamani, who is some years younger, their daughter Tepivai and her husband and child, their daughter Tuhipa and her husband, and their son Tapanga. Tukaoko's and Hamani's marriage is neither a civil nor an ecclesiastical union.

Hamani in her young days lived with a man from another island, to whom she was married in a Mormon church. After that she lived with a number of Raroian men, each time not being either civilly or ecclesiastically married to any one of them. At last she went through a civil marriage ceremony with a man from a neighboring island. She is still married to him, but has been living with Tukaoko for twenty years. She had two children by her earlier marriages, both of whom were adopted by other people.

Tukaoko has never been either civilly or ecclesiastically married to anyone. He does not remember how many women he has lived with and has only a vague idea of the number of children he has fathered. He and Hamani have had five children, two of whom died young.

Tapanga, their son, when he was fifteen, married a girl of fourteen because she was expecting a child. Both child and mother died immediately after the delivery, and since then Tapanga has been a bachelor. The daughter Tepivai has had five children, four of whom died in their first year. The fifth has been adopted by Tepivai's half-sister, who was herself adopted by another family. Tepivai has been ecclesiastically married to a Tahitian for some years. The other daughter, Tuhipa, has no children and has for some time been living with Vananga, who is legally married to another woman who is living with a Tahitian whose wife deserted him! I could add a good deal about the earlier connections of the sons-in-law, but that would only be a wearisome repetition of the general pattern.

These continual changes of partners seem generally to take place in a quiet and peaceful manner. Most of the people we asked explained that they simply got tired of one another and therefore separated. The only story of near-passion the Raroians can remember is that of Maru and Tefau.

Maru's parents wanted her to make a good match and therefore promised her to the son of the merchant Temake. This did not suit Maru, and she began to live with Kainui instead, to the annoyance of her family. The two young people succeeded in being faithful to one another for more than a year; their parents thought this so remarkable that their hearts softened, and they decided to arrange a proper wedding between Maru and Kainui before the priest and the chief. The Raroians shook their heads, saying that it was too much all at once and that an ordinary feast would be enough; but the parents persisted. To celebrate this unusual event both parties' families invited relations and friends from all the islands of French Oceania, and soon the schooners were compelled to make extra stops at Raroia.

Kainui's brother, Tefau, came back from Tahiti to be best man. He had been at school in Papeete for a long time and so had not seen Maru for many years. But one look was enough to make him realize that he loved her, and one look was enough to tell Maru, too, that she had found the right man. Just as the wedding guests had assembled outside the church Tefau and Maru disappeared. A search was instituted at once, headed by the bridegroom, but not a trace of the runaways could be found.

Only when the last wedding guest had left, and the anger of the parents and the ex-bridegroom had subsided, did Tefau and Maru return from their hiding place on one of the small islands on the other side of the lagoon. This happened more than five years ago, and they are still living together and look just as happy as if they had run away yesterday.

In contrast to what we are accustomed to, a marriage on Raroia—irrespective of how long it lasts and how often the parties change—hardly means any increase in responsibility or more work. Rather the contrary.

In the first place, the newly married couple receive a piece of land as a gift from their parents and so become

Chart Showing How a Raroian Family Spends Its Time

Members of Family	Monday A.M.	Monday P.M.	Tuesday A.M.	Tuesday P.M.	Wednesday A.M.	Wednesday P.M.	Thursday A.M.	Thursday P.M.	Friday A.M.	Friday P.M.	Saturday A.M.	Saturday P.M.	Sunday A.M.	Sunday P.M.
Tapakia 38, husband	Made copra	Rested	Talked to friends	Fished	Rested	Talked to friends	Read Bible	Talked to friends	Made copra	Rested	Rested	Talked to friends	Church	Talked to friends
Terou 36, wife	Household work	Talked to friends	Rested	Household work	Looked after children	Rested	Made clothes	Talked to friends	Household work	Rested	Made clothes	Talked to friends	Church	Read Bible
Terii 19, son	Rested	Talked to friends	Made copra	Rested	Made copra	Fished	Fished	Talked to friends	Made copra	Played football	Fetched wood	Singing	Church	Music and Singing
Tepava 16, son	Rested	Household work	Made copra	Rested	Fished	Fetched wood	Made copra	Household work	Made copra	Played football	Household work	Singing	Church	Music and Singing
Tekeho 14, daughter	Household work	Household work	Household work	Talked to friends	Household Work	Rested	Household work	Household work	Talked to friends	Household work	Household work	Singing	Church	Music and Singing
Rari 10, daughter	Looked after children	Talked to friends	Household work	Household work	Played	Household work	Household work	Talked to friends	Rested	Household work	Played	Household work	Church	Music and Singing
3 girls aged 2–6	Played	Fetched water	Played	Played	Fetched water	Played	Played	Ran errands	Fetched water	Played	Played	Played	Church	Played

at last quite independent of them. Further, they adopt one or a couple of children, who take charge of the housekeeping and do all the work of a servant—for no wages. Thus the most important problems are solved. As time passes and the children (adopted and their own) grow up, the parents' existence becomes more and more pleasant, and as soon as the children have reached their teens they can even hand over most of the tedious copra-making to them.

The women in particular have an astonishingly free and idle existence. As long as there is a child in the neighborhood, a married woman does as little as possible in her home; and as the land she has got from her parents is her private property, she is seldom economically dependent upon her husband. Her most important occupation, in fact, is gossiping with women friends and making new clothes. There is a sewing machine in every home, and a self-respecting woman makes a couple of new dresses every time a schooner comes with cloth—at least once a month.

How a family spends its time is shown in detail on the chart on page 159, based on observations of a "normal family" during one week. The youngsters clearly take the brunt of the work.

Week after week, month after month, year after year, the Raroians' life flows on in this idyllic manner. The interruptions are few and insignificant. Going to church of course means some change—especially as it serves as a pretext for brilliant fashion parades—but the schooners' visits are even more highly appreciated. As a rule one schooner a month comes to Raroia, and her arrival is always greeted with loud shouts and great joy.

The schooners seldom stay more than one day, but that is enough for the Raroians to be able to buy a piece of

Old Te Iho, the last sage on the island. With his light complexion and snow-white hair and beard, he could easily play Santa Claus in any American home.

Soon after Te Iho's story of the old times, I went down to the landing place on the bay and sat upon the chief's seat at the stone-built *marae,* or cult site.

The girls often work more than the women. The young girl astride the stool (*above*) is grating coconut on the crescent-shaped piece of iron, while one of our cats helps himself to a free lunch. Two younger girls (*below, left*) are fetching water, and an older girl (*below, right*) is doing the family wash.

In spite of all the manufactured goods available to the Raroians, they still use the palm leaf for a variety of purposes, and all the women are able to braid together a leaf mat in a few minutes.

Marie-Thérèse, in native costume, splits a palm leaf, as she prepares to plait a palm-leaf mat.

Polynesian women have a reputation for attractiveness, and many are astonishingly comely. None consider themselves well-dressed without a *tiare* bloom behind the ear.

Back to the old times when weapons were made of wood — a spear sharpened at both ends and a heavy club!

cloth or a few bottles of rum and hear the latest gossip from Tahiti. A wedding, or a visit from relations from some other island, is also a possible interruption; but young people of a marriageable age are sadly few, and the relations live the same simple life as the Raroians themselves and so rarely have any particularly interesting news to tell. It is not surprising, therefore, that some grow tired of their monotonous life, and at least for a time, seek adventures elsewhere.

The women usually go to Papeete. The men, on the contrary, have several possibilities to choose from. They can either ship on board a schooner, try to find work in Tahiti, or become divers on one of the pearl or mother-of-pearl islands. Most of them have no definite plans, but go off to see what will turn up. Tehei's case is typical. He related his adventures to us as follows:

"One day a big yacht came to Raroia. A tall stout *popaa,* who smoked cigars and drank strong spirits, was obviously the chief. Everything on board was clean and scrubbed; she was the finest boat I've ever seen. None of the strangers talked any language I understood, but I think they were Americans. The yacht stayed a week and I was pilot to the fat man all the time. He often gave me queer things to eat which I had never seen before, and he seemed a good sort.

"When the yacht was going to leave Raroia I took my pandanus mat and went on board and showed by signs that I wanted to go, too. They all laughed and nodded, and soon we were out at sea. I tried to ask where we were going, but no one understood me. We cruised round for a long time among the Tuamotu Islands, but at Takaroa two more men came on board and were also allowed to stay.

"We went on to the Marquesas Islands and visited nearly all the other islands in French Oceania. At last we came to Papeete and there the fat man told me by signs that I was to go ashore. I wanted to go still farther with them to see the whole world, but he would not agree to that. When I tried to hide down below, they threw me into the sea. All the Papeete people laughed at me when they saw me floating in the harbor with my pandanus mat.

"I swam in to the quay and lay down to dry myself in the sun. It was the first time I had been in Papeete, and for several weeks I went round the bars all day and went to the movies every evening. I slept in the streets at night, for I had no relations in Papeete to stay with. At last I had no money left, and then I went down to the harbor to see if there wasn't some boat which wanted a man.

"Another American yacht had just come in and on board her was another fat *popaa,* who also smoked cigars and drank strong spirits. He had an interpreter who talked Tahitian. The interpreter explained that the fat man would give me 6,000 francs ($96) a month to have photographs taken of me. Of course I was pleased and said that he could take as many photographs as he liked for 6,000 francs.

"I went on board the yacht to one of the Tuamotu Islands which is called Marokau, and there the fat *popaa* began to put the apparatus and machines in order. Then he told me to climb up the mast and jump into the sea. I thought this was a funny way of taking photographs, for in Papeete you always sit still on a chair when the photographer is taking you, but anyhow I did as he told me.

"'Good,' said the *popaa* when that was finished. 'Now get hold of a shark and fight with it.'

"I told him it was dangerous to fight with sharks and that I didn't want to lose my arms and legs. He thought for a minute or two and then he said:

" 'If we haul up a shark and tie up its mouth with a fishing line, will you fight with it then?'

"There shouldn't be any danger in that, I thought, so we hauled up a big fellow and tied up his mouth. Then I jumped in with the shark and the *popaa* began to take photographs. But there were a lot of other sharks in the sea, and in a little while I didn't know which was the right one. I didn't want to seem afraid, so I went on. The *popaa* was pleased and said the photographs were good.

"We stayed on Marokau two months, and I swam through the breakers, climbed up the palms, dived for giant mussels, and did a lot of other dangerous things. Sometimes I had to dress up and act with other *popaa* who were dressed up too, and once they bound me hand and foot and threw me into the sea. They only just saved me before I was full of water.

"At last the fat man had taken all the photographs he wanted, and then he went back to Papeete. There was no one else who would pay me for being photographed, so I began to work in the harbor. After a month I couldn't stand it any longer, and as I had no more money and couldn't get any other work, I came home to Raroia."

Most of the men, like Tehei, return to Raroia sooner or later. When their eagerness for adventure has subsided, they find that the world is considerably harder and more ruthless than they had imagined; and at last they begin to realize how happy life on their island really is. Taught by experience, they prefer in the future to stay in the only place where they have land and incomes and are their own masters. The city, of course, continues to attract them, but they content themselves with a visit now and then, when they are flush with money, and no longer dream of settling down and finding work there. They have become good local patriots who—certainly quite rightly—have become convinced that there is no better place on earth than Raroia.

The women who seek adventures in Papeete fare differently. As long as they are young and attractive, they can always find someone to keep them, or they can become prostitutes. Most of them regard this as an ideal and pleasant existence, and so they find no reason to go back to Raroia, where life is dull and monotonous. As they grow older, they do find it harder to get along, but most often they are loath to admit defeat and return, or else they have become so fascinated by town life that they cannot tear themselves away; so they prefer to stay and take a poor-paying job. The result has been the present unfortunate disproportion between men and women on Raroia.

After the Raroians have come safely through their last "Papeete crisis" and settled down for good on their island, there is scarcely anything to add. Days and years pass, rain and sunshine follow each other, the coconuts ripen and fall to the ground, but the people, wise with age and experience, continue to live their quiet, secure lives. They make a little copra now and then, fish in the lagoon, and talk, sing, and dance for the rest of the time. Without themselves noticing it or thinking about it, they slowly grow old, and suddenly one day they find their relations beginning to talk about their infirmities and approaching death. There is no pretense even on these subjects—they are broached as candidly as any other topic.

We found this out for the first time when Maiata, a wrinkled little old woman, believed to be the oldest woman on Raroia, asked us to look at her daughter Tehina, who had a toothache. The case proved to be hopeless, as nearly all

Tehina's teeth were broken and black; and we therefore advised her to go to Papeete and have them all taken out by a dentist and a false set put in their stead. Tehina considered our proposal for a long time, and then said:

"That's a good idea all right, but I won't go now, for my mamma is old, and may die while I'm away, and then who will take care of the children?"

"I shan't die now," the old woman, who stood close by, protested. "You go."

"You've been coughing a lot lately," Tehina said emphatically, "and that's always a bad sign."

After a thorough and realistic discussion of the old woman's health and life expectancy, the two at last agreed that Tehina should go.

Their calculations were right. Three or four months passed before Maiata at last died quietly and peacefully in her sleep. Tehina and her relations wept bitterly for a day and a night, and the village rang with lamentation. But the day after the funeral all were laughing and singing again. We thought for a long time that this particular instance must be a little unusual and abnormal; but several other deaths which occurred afterward taught us that the Raroians do in fact leave life in the same simple and inconspicuous manner in which they begin it.

The Governor's Visit

THE merchant Temake had wanted a radio for a long time. If it had been only a question of money, of course he could have obtained several dozen sets; but unfortunately it was not so simple as that. The difficulties which had done most to prevent the realization of his dream were of quite another kind.

In the first place, he did not know how to manage a radio; in the second, he had no idea how he should go about getting one. We assured him that no more was involved in starting a radio than in turning a key in a door. This gave him fresh hope, though he did confess that it was not always so easy to lock or unlock a door, and that he often ruined his keys by turning them the wrong way. We therefore added that, to make things quite safe, there were marks on radios showing which way the knobs should be turned.

The only remaining question, therefore, was where he would find a set. On his visits to Papeete he had tried several times to get one, but unfortunately they had always been sold out. When we offered to write directly to an importer and asked him to order a radio in France, Temake —and the population as a whole—was overjoyed.

Several months of impatient waiting followed, but at last news came from Papeete that the radio had arrived. The cost, including customs duty, shipping costs, and the importer's commission, would be 15,000 Tahiti francs or $240. We were left speechless at the price, but Temake declared that it was a trifle and that he would gladly pay double if necessary. To prevent Temake from increasing the price out of sheer enthusiasm, we wrote to the importer telling him to send the radio out to Raroia as quickly as possible. The radio had two batteries. To charge them Temake needed a motor. We had already explained this to him and pointed out that Tutepo's fine motor would now be of some use; but Temake had got it into his head that he should have his own motor and ordered one from Papeete by return mail—of course twice as large as was necessary. It cost as much as the radio and this Temake thought was splendid.

During the weeks that followed the whole population made a morning and evening pilgrimage to the lookout point on the west side of the island, all chattering eagerly about the anticipated joys of tuning in. When at last the *Florence*'s battered sails appeared above the horizon, all broke into such impetuous cheering that Marie-Thérèse and I almost thought they had returned to the savage customs of their ancestors and were about to hold a cannibal feast.

The whole crowd came rushing at a furious gallop into the village, up to our veranda, where we were eating our breakfast in solitude. First came some of the boys and the young men, then some of the girls and the older men, followed by a long trail of old men and old women with Matapu, aged seventy-five, bringing up the rear. They all bounded and scuttled along between branches of trees and heaps of copra with such amazing lightness and agility that several of the oldest dogs found it hard to keep up with them. When they had all in turn imparted to us the sensational news that the *Florence* and the radio had at last come, they all rushed back to the lookout point to be sure they had not seen a vision.

As soon as the schooner had cast anchor in the lagoon off the village, Temake hurried on board to fetch his treasures. He clasped the radio set with an embracing sweep and carried it tenderly ashore, while Tufaka took charge of the batteries. Tehei seized the motor, and some of the children collected the small parcels. The procession disappeared slowly and ceremoniously into Temake's house amid prolonged cheering from the populace.

"Please start the radio," Temake said to me, as soon as he had set down his precious burden.

I explained that it was best to put up an aerial and ground it first, and that the batteries would certainly be none the worse for being charged. The Raroians, remembering that the *Kon-Tiki* crew had put up an aerial in one of the tallest palms, decided at once to better the *Kon-Tiki* aerial. They attacked their task so energetically that they had spliced together a hundred yards of wire, felled three palms, and put up sticks in most of the treetops round Temake's house before I could stop them. Meanwhile the captain of the schooner and I charged the batteries.

About seven o'clock in the evening everything was ready for the first program. I selected the Papeete station and asked Temake to turn on the instrument. Amid a reverent silence he took hold of the knob, which almost disappeared in his giant paw, and turned it halfway round to the right. This was evidently the right way, for a faint buzzing was heard, followed by a machine-gun-like sputter. Then suddenly a voice came through. It was the Tahitian announcer at the Papeete radio station. The station was extremely weak and there were continual disturbances, but that made no difference to our friends. Temake and the other Raroians listened to the program, which consisted of a news report in Tahitian and local music, with an expression of beatitude on their faces. In one voice they declared the entertainment superlatively good. Unfortunately the program lasted only an hour. There were, however, masses of American stations to choose from; I soon found one with languishing music, which was ten times louder and clearer than the Papeete station, and retired discreetly to let Temake enjoy his triumph alone.

But in a little while he came and knocked at our door. He looked worried.

"Can you come and change the music?" he asked. "It isn't good."

I had just heard the announcer say that the piece was the vastly popular song, "I Want but You Don't"—or something like that—which everyone was completely mad about, and explained this to Temake. He assured me that, however many people might be mad about this song, the Raroians at any rate did not like it. They were tired of all kinds of modern dance music, he added.

I tried symphonies, violin music, piano, operas, and yodeling. The yodeling went well, but everything else the Raroians rejected with unmistakable signs of disapproval. Unfortunately there were not many stations with yodeling on their programs, and the Raroians' spirits were at zero when the party broke up.

Our attempts to entertain the Raroians with the phonograph had taught us long before that the only kinds of music they really appreciated were Hawaiian music and cowboy songs. The next day I made concentrated efforts to find some station which was sending out programs of this kind. Now and then, of course, I found some tunes which the listeners liked, but at least three-quarters of all the programs consisted of dance music, commercials, news, and plays. This was a snag which, unfortunately, I had not considered. Temake, who had expected it would be as easy to find Hawaiian music and cowboy songs as to put on a phonograph record, was bitterly disappointed.

Days passed, but the results of my dial-twisting remained as meager as ever, and I began to feel that the whole of my prestige was at stake. Temake had already begun to talk of getting another radio with better music when, by chance, I found in an American magazine an advertisement of a radio station which seemed to specialize in cowboy songs. This was clearly salvation!

That very evening I tried to get it on the short-wave length, and to my unbounded joy and relief "Give Me Back My Boots and Saddle" immediately flowed through Temake's house. I waited eagerly for the next number. That was a cowboy song, too. And the next, and the next. An hour passed. Still nothing but cowboy songs. The villagers were delighted, and Temake at last began to feel that he owned a radio.

But the station had one drawback. It was supported by a correspondence school which wanted to advertise its curriculum. In between the cowboy songs a loud enthusiastic

voice talked for a few minutes of the advantages of studying at the "Never-Too-Late School." The gist of the com-
mercial was always the same and ran more or less like this:

"Have you got a high-school education? Have *you* got a
high-school education? If not, remember that the Never-
Too-Late School offers you the best, quickest, and cheapest
courses. Five dollars cash, the rest in installments. You can
study when you like, where you like, and how you like.
Do you want to get on in life?—and you sure do—do you
want to earn more money?—and who doesn't?—remember
that the best way is to get a certificate. Get your high-school
diploma at the Never-Too-Late School! Do you want to
make a dream reality? Get your high-school diploma!
Do you want a higher salary? Get your high-school
diploma! Do you want to take part in building the world
of tomorrow? Get your high-school diploma! The Never-
Too-Late School is for you, whoever you are, wherever you
are. Five dollars cash, the rest in installments. You can
study when you like, where you like, and how you like.
Write to the Never-Too-Late School—RIGHT NOW!"

When Temake explained to the audience that the announcer was a real cowboy telling of his latest exploits, the
Raroians accepted the interruptions without a murmur.
Their mouths half open and eyes closed, they listened to
the brisk cheerful voice with the same interest and enthusiasm as the songs.

Time passed, and the Raroians continued to assemble
round the radio as faithfully as ever. But Marie-Thérèse and
I soon grew more than a little weary of these "Wild West"
programs and decided to have a rest from it all. Most of
the Raroians were aghast at our indifference to world
events; so they came from time to time and told us the

most important news. As usual it was a little difficult for them to evaluate news in the proper perspective. For instance, one evening Tapakia came rushing in, highly agitated, and cried:

"Have you heard, have you heard what's happened on Pukapuka? [Another island in the Tuamotu group about 130 miles east of Raroia.] The schoolteacher's been murdered! Her husband did it. When he came home from fishing, she was with another man, and he was so angry that he stuck his harpoon into her. He stuck it into her three times, and she died soon afterward."

"That is awful," we both said, sincerely meaning it.

"Yes, isn't it?" Tapakia went on. "He ought to have hit her with his fists or a log of wood instead. That's what we do on Raroia. But on some of the eastern islands they often use harpoons to fight with. That's bad."

We discussed the incident long and thoroughly. At last there was nothing more to be added, so we asked Tapakia if he had no other interesting news to tell us.

"Let me see," he said. "Yes, two schooners are coming to Raroia in a week. On Tahiti they're arranging a ball with *two* bands, and a great war has begun in Europe."

"What?" I cried, catching hold of his arm in alarm. "What did you say? Who has started a war?"

"Let me see," said Tapakia, scratching his head, "either it was Germany and Russia against America and some other countries, or else it was Russia and America against Germany and England and maybe some other countries. I don't remember exactly. But anyhow it's a big war."

We waited anxiously for the next news report, but did not need to listen long to find that Tapakia's version of events in Europe was misleading, to say the least. But we did not dare interrupt him to give him a correct account of what had happened. He was in the middle of an animated discussion with Temake about the murder on Pukapuka and the ball at Papeete.

Many days passed with no more startling news—neither murders nor wars. Then Chief Teka came quite unexpectedly one day and informed us that the governor was coming to the Tuamotu Islands on a tour of inspection. This was truly great news, for Raroia had not been honored with a visit from a governor since 1910! The Raroians, who even consider the *mutoi,* or policeman, a person of high standing, were almost panic-stricken at this announcement, and some of the most inventive immediately proposed that the whole population should hide on the islands on the other side of the lagoon.

Teka, however, showed himself equal to the situation and made a shrewd appeal to their local patriotism. He got up and made a long speech in which he pointed out that the Raroians, instead of going and hiding, ought to take the opportunity to distinguish themselves. On most of the islands in the Tuamotu group, he pointed out, there was no radio, and there would therefore be no expectation of, and no preparations for, the governor's visit. On Raroia, thanks to Temake's radio, everyone was now warned, and it would be possible to give the governor a reception such as he had never experienced. Thus the Raroians would gain not only his favor, but prestige and honor among all the Tuamotu Islanders.

The response was as Teka intended. All were filled with enthusiasm and forgot their fear of the exalted person. At a public meeting which was held on the following day several of the villagers proposed lavish plans for the reception. Taipuhia, for example, wanted to decorate the whole "main street" with triumphal arches of roses, while Maono eagerly advocated a gigantic fireworks display. As there were neither roses nor pyrotechnic pieces on the island, and there was no time to send for any (details which Taipuhia and Maono willingly agreed that they had forgotten in their zeal), the islanders unanimously accepted Tekura's proposal to clean up the village, paint the flagstaff, and organize a feast with genuine Polynesian songs and dances.

The village had not been thoroughly cleaned up for a long time, but the whole population flung itself into the task with such energy that only a few days later all the "streets" were cleaned of weeds, all hedges clipped, and all the tumble-down houses propped up. Taupua, our "mother," undoubtedly showed the greatest zeal, for she pulled up not only the weeds, but all the flowers and other plants which grew in her garden. It finally resembled a newly plowed field more than anything.

"But why are you pulling up all the flowers?" we asked her while she was devastating the garden.

"Oh," she said, "simple flowers like these will certainly seem no better than weeds to the governor."

So saying, she seized the next clump with concentrated energy and pulled it up by the roots.

When the Raroians had finished cleaning up the village, a huge mountain of empty bottles bore witness to their monumental thirst. Rehua, who was almost as much interested in empty bottles as in full ones and has the prettiest "beer bed" on the island, proposed that they should be planted along the "main street" of the village as a kind of triumphal avenue for the governor. Fortunately, we succeeded in preventing his plans from being carried out.

Teka pointed out quite rightly that the quay was in a lamentable state and that the governor's first impression would therefore be very bad, which could have most unfortunate consequences. To repair the quay was, however, a big job, especially as the necessary sand and coral had to be fetched from the outskirts of the village—and the Raroians had no desire to undertake such severe exertions, even for the governor's sake.

Teka now gave proof once more of his superior knowledge of humanity. He immediately announced a work game. He divided the population into several groups, each of which fetched a handcart. Then he had all the carts drawn up in a line and declared that the team which was the first to load its cart and push it to the quay should get half-a-dozen bottles of beer.

This was a method of work which the Raroians understood. For two whole days the village rang with laughter and shrieking from morning to late in the evening, and the quay grew rapidly in both breadth and length. Certainly it was more tiring to work in this manner, and certainly several of the carts were smashed, but what did that matter? It was jolly work anyhow, and that was the most important thing. Anyone who thinks that the Polynesians' idleness is unconquerable would have changed his mind with this display of energy. During the two days the work lasted, the Raroians only knocked off for a half-hour at dinner-time—when the sun was at its highest—and that was not to eat but to divert themselves with a short game of football!

Not till the quay was finished did they begin to rehearse the songs and dances which were to form part of the festive program. As there were no good leaders among the young people, Te Iho was summoned and for a time he seemed to liven up again and regain his youth and energy. I remember particularly the first evening when, along with all the Raroians who could walk or crawl, we went out to a glade outside the village to see the rehearsals.

Every spectator had with him a lamp or torch, and they at once formed a wide ring of light within which the participants took their stand. The "band" took its place under a palm close by. It consisted of five men with empty kerosene cans for drums. Te Iho first showed how the dances should be done, and then, marking time to the sound of the drums, the little troupe of men and women began to move backward and forward on the dance floor of coral sand.

As the hours passed Te Iho became more and more inspired and the dancing livelier and wilder. The shadows leaped and danced among the palm trunks in the flickering, shifting light, like ghosts and spirits from a past age, wakened to life by the primitive exciting music. Breakers rumbled dully in the background. We could not help being affected by the strange atmosphere and felt ourselves suddenly carried hundreds of years back in time.

During the first evening rehearsals no fine dresses had yet been made for the participants, but soon more and more of the men and women began to appear in loincloths and crowns of plaited pandanus leaves. When finally all the performers looked as heathenish as their ancestors, the band decided that the kerosene cans were a trifle unsuitable and replaced them with real wooden drums, made for the occasion by hollowing out a few branches of hard *tou* wood.

When the dancers collapsed, exhausted, and the drummers could no longer move a finger, they rehearsed their songs. In addition to the old, well-known songs and ballads, they decided one evening to make up a new song, as is

The women practiced long and hard in order to perfect a special dance for the festivities planned for the governor's visit . . . .

. . . . and the men made special gifts for the long-awaited governor. They carved a walking stick, inlaid with mother-of-pearl, and fashioned the head in the form of a turtle. The other gift was a fiber crown.

Dressed in native costume, I tried on a palm-leaf crown, the type usually worn as a sunshade.

When copra is to be made on Raro, a great distance from the village, the whole family sets out in one canoe, loaded down with supplies, and sometimes they even take their galvanized-iron houses.

A wheelbarrow loaded with provisions to be taken to the lagoon islands for the stay while making copra. Note the pups in the basin.

At the lagoon islands, after the nuts have been split with an ax, the halves are piled up, with the coconut meat facing downward, and left to dry.

After the heaped-up nuts have dried, the copra is removed with a special knife (*above*). A boy drinks the coconut water from one of the three eyes (*below, left*). Raroians now make fire by rubbing two sticks only when matches are not available (*below, right*).

usual on all important occasions. First they agreed on a familiar tune, and then one of the men was chosen, by vote, to compose the words. He did not use pen and paper, but instead in real Polynesian style read the verses aloud as he composed them, and those who sat round repeated them quietly to themselves. Every verse ended with the words, "it takes a long time for the governor to come to Raroia, he's been on his way for forty years." When the song was finally composed (in about an hour), one of the girls got up and sang it from beginning to end without a mistake. When it was next rehearsed, everyone knew it.

We begged Te Iho, half in fun and half in earnest, to invent a new dance. He did not hesitate for a moment, but asked at once what kind of dance we wanted. He had often shown us how the Polynesians make fire by friction, and we had found his movements surprisingly harmonious and rhythmical. We therefore asked him if he could do a "fire-making" dance. An hour later he had devised a new dance, so fascinating and symbolic that even a spectator of moderate imagination could have read into it the whole drama of man's eternal striving for clarity and light.

After two weeks' hard work and diligent practice everything was ready—with one important exception. The men had not yet been able to agree as to who was to deliver the speech of welcome to the governor. But the day the radio announced that the governor had left Papeete, they decided in true Solomonic style that Taipuhia should deliver the speech, as he was the only man who at the moment was neither hoarse nor suffering from a cold.

Taipuhia took the task seriously, for he shut himself into a palm-leaf house (specially built for this purpose) with a copybook and a pen borrowed from the schoolmistress, and did not come out till he had written a speech which extended from one cover to the other. That it might be really perfect, he asked me to type it for him. When at last the masterpiece was finished, it occupied eight closely typed pages, although I had taken pains to omit some of Taipuhia's wildest extravagances of style. He looked as radiantly happy as an author who sees the result of his efforts in print for the first time.

Next day, however, he stood in the doorway again, twisting his hat in slight embarrassment.

"What is it now?" I sighed. "Have you written a new speech?"

"No, not really," he replied, "but I'd like you to write the old speech again."

He fished up a dirty ball of paper from one of his trouser pockets.

"Look, I lent people the speech, and when I got it back it looked like this."

I retyped it from beginning to end and for safety's sake made a carbon copy for the Raroians' use.

The same evening on which the new version of Taipuhia's speech began to circulate, a fresh council was held to discuss what else ought to be done. All agreed that the most important thing which remained was to find some presents for the governor, and finally Manumea and Rehua were commissioned to make a stick and a coconut-fiber crown— the old symbols of chieftaincy in the Tuamotu group.

We knew that both Manumea and Rehua were skilled woodcarvers, but the stick they showed us a few days later really exceeded all our expectations. It was carved from the finest *tamanu*—a kind of wood which is called Tahitian mahogany—and inlaid with mother-of-pearl shells which cast a golden shimmer (a rare variety). The shape was simple and dignified and the stick ended at the top in a graceful handle formed like a turtle, the Tuamotuans' sacred animal in the old heathen times. It was indeed a masterpiece!

The coconut-fiber crown was also a work of art, but it had one serious defect. It was so large that it would most certainly fall down onto the governor's nose. Rehua had the bright idea of threading a string through it, and declared that he would take the measure of the governor's head with his eyes as soon as he stepped ashore and pull the string of the crown till it was the right size. We thought this a slightly risky solution, but the Raroians showed no misgivings, so we went along with it.

The stick and the crown were substantially gifts from the men. The women did not want to be outdone, so they divided themselves into working parties and began to plait a pandanus mat.

An ordinary pandanus mat is about 6 by 6 feet in size, but before we could wink an eyelid the governor's mat was at least 15 by 30 feet. As we quickly discovered, its gigantic dimensions were due not only to the women's desire to surpass all other pandanus mats which the governor could imaginably receive, but also to practical considerations. On Maihotu's proposal it had been decided to plait a text into the mat with the aid of red ribbons—and this text consisted of a whole verse of the Bible in letters three feet high!

While all this was going on, Tepava and Teka listened regularly to the radio, which had some news about the governor's tour of inspection almost every day. Among other things they heard that the governor's wife was also on board the ship. It would, of course, be impolite to forget her when the presents were being made, so the Raroians at once began to worry their heads to find something suitable for her. At last Marie-Thérèse remembered she collected shells. That was the solution. There were masses of shells on the beaches, and it would take no time to make a nice collection. However, our friends were dubious.

"Pooh, ordinary shells aren't a thing to give to the governor's wife," one said.

"If only we could gild them," said another.

"What does she want the shells for?" said a third. "Does she eat them?"

"She'll laugh at us," said a fourth. "Let's try to embroider a tablecloth instead."

We stood our ground and explained that she had many shells from other places but none as yet from the Tuamotu Islands, and that she would be glad to get as many new ones as possible. No one seemed really convinced by our arguments, but they all frankly admitted that we ought to understand *popaa* affairs better than they, as we ourselves were *popaa,* and at last they agreed to collect shells. Next morning a heap of shells began to form on our veranda. There were small shells and large shells, round shells and twisted shells, white shells and colored shells, but all had one thing in common—they were unusually pretty and bright. The situation was saved.

On the afternoon of the same day Teka made a tour of inspection through the village. Everything seemed to be in perfect order. The streets of the village were freshly sanded and raked, there were gay flower beds here and there among the palms, and many of the houses were newly painted. The village indeed looked really smart. But suddenly Teka stopped. Tauroa had obviously done nothing to his tumbledown shanty of rusty galvanized iron and wooden boxes—

and his house was conspicuously opposite the village assembly house.

The chief summoned Tauroa, who declared that he had indeed meant to paint the house, but that it had not been done simply because he had no paint. When Teka pressed him a little, he admitted that he ought to have asked someone to lend him some paint, but added, probably with truth, that he had not thought of this until it was too late. Teka ordered a search of the village, but unfortunately there was not enough paint left even to paint Tauroa red, which Tunui proposed as a suitable punishment.

At last Tauroa hit upon what seemed to him an excellent solution to the problem. He maintained that it did not matter so much if the house was tumble-down and a trifle paintless, for he would seat himself at the door and entertain the governor in such a fascinating manner that the latter would not notice what the house looked like.

No one, however, had any great confidence in Tauroa's charm, and so the inhabitants decided at once to do the only possible thing—to move the house. There was no time to be lost, and the men fetched wooden rollers, which they pushed under the house. The whole population helped, and despite Tauroa's vigorous protests the house soon disappeared into a clump of trees a few hundred yards away. Tauroa stood in the doorway till the last moment, attempting with eloquent pantomime to show how urbanely he would receive the governor, if only the house might stay where it was.

Several days passed. Early each morning Teka sent a party of boys over to the west side of the island to keep a lookout for the government vessel, and he ordered them to climb up into the palm tops that they might see her as soon as possible. They stayed there as a rule till late at night, when fear of the dark at last drove them home. He himself constantly inspected the village and assembled the population daily to practice the reception ceremony down on the quay.

To make as effective an impression as possible we had decided that I was to play a phonograph record of the *"Marseillaise"* at the moment when Teka said in a loud voice, "Welcome to Raroia, Your Excellency!" Immediately afterward the population would join in the song. Not till the national anthem was over would the turn of Taipuhia, the singers, and all the rest come.

All the rehearsals went splendidly. Old and young knew their parts by heart. Teka bellowed, "Welcome, Your Excellency!" like the fiercest drill sergeant, and the whole crowd sang the *"Marseillaise"* with spirit and gusto, although of course none of them knew the words very well.

We had just finished rehearsing the ceremony for the fifth or sixth time when one of the scouts came running and breathlessly announced that a ship was in sight on the horizon to northward. We all hurried over to the lookout point. The sails grew in size quickly, and there was no doubt that it was the government schooner. When the gleaming white ship dropped anchor in the lagoon a half-hour later, we were assembled on the quay, confident and expectant.

But one thing struck me at once. All was so curiously silent and still on board the vessel. No gold-braided personages were to be seen, and no orders were heard. We all began to be uneasy and nervous. Something was wrong. Five minutes, ten minutes, a quarter of an hour passed without anything happening. At last a rowboat cast off from the ship and slowly approached the quay. In the stern sat a subordinate official, holding a portfolio. *He was alone!* Not even the administrators of the Tuamotus had come.

"What shall we do now?" said Taipuhia in despair, fingering his fine typewritten speech.

"The only thing we can do is to carry out the entire reception program," Teka replied. "It's too late to draw back."

So as soon as the rowboat scraped against the quay I set the *"Marseillaise"* going, and Teka drew himself up and bellowed: "Welcome, Your Excellency!"

The official was so overwhelmed at this unexpected reception that he could not utter a word, but the many verses of the *"Marseillaise"* gave him time to pull himself together, and the last notes had scarcely died away when he raised his voice and said: "But what on earth are you doing?"

"Doing?" replied Teka. "We're waiting for the governor. Isn't he on board?"

"No," said the official. "He's on board a destroyer. What made you suppose he was coming?"

"Temake's fine new radio said he was," Teka answered, and for the first time he sounded a little uneasy.

"It was said that he was coming to the Tuamotu group on a tour of inspection. That is correct. But the Tuamotu group is large. There are seventy-eight islands and he cannot visit them all. For that matter he has already visited as many islands as he can, and he is on his way back to Papeete now."

The official looked round, shook his head, and added:

"Hurry up and get out your reports and books, for we must go on to Takume at once."

Poor Teka! He had never imagined that the governor could make a tour of inspection among the Tuamotu Islands without visiting Raroia. Poor Raroians! They, too, had assumed that Raroia and Tuamotu meant the same thing, although the announcer had not positively said so. Poor boys and girls who had practiced songs and dances all for nothing! Poor children who had expected to be present at real festivities!

Marie-Thérèse and I felt very sorry for our friends and realized that something must be done. But what? Suddenly I had an idea. I called to Teka:

"Sound the village drum. We'll have a sports contest."

"Sports contest—what's that?" asked Teka, bewildered.

"You'll see. Collect the people."

The natives immediately greeted our proposal with visible and audible delight, and after eager discussion and demonstration we finally agreed to hold a popular festival, the main features of which would be folk dances, tossing the caber, and throwing the discus. No one had ever heard of these games, but they were anxious to try them after I explained them. As a finale, a real Polynesian dinner would be served. There was no time to lose, and while the Raroians ran home and kicked off their shoes and got out of their Sunday clothes, Marie-Thérèse and I began to measure out the ground for the contests in the open space in front of the assembly house.

To find logs for tossing the caber, the men felled a few young palms and cut them into pieces about fifteen feet long, so heavy that I could only just lift them. But amid cheers and wild cries of *ke-ke-ke-ke-te-hu-ru-hu-ru* the strong men of Raroia tossed them a good thirty feet. When Taipuhia had shown his superiority three times in succession, we went on to throwing the discus, which was open to all comers.

We had difficulty in finding stones suitable for discuses, and it was not until Hamani discovered that mussels' shells were suited to this purpose that the game really got going. For a good hour the shells flew through the air like projectiles, in which the sun was mirrored and refracted in all the colors of the rainbow. It was rather hard to decide who were the winners in the different groups, as they all cheated as soon as our backs were turned, but we finally managed to pick out three boys, two women, and one old man for the final which one of the women won with surprising fairness.

Then we went on to the folk dances. In honor of the occasion the Raroians composed new words, which were about as much like the original as a soldiers' song is like a nursery rhyme!

As the general excitement had reached undreamed-of heights, and nobody wanted to stop, we thought we had better think of some new items for the program and proposed an obstacle race. Fresh enthusiasm hailed the new diversion, and in no time an obstacle course of boxes, school benches, and furniture—the course will long be remembered —was made round the assembly house. The most difficult obstacle was Ruto's carpenter's shop, which we had turned upside down and filled with old chairs. It was certainly no child's play to clear it, and one or two of the stoutest women got so hopelessly trapped that they did not succeed in getting out till the race was over.

After we had all rested a little, Tehei suggested a genuine Polynesian contest. Marie-Thérèse and I were delighted. The men at last settled on a spear-throwing contest, an old Polynesian sport about which we had heard a great deal.

While the other men were fetching their fishing spears, Tehei placed a coconut on top of a stake, about twice his own height. Then he stepped out twenty-five yards and drew a line on the ground. By now the competitors had begun to assemble. Each of them had ten thin, supple spears with iron points, each spear marked with its owner's name. Tehei announced that the competitors could throw their spears when they liked and in what order they liked. The man who scored the most hits would, of course, be the winner.

The participants crouched down with every muscle taut, holding their spears in position. Then Tehei gave a sign and the spears began to whistle through the air. All the competitors held the spear by the butt and aimed with the point, and all showed an equally astonishing sureness of aim. When the contest was over, seventeen quivering spears were fixed in the coconut, and as many had struck it but had broken loose and fallen to the ground. The fifteen participants had used 150 spears in all; considering that the distance was a good twenty-five yards and the coconut no bigger than a man's head, the percentage of hits was truly stupendous!

After this brilliant exhibition we thought it was time for dinner and the distribution of prizes. Our friends, however, were enjoying themselves too much to stop so soon, and they insisted on a sack race and last-couple-out. Marie-Thérèse and I marveled when our "mother," Taupua, who was certainly at least sixty, won both these events.

Afterward she disclosed the secret of her successes. During her frequent jaunts to Tahiti she had learned the knack of these games, and she had even on one occasion been woman champion of French Oceania in copra-sack racing. If the good Raroians had ever heard of the difference between an amateur and a professional, they would certainly have insisted on Taupua being declared a professional, but they were happily ignorant of this burning problem and were only delighted at her successes.

Not even when darkness began to fall would the Raroians stop, and it was not till we had announced a drinking contest (with coconuts) that they began to take a serious interest in the feast. But once they had sat down to huge helpings of roast pork and breadfruit, a deep weariness overcame them, and we could proceed to distribute the prizes in peace and quiet. Besides Teka's beer bottles the prizes consisted of raisins—a rare delicacy—chocolate cookies, and old magazines. To our surprise the magazines proved to be the most popular prizes. It even happened that Tapakia, who had won the spear-throwing contest, came and asked if he could not exchange half-a-dozen bottles of beer for a bundle of magazines! This must be regarded as a unique occurrence, for Tapakia had the reputation of being the thirstiest individual on the island!

But the finest and most notable prizes we ourselves received. In the middle of dinner Tupuhoe rose and handed over to us the Raroian prize of honor—the governor's coconut-fiber crown and mother-of-pearl stick. I tried to persuade him to keep the treasures till the governor really visited the island, but Tupuhoe would not yield. He said, in tones which betrayed a certain disappointment, that the Raroians had been waiting for a visit from the governor for forty years and that they would probably have to wait another forty. I therefore gave way at last and accepted the presents.

The coconut-fiber crown came to a sad end (it was blown away one stormy night, when the wind turned our house inside out), but I still have the stick and often use it on formal occasions. Whenever I take it out, I cannot help but wonder if there is not more than one reason why the handle of the stick which the Raroians meant to give their long desired governor should take the form of a turtle. Our brown-skinned friends do not lack a sense of humor!

The Rustling Palms

A MISSIONARY on one of the Tuamotu Islands once wrote: "There is scarcely any part of the coconut palm which the South Seas natives cannot utilize, and to describe all the riches with which the Creator has endowed this tree is to sing a hymn in His praise."

Indeed, the rustling palm whose soft murmurings are heard on every South Sea island serves the natives well.

To begin at the bottom of the tree, the dry root fibers are used to make the finest kind of dance skirt. The women collect a great bunch of these fibers, which are unusually thin and fine, soak them for a week, then beat them with a wooden club until they are soft and pliable, and finally plait them.

The trunk of the palm is well suited for house posts, and many people throw a house together quickly and gaily, simply by driving four posts down into the earth and nailing galvanized iron or planks between them. The pith itself is soft and floury, and consequently the tree is not suitable for sawing up into planks. But the outer layers of the trunk consist of a hard heavy wood, which in old times was used for making lances and war clubs and is now the principal material employed in furniture-making and the more delicate types of carpentering.

Even more useful than the roots and trunk are the leaves. Every leaf on a coconut palm consists of a stiff central nerve, many feet in length, along which the fronds are fixed. By splitting the central nerve lengthwise and plaiting together the fronds on the two halves a convenient mat is made, which is usually eight feet long and two feet wide. These palm-leaf mats have been a household necessity throughout the people's whole history, and the Raroians often make quantities of them to keep in stock. They can serve as enclosures, coverings for the copra, house walls, and sheds. Otherwise the palm leaves are used in more or less the same way as we use paper, and all the men, women, and children can make a leaf parcel or plait a basket in the twinkling of an eye.

The most valuable part of the palm is the coconut itself. When ripe, a nut is about the size of a man's head and weighs ten pounds or more. Outwardly it looks smooth and polished, but if you cut it in half, you discover that under the smooth surface there is an inner layer of soft fibers which resemble horsehair. Embedded in this layer of fiber, which measures from two to four inches thick, lies the actual nut. It consists of a hard shell filled with coconut water, which as the nut ripens gives off a thicker and thicker deposit of grease—the coconut meat.

Marie-Thérèse and I had always thought that a coconut was a coconut, but after a few weeks on Raroia, we found we had been mistaken. Although the palms themselves are alike, there are nearly as many different kinds of nut as there are pears or apples. For the Raroians, as for all Polynesians, the differences are more important than the similarities, and characteristically enough they have no word which corresponds to our "coconut"—only names for the different kinds.

Once when we asked Tufaka, who has had four years' schooling and speaks French fluently, to fetch a *noix de coco,* he was completely baffled and finally explained that a coconut as a general term did not exist and that we must say which sort of nut we wanted.

An important and natural way of classifying the nuts is by size and ripeness. Five types are usually distinguished. The smallest, newly formed nuts are called *puriri*. They are never picked and are valuable only because they will grow into larger nuts. During violent squalls the wind blows down masses of *puriri* nuts, and the children often collect them for mock battle, in the same way that American boys play war with acorns.

The next stage of development is the *rehi*. A *rehi* is an almost full-sized nut in which the coconut water has begun to give off a thin deposit of grease. The water is drinkable, but it does not taste really good until the next stage, when the nut is called *viavia*. The deposit of grease is still insignificant at this point, and only in the full-sized nut, *omoto,* does it measure nearly half an inch. Finally, in the last stage, the nut is called *ngora*. It is dark brown in color and sometimes has a rather shriveled appearance; the water is sour and unpleasant to taste, and the kernel of the nut has reached its maximum thickness, about one inch.

The *ngora* nuts fall as soon as they are ripe. The remainder of the nuts have to be picked, a task performed in several different ways. The classical method, of course, is to climb the palm trees for them. Much nonsense has been written about the natives' wonderful climbing powers. In reality it is no more difficult to climb a palm tree than to swarm up a rope, which American schoolboys and schoolgirls learn without any difficulty. If anything it is easier, for the palms have round rings on the trunks which give good support to the feet. To study the climbing technique more closely, however, we took some small boys with us one day and found a straight palm which was about eighty feet high.

Ten-year-old Mataroa, who was considered to be the smartest climber, had the honor of beginning. He clasped the trunk with both hands and hung straight down. Then he drew up his legs as high as he could and got a hold on the trunk with his feet; he then arched his back like a cat and stretched out his legs, moving his arms up at the same time. He was now a good many feet up the trunk, and by continually repeating the same series of movements he shot quickly toward the top. The other boys followed, having first for safety's sake drawn a ring of plaited palm leaves around their ankles to keep their feet from slipping too far apart.

In addition to this climbing technique the Raroians use another more exacting method. By catching hold with one hand a little above the other and moving an arm and a leg alternately, they clamber up just as we would ascend a ladder. The small but decisive difference is that they must catch hold with their hands *behind* the trunk, which requires a considerably stronger grip than climbing a ladder.

Climbing palms, however, has become old-fashioned, like so much else on Raroia. It may be all right for small boys or for an emergency, but for general practice the islanders have found an easier method of getting at the nuts. Every household possesses a long wooden pole with an iron hook at one end, and with its help the Raroians can in a moment tear down as many nuts as they want without consuming any unnecessary energy. And the leisurely Raroians have put this pole to further use. By tying the nuts together in pairs and hanging them over the pole, now balanced on the shoulder, a man can easily carry several dozen home.

Although picking a nut involves little difficulty, a good deal of skill is required to open it—at any rate if one wants to keep the coconut water. One way is, of course, to cut off the top, fiber and all. But this method the Raroians consider both impractical and clumsy. It is difficult to cut a piece off neatly; moreover, the nut is always heavy and unwieldy so long as the fiber is on it, and no matter how one holds it, some of the water is bound to spill on the ground. The Raroians, therefore, always remove the fiber before they open a nut, and this they do rather cleverly. They sharpen a thick stick of wood about three feet long and drive it into the ground. Then they grasp the nut with both hands and press it against the upstanding point till it penetrates the husk to a depth of two or three inches. It is then easy, by carefully working the nut sideways, to loosen a strip of the husk. Strip after strip is peeled off in the same way until only the nut itself remains.

At one end of the nut there are the three eyes. If it is a drinking nut intended for children, one of these holes is usually opened. But an adult seldom likes to drink a nut in this manner. He prefers to cut a square hole in the opposite end and empty the nut as if it were a giant champagne glass! (Whether this habit has contributed to the Raroians' tendency to curved glasses and French wines I could not say.)

The division of the nuts into *puriri, rehi, viavia, omoto,* and *ngora* corresponding to different stages of maturity is, however, insufficient. All *rehi* do not taste the same, nor do all *viavia* or *omoto* have exactly the same characteristics. The Raroians, therefore, have terms which signify different varieties. These can generally be defined by shades of color, and the three most important are *mamangu, kekeho,* and *kurakura* — green, light yellowish-brown, and red-brown nuts, respectively.

By combining these two series of names the Raroians can exactly describe the characteristics and appearance of a nut, and they need never be afraid of suffering what happened to us at the beginning of our stay when children often came back with a sour inedible nut instead of a fresh one.

The experience of centuries has also told the Raroians how the different varieties should best be used. The best drinking nut is a *viavia kekeho.* It has a faintly sweet taste and often has small air bubbles like soda water a day old. The coconut water is best and coolest if the nut is picked early in the morning, but is quite drinkable all day, as the thick fiber covering acts as an insulation. A *viavia mamangu* is also drinkable, but rather bitter. It is therefore best suited for a beverage while at work, as the sweeter *viavia kekeho* tends to increase thirst rather than diminish it.

While the coconut water is used exclusively for drinking, the meat of the coconut is put to much more varied uses. As early as the *rehi* stage the nut is sought and eaten straight out of the shell. Its consistency is roughly that of soft cheese, and Raroians consider it a great delicacy. As a rule this kind of nut meat is the first solid food a child gets, and when a child is two or three years old, it plays a large part in his bill of fare. But the nut with the most valuable meat is undoubtedly the mature *ngora* nut. The nuts found in American groceries are of this type, for the simple reason that it is the only sort of nut which can be transported for a long distance without rotting. The coconut water in these nuts is sour and the meat generally hard and thick.

The Raroians, like the Polynesians in general, use the *ngora* nuts exclusively in the grated form for different dishes or for making sauce. Every household consumes at least half-a-dozen *ngora* nuts a day, and they are still grated in the primitive Polynesian manner. The instrument used is an *ana,* a four-legged wooden stool which has a projecting wooden arm; it resembles most closely a hobbyhorse. A crescent-shaped piece of iron (formerly a piece of mother-of-pearl) is nailed firmly to the "head," or wooden arm, of the stool.

When a woman wants to grate a nut, she first cuts it in half across the middle, then she takes a half in one hand, sits astride the stool, and presses the nut against the cutting iron, while at the same time she spins it round with the other hand. The thin, finely separated flakes fall straight down into a dish on the ground.

The famous coconut milk is made from this grated coconut pulp. The recipe is very simple. Take a piece of cloth—or lacking a cloth, the fibrous tissue which surrounds the leafstalks on young palms—wrap the coconut pulp in it, and press with great force till the coconut milk begins to trickle out. That is all. The liquid is exactly like ordinary milk in appearance, but is never drunk. Instead it is very often used as a sauce, and every well-provided dinner table bears a bowl of coconut milk mixed with sea water, in which the Raroians dip all their food, whatever it may be—breadfruit, fish, corned beef, or bread—before they pop it into their mouths.

In America and in most European countries, the term "coconut milk" is used for the clear liquid inside a coconut. This liquid, however, should be called "coconut water," and the term "coconut milk" reserved only for the greasy juice which is pressed out of the grated coconut meat. The earliest Pacific explorers appropriately called this white sauce "coconut milk," but later on botanists and South Sea enthusiasts who had never seen a coconut made the mistake of using this term for what should properly be called "coconut water," and the mistake still stubbornly persists.

But the coconut water and the meat are by no means the only parts of the nut which are utilized. From the shells themselves scoops and bowls are made, which after a little polishing with a coral stone acquire a beautiful dark-brown sheen. In recent times the natives have devised another original use. They make charcoal from them. Comically enough, their conversion at the end of the last century created this need. Previously they had only worn a few scraps of clothing of plaited pandanus, or gone about quite naked. This, of course, the missionaries considered incompatible with Christian morality, and at last they succeeded in persuading the people to get themselves at least a pair of trousers or a dress.

After they had rigged themselves out in *popaa* clothes, they also wanted, in *popaa* style, to increase their elegance by pressing their clothes. For this they required flatirons. The only irons for sale on board the schooners were of an old-fashioned English make, heated by charcoal which was stuffed into an inside container. Thus the Raroians came to need charcoal, and after a short period of experiment, they found that coconut shells were the best raw material. As we see, it is not always necessity which is the mother of invention!

There is still another part of the nut which has not yet been mentioned. If one lets a *ngora* nut grow till the leaf begins to appear, the nut is filled up with a porous, fibrous pulp. This pulp is called *nounou* and is highly valued for two reasons. First and foremost, it can be eaten in a raw state, when it most resembles a gigantic sweet and mealy apple. On Raroia, therefore, *nounou* plays roughly the same part as candy with us. The only difference is that the Raroian children get their sweets more easily. They need neither money nor candy counters, but have only to pick up and open a few of the nuts which lie about on the ground.

In recent years, however, the adults too have begun to take more and more interest in the *nounou* nuts. They have discovered that a strong beer can be made from the contents of these nuts, and they use this substitute extensively since the export of hard liquor and beer to the Tuamotu Islands has been forbidden.

As the Raroians see everything on a large scale, they always brew at least a cask of beer at a time. The cask invariably contains fifty gallons and is usually a gasoline drum; it is placed right over the fire and filled with *nounou* and water. After a few hours' boiling the *nounou* pulp is taken out and yeast, sugar, and rice added; then everything is allowed to boil for some time longer. The drink has a fresh fruity taste, but is so strong that it often takes several days for the population to empty one of these casks, although they all certainly do their best.

There remains the husk. Its primary importance is as fuel, since there are few trees on the island and those which exist are needed for house-building and carpentering. The Raroians generally kill two birds with one stone when they cut up a few coconuts for a meal. The meat and coconut water are used for food and drink, and the husk to make a fire under the cooking pots and saucepans.

In old (and perhaps also good) times all rope and string were made of coconut husk, but since the schooners have begun to sell hemp ropes and cotton string, the Raroians have naturally abandoned the native material, although it is better and more durable. Many of the islanders have found, however, that coconut husk makes excellent stuffing for a mattress and in their delight at this have stuffed their mattresses so full that they are as round as sausages. Of course, no one can lie on these sausagelike affairs, but that doesn't matter, as the beds are there only for show, to impress the neighbors.

As the trees are groaning under the weight of coconuts and large heaps of cut-up husk lie about everywhere copra is made, I was surprised that all the Raroians did not have mattresses of the much-admired sausage shape. This mystery was cleared up for me when I asked Tunui why he, too, did not make himself a mattress.

"I'd like to have a little shredded husk fiber," he replied, "but it's hard to find new crabs' holes."

"Crabs' holes?" I exclaimed in amazement. "What have crabs' holes to do with coconut husk?"

"Don't you know?" Tunui asked, every bit as astonished as myself. "There's a kind of large crab here in the Tuamotu Islands that lives on coconuts. They've two big claws as sharp as knives. To get at the kernel of the nut they tear the fiber away thread by thread and leave the nut in the sun till it cracks. So there are always masses of torn-off husk, ready for use, outside the crabs' holes. As soon as I find some new crabs' holes I shall stuff my mattress."

I suggested to Tunui that he should tear off a little coconut fiber himself, but this he considered an unthinkable solution.

A further original use of the coconut husk—or, to be more correct, of the outer covering of certain nuts which for one reason or another had not become fibrous—should perhaps be mentioned before we leave this subject. The word *kaipoa* is applied by the Raroians to a *rehi* or *viavia* nut which has a thick outer covering of about the same consistency as a sugar beet or turnip. The remarkable thing about this covering is that it is edible and a great thirst quencher. So when we wanted a little fresh food, we simply got a *kaipoa* nut, cut it up, and we had a first-class salad!

This short account (naturally far from complete) will perhaps give some idea of the important part which the coconut palm plays in the life of the Raroians and of all other Polynesian peoples confined to the meager resources of an atoll. But the importance of all these foodstuffs and other necessities with which the coconut palm provides the Raroians *directly* is small compared with the prosperity it brings them *indirectly* through copra. While the nuts could formerly only be used for food and drink, through the development of the copra trade coconuts have become a kind of money growing on trees, enabling the Raroians to satisfy all their wishes and caprices.

Our first initiation into the mysteries of copra preparation took place one day at the beginning of the year when we accompanied the Raroians to their plantations on the numerous islets south of the village. Everyone, of course, had assembled in the village during Christmas, but as soon as the

Epiphany was past many began to talk of going off, "as the price of copra might fall any day." But a visit from a schooner, a miraculous haul of fish, a feast, and a few illustrated magazines, which we had received by mail, detained them all; indeed, a whole month passed before anyone recollected his intention of hurrying away.

We had asked Rauri to tell us when it was time to get ready, and early one afternoon at the beginning of February he suddenly appeared and informed us that the departure would take place next morning.

"Why didn't you tell us before?" I said in a tone of mild reproach. "There's a lot of work to do, packing and clearing up everything, if we're to stay a month on the southern part of the island."

"I'd have told you earlier with pleasure," Rauri replied laughing. "But it wasn't decided till now. When a Raroian gets an idea, it's like a stroke of lightning. It comes suddenly and unexpectedly, and if it doesn't catch on at once it never will. So I should advise you to have everything ready early tomorrow morning."

Rauri's advice was well founded, for next morning there was a regular break-up atmosphere. When we came trudging down with our sailors' duffel bags on our backs, almost all the Raroians were assembled down on the beach and ten outrigger canoes already lay rocking on the waves with their sails flapping merrily in the wind. We got into Rauri's canoe, into which Taupua, Ruarangi, Tarakeha, Nganahoa, Ihi, Rauri junior, and Rari (the whole of our family-by-adoption) had already crammed themselves. The hold had naturally been loaded to capacity long before, and on deck there was a glorious muddle of household equipment, clothes, axes, and puppies (the provisions!). We may have looked a little uneasy as we sat down on the outrigger arm, for Rauri at once said soothingly:

"There's no danger for us. The canoe is new and the rail is always a hand's span above the water. Be glad that you're not in Tapakia's canoe, for that's old and rotten; besides, he always takes his house with him when he goes to the lagoon islands."

"Takes his house with him?" I asked in astonishment.

"Yes. He's too lazy to make a house of plaited coconut leaves every time he comes to a new lagoon island, and so he takes his iron house to pieces and takes it with him."

On closer inspection we did find that Tapakia's canoe was so packed with children and shining galvanized iron that it was on the verge of capsizing.

Soon the whole flotilla was on its way, south bound for Raro (the southwestern part of the atoll). Some of the passengers had taken their guitars, and while the canoes plowed forward through the waves, one of the young men in the leading canoe struck up an ancient travel song, which was in fact a trustful prayer to the gods to grant a fair wind and a safe passage. The wind carried the song on from canoe to canoe, and soon a mighty chorus of voices blended with the rushing of the waves and the crying of the gulls. The words and tune were simple, and Marie-Thérèse and I soon could blend our voices into the cheerful refrain:

> *"Hoe mai ra, hoe atu ra,*
> *Hoe mai te vaka nei,*
> *Na te vaka i tapiri to tatou fenua!"*

> "Let us paddle here, let us paddle there,
> Let us paddle this canoe,
> The canoe which nears our land!"

After a good hour's sail we arrived at Raro, which proved to be a string of small islets several miles long, separated by channels of varying depth. While the other canoes went on, Rauri steered into a bay on the largest island, which may have been three-quarters of a mile long and certainly was not more than a few hundred yards wide. We cast anchor in the light-green water of the bay and waded in toward the shore, where a house was visible among the palms. It consisted of a single room without windows and was built in the old Tuamotu style.

While Ruarangi and Taupua swiftly plaited some palm leaves together to repair a few holes in the roof, the rest of us fetched dry ferns, which we spread out on the floor of crushed coral. This completed the furnishings, and we went on to arrange the kitchen. Tarakeha drove two cleft wooden sticks into the ground and laid the branch of a tree along them, on which he hung up two cooking pans and a coffee-pot. Then Rauri fetched the rest of the household utensils and hung them up on a bush in the vicinity, while the rest of us collected coconut husk and other fuel. The kitchen was now ready, and we proceeded with other more important matters.

A round of visits to our neighbors on the nearest islets, which we paid with Rauri on the two following days, showed us that our dwelling was very well equipped and comfortable in comparison with those of many others. Rakenui and Vananga, for example, who were at work making copra a little farther south, had only a low tentlike house and a carton of canned goods which they heated right over the fire, while Tukaoko had neither canned goods nor cooking pans.

But Heiao's way of life was the most primitive of all.

He slept behind a wind screen, a roof of plaited palm leaves which reached down to the ground, and had no household equipment with him. He began his day by emptying two coconuts and then at once set about making copra. About midday he quenched his thirst with two more nuts and slept for a few hours until the worst heat was over, when he set to work again. Not till dusk began to fall did he knock off and harpoon a couple of fish, which he fried on the coals. He may have taken an afternoon off now and then to catch sea birds and lobsters or to collect birds' eggs, but these were the only breaks in his simple existence.

"If I build a wind screen on every island where I make copra, I am never far from home," Heiao explained. "Rauri has a fine house all right, but often it may be a half-hour's or an hour's walk from the plantation where he's working. There's no point in bringing a lot of belongings with one either. One can't take them about everywhere to one's different working places, and if they're left in the house, one has to go back to every meal. It's too much trouble."

Rauri pointed out that the advantage of having a house and being properly established was that a man could take his family with him, but Heiao, like most of those who subscribed to his method of work, seemed to have difficulty in seeing the importance of this. Apparently he found it rather a relief to get away from his wife and children for a time.

I asked Heiao what equipment he considered absolutely necessary.

"A pair of shorts, a *pareu* [loincloth], an ax, a copra knife, and a fishing spear," he replied unhesitatingly. "I seldom have with me more than that."

"But what about matches?" I objected. "You won't want to eat all your fish raw?"

"Matches are a good thing to have," Heiao answered quietly, "but not absolutely necessary. If I haven't any, or if they get wet, I do this."

Without rising he broke off a dry branch from a bush close by and cut it lengthwise with his copra knife. He laid one half on the ground before him, and gripped the other firmly with both hands. Then he put the point of the stick he held in his hands against the groove down the middle of the other, which was full of a dry pithlike sawdust, and moved it carefully to and fro several times. When the fine dust had collected in a small heap at the farther end of the groove, he increased the tempo and at the same time put more vigor into his movement. In a minute the groove down the middle of the lower stick began to assume a brownish color, and in a little while we could clearly detect the smell of burned wood.

Sweat was dripping from Heiao's forehead and his whole body was trembling with the strain. Suddenly a light smoke rose from the little heap of fuel, and we could see the glow of sparks as well. Heiao laid aside the rubbing stick and blew energetically on the smoldering fire. Little flames sprang up and he quickly held a piece of coconut husk over them. In a few minutes a fire was blazing before us. Heiao's answer was clear enough.

Many of our friends whom we visited during our stay on Raro lived lives as solitary and isolated as Heiao's, and it sometimes happened that they did not see any other human being for several weeks. Several of the families divided into smaller groups in order to get on with the work more quickly.

It seemed to me, therefore, rather curious that the worthy Raroians had been so particular about all beginning work on the copra at the same time and going to the same location together. I asked Rauri if it was always done this way, and he said it was. He also told me that the island was divided into three districts, in which copra was made in turn during defined periods.

"But when everyone makes copra by himself, why has the island been divided into districts and why do you all go to and from work together?" I asked.

"Well, that's hard to say, but it's always like that with everything on Raroia," Rauri answered. "If someone goes off to catch turtle, everyone immediately wants to catch turtle. If someone buys a red *pareu,* all the others immediately want to have a red *pareu.* Once Maono bought a pair of dark glasses on board a schooner. Next time a schooner came everyone bought dark glasses. The lenses were almost black and we had to take them off if we wanted to see properly, but the main thing was that we all had dark glasses like Maono's."

But there was another and considerably more rational explanation for this mass migration, which Rauri had evidently been ashamed to mention. The Raroians are afraid of being robbed by their neighbors if they do not keep an eye on their plantations; so either everyone goes to the lagoon islets, or no one is allowed to go!

There are undeniably some grounds for this fear, and the senseless division of the land is certainly the main reason why the Raroians, otherwise so honest, are a trifle light-fingered in the matter of copra nuts. According to prevailing custom the parents give their children a piece of land when they marry. Naturally, the land is also divided up in the same way when inherited. With each generation, therefore, the pieces of land have diminished in size and increased in number and each property owner has small holdings scattered over the island.

The situation was the same in medieval Europe, but the difficulties were gradually overcome by exchange and purchase. The Raroians, however, have opposed all attempts at reform and obstinately refuse to believe that any other patch of land could be as good as that which they have inherited from their fathers. The consequence has been that most of the islets are divided among ten, twenty, or thirty owners, and that there is not a single islet, however small, which is owned by one man alone.

These irrational conditions naturally impede copra production since most people are obliged to make perhaps half-a-dozen journeys to different lagoon islands to procure the same amount of copra they could make in half the time if they had all their land in one place. It is hardly surprising, therefore, that many people would pick as many nuts as they could get hold of, without bothering about boundaries, if the owners of the neighboring patches were not near.

The Raroians are as unwilling to exchange their land as to sell it. The natural consequence has been an unequal distribution of the land. While in one family there might have been many offspring for several generations, others would have only a few. With this general unwillingness to sell land, the only way in which those who have fared badly can hope to better their position is through an advantageous marriage. But this is no easier on Raroia than elsewhere, and the difference between the large and small owners of land tends to increase rather than to diminish.

Exactly how much land each man has is rather difficult to judge, but in any case there is a small "upper class" of five or six persons who have more than twice as much land as the average holder, and there are about the same number who have only just enough (by Raroian standards). In practice this has no very great importance, as those who are rich in land are unable to harvest all their copra themselves and are only too thankful to be able to employ those who have not land enough. The conditions of these agreements are very generous, and the landowner and workman always share the net takings equally. A hard-working person could, therefore, easily earn a small fortune in this way without owning a single coconut palm himself. But, of course, no such person exists on Raroia!

Another evil of the outmoded land division is, naturally, legal disputes. Far back in pre-European times there were already fights about land, and these became more and more common when the copra schooners began to appear and the nuts acquired an enhanced value. At last the authorities grew tired of the continual bickering and resolved to settle all the disputed cases once and for all and issue title deeds to all the landowners who could make their claims good.

The Tuamotuans' thorough knowledge of their family genealogies made this work considerably easier than it would otherwise have been. By calling councils, in which all of the older people took part, it was possible on most of the islands to clear up the complicated relationships, and therewith to determine the right to possession, fairly quickly. So far so good. But how could one fix the size and location of the pieces of land on those islands which had never been surveyed and mapped?

As the authorities had no surveyors at their disposal, they contented themselves with giving orders to the chiefs on all the Tuamotu Islands to measure out the land at once and send to Papeete a list of the owners' names. This was done on most of the islands in the same way as on Raroia. After a few days the chief got tired of crawling around measuring pieces of land which were not his own, and relieved himself of the troublesome task in the same way as his superiors—by delegating it to others. He simply called the inhabitants together, gave each a few hundred yards of string, and sent them out to measure their land themselves.

The result can easily be imagined, and one of the old men who took part in this famous survey told the following story:

"You'll understand," he said, "that it was a bit difficult, as many of us could neither count nor write, and no one had ever measured land before. But in spite of this everything might have gone well if it had not been for the bushes. On most of the islands there are masses of scrub, as you know. To be able to measure properly, of course, we should have cleared away the scrub. But we all thought that was too much trouble and found another way out.

"We fastened a bit of coral to one end of a string and flung it over the bushes. When we got back to the village, the chief measured the strings and calculated how large our pieces of land were. He wrote the result down in a big book which he sent to Papeete, and after a time we got our title deeds.

"All went well till Tara began to clear his piece of land. When he measured his land afterward to check up, it was naturally much less than when he had measured it with the bushes on it. Then at last we began to realize that we had deceived ourselves. We had indeed the title to the land— but we had the title to more land than there was on the whole island! As no one would give way, disputes became even commoner and more violent than before, and the situation is still more or less the same!"

During the month in which we lived with Rauri and our family-by-adoption on the lagoon islands, we had many opportunities to see how copra was made. The work was the simplest imaginable, and the whole family always took part in it. While the children and old people collected the *ngora* nuts which had fallen during the last few months, Rauri and Tarakeha took out their long-handled axes. A lifetime of practice had given them such certainty and skill that they cleft nuts into two exactly equal halves with a single, well-directed blow, never missing; and so sure and automatic were their movements, they could laugh and chat together all the while.

As soon as the nuts had been cut in half they poured out the last drops of the sour and worthless coconut water and piled up the halves of the nuts in neat little heaps with the convex outside upward and the hollow inside with the white coconut meat downward. In this simple way the nut meat was protected against rain (which causes it to rot), while at the same time the air could circulate freely. Rauri and his family left the nuts in heaps and moved on to another place, to continue the same work.

After all the working places had been visited, which took about a week, we returned to the first place. The nut meat was dry and ready to be collected. Everyone sat down in front of a heap of nut halves and with an *S*-shaped knife began to take out the copra, as the nut meat is called in the dry state. To get the copra out, it was, as a rule, sufficient to insert the knife and spin the half-nut vigorously once—easy and quick work. Rauri's family completed the circuit of the different working places in one or two days; and after the nuts were cut up, it had taken another week. The finished copra was poured into sacks, ready for export at once!

The general calculation on Raroia is that a man who, like Rauri, has the whole family to help him can easily make three tons of copra a month, while one man alone can manage at least two tons a month. This tempo, which is considered quite satisfactory on Raroia, is anything but severe, for it has happened on several occasions that Tahitian hired laborers have made as much as a ton a week. The Raroians, however, afraid of being affected by this unnecessary display of energy, promptly returned these record breakers to their native island and engaged more steady-going Tuamotuans.

Even more simple than the preparation of copra is the care of the copra plantations, or to be more correct, the Raroians' way of taking care of their plantations. Here, too, they follow their usual policy of doing as little as possible. They may plant a palm—dig a hole and throw in a nut— but from the moment it has taken root they pay no further attention to it.

The palm is a remarkable tree, however, and as a rule it looks after itself quite well. After only five or six years it has reached a height of between fifteen and thirty feet and is beginning to bear fruit. It then bears regularly for at least fifty years, and often up to eighty—still, of course, without receiving any care. If one adds that there is no season, but that the nuts ripen and fall in regular succession all the year round, one understands that the palm is the ideal tree for the Raroians.

The size of the yield naturally depends on many different factors, but as a rule one can calculate that each palm should give about fifty nuts a year. As four nuts are needed to make a kilo (2.2 pounds) of copra, and there are about eighty palms to every hectare (nearly two-and-one-half acres), this would correspond to about a ton of copra per hectare every year. In reality the Raroians' annual production is considerably more modest because the palms stand too close together and the nuts rot, or are eaten by rats.

No nuts, of course, would need to rot if the plantations were cleared regularly, but this is both hard and monotonous work! Therefore, the Raroians prefer to let the brush grow freely and spread as it pleases. The natural consequence is that masses of nuts simply disappear into the tangle of leaves and boughs. I once asked Tarakeha cautiously why he did not take the trouble to tidy up a little, and his reply was most illuminating.

"Why should I?" he said. "I can't even cut up all the nuts I get without any effort. To clear away the scrub to get more nuts would only mean unnecessary trouble."

"But why not employ a few laborers when you've so many nuts?" I asked.

"That would be an idea, of course. But it's almost impossible to get hold of any laborers nowadays; besides, I'm satisfied with everything as it is."

All over the small islands quantities of empty nuts lie about, with a round hole close to the stalk where the fiber is thinnest. This is the work of rats. Most of them simply live in the palm tops, where they alternately eat holes in the nuts and feast on the contents. When they have finished off the nuts on one tree, they go on to the next. The best way to protect the palms is to fasten a broad iron ring round the trunk. This method is practiced extensively in Tahiti, where on many plantations rats have disappeared completely. I pointed this out to Rauri and asked him why he did not put iron rings round the trees.

"No, that's no good here on Raroia," he replied. "The rats jump over."

"Then you must make broader iron rings."

"They'll jump over anyway."

"The rats never jump over the rings in Tahiti," I stubbornly persisted.

But this had no effect on Rauri.

"Perhaps," he answered, "but here on Raroia we have different rats."

I gave up, for of course it was really the same with the rats as with the brush. Why should the Raroians protect their palms against rats, when they have more nuts than they can deal with in any case? They have achieved what they consider the right balance between work and income, and they have no desire to imperil it. The best proof of this, by the way, is that on Raroia, in contrast to most places in the world, production goes down as soon as the price goes up!

I have often amused myself by trying to imagine what would happen if a man with business sense took over the copra plantations on Raroia. The first thing he would do would certainly be to solve the labor problem in one way or another. After that he would presumably see that the natural sources of power were utilized. Although the islanders do not know it, there are two first-class sources of power on Raroia: the ceaseless trade wind and the strong current in the entrance to the lagoon. These should be able to supply electricity for the machines which would facilitate the manufacture of copra—for example, drying apparatus and saws.

A real businessman would also find new and better ways of utilizing the wealth of the coconut palm. He would certainly make ropes, mats, and similar articles from the husk, and he might also be tempted to try to export canned coconut milk and coconut water. And he would have no difficulty in finding uses for leaves and roots, not to speak of the shells.

But all this would only be a beginning, for sooner or later the day would come when this businessman would ponder whether many of the products of copra which are now made in Europe and America—soap, margarine, and oil—could not be made at a considerably lower cost on Raroia or at any rate in French Oceania. Overwhelmed by the immense possibilities which I see opening before me, I will stop here and carry the train of thought no further.

It need hardly be added that we hope, for our own sake and that of our friends, that no such man with business sense will ever appear on the island, for it would inevitably mean the end of the cheerful, happy existence which we learned to love and cherish as much as the Raroians themselves.

Our Daily Fish

"OUR Father who art in heaven, hallowed be thy name. Thy kingdom come. Thy will be done on earth as it is in heaven. Give us this day our daily *fish* . . ."

Thus a little girl on Raroia once prayed. And considering her daily menu, she was perfectly right, for on Raroia fish plays an incomparably more important part than bread. Many people never eat bread, and those who do bake only occasionally—for example, at Christmas, Easter, or some other principal festival. Fish, on the other hand, the Raroians eat practically every day, and their favorite dishes all consist of sea food in different forms.

It would be hard to expect anything else from a people living on a level with the sea's surface in the middle of the world's greatest ocean on an island which forms a gigantic natural fish basket. Every day thousands and ten thousands of fish stream with the tide into the relatively shallow lagoon, and many stay behind and multiply there. Others seem to have lived there for countless generations and thrive nowhere else than among the coral shallows and seaweed. (How they originally came there I leave it to the ichthyologists to explain.)

The island's resemblance to an ordinary fish basket is only partial, of course, as fish are easily obtained not only inside the Raroia basin but also outside. The broad shelf-like outer reef is a popular feeding ground for many kinds of fish, and all along the barrier formed by the reef other fish continually dart in and out through holes and chinks. The whole place is crammed with fish, and the Raroians can literally scoop up as many as they like without the supply being perceptibly diminished.

How many kinds of fish there are in the Raroia lagoon and in the sea round the island no one knows for certain, but I have been able, without any special effort, to draw up a list containing over two hundred fishes' names—and there are at least as many more.

Even if all these names do not really represent a corresponding number of different species as recognized by science—for the Raroians often use different names for a large, a medium-sized, and a small fish of the same kind—it is still a fairly impressive total. As the temperature of the water is between 80° and 86° all the year round, the fish are naturally quite unlike those found in northern latitudes; indeed, we have not yet found a single fish that we knew before.

Some of the fish are five feet long and weigh as much as a full-grown man, others are so small that there is room for several hundred in an ordinary deep dish. Some have great pointed noses, others have fins which look like angels' wings, and some have spikes like a hedgehog—but all have a lovely sheen and reflect every imaginable color.

Some have patterns not even dreamed of by surrealists. A common fish which is called *karava* (of the genus Balistes), displays an almost bewildering orgy of coloring: round the mouth, light-red lines giving the impression of a careless make-up; on the upper part of the head, a brown triangle containing a large, stupid eye, not unlike a symbol frequently used by certain theosophical societies; on the lower part of the head (the chin, if the expression may be allowed), pale-green spots which have a depressing effect; on the back, transparent pale-green fins; on the hind part of the body, orange-colored zebra stripes on a light-brown background; on the tail fin, a blue labyrinth with yellow spots which seem to be going round and round without being able to find the way out. Not even Dali could surpass this!

The Raroians do not care in the least about the appearance of the fish; the most important thing for them is, that it can be eaten. With some few exceptions (well-known to everyone) most of the fish are not only edible but extraordinarily good. Some taste exactly like Baltic herrings, others like haddock or cod, while the taste of many was a new but delightful experience for us. The best thing, however, is that no two kinds of fish taste alike—the principal reason why we, like the Raroians, could eat fish at least five or six times a week without growing tired of it.

To make a fish diet varied, one must, of course, be sure of catching different sorts at will. The Raroians have solved this problem perfectly, and they are never disappointed with the results of a fishing expedition. In contrast to our Sunday fishermen, they never fish on chance, but always decide first what sort of fish they want and choose the implements and localities which they know by experience to be the best for just that kind. As marine life and natural conditions have not changed in the last few thousand years, most of the methods of fishing employed by the Raroians have not changed either since heathen times.

Of course, many types of fishing have been abandoned; for example, the huge stone traps which one encounters here and there along the shore of the lagoon are no longer used. These traps—often with arms several hundred yards long and a labyrinth of compartments in which the fish easily lose their way—provided the islanders with quantities of food in old times. Although they could be put into working order with comparative ease, no one lifts a finger to repair them. The reason is quite simple: the old communal spirit and solidarity have disappeared since there is no longer any strong temporal or religious authority to compel the Raroians to collaborate.

"There's no point in trying to repair the stone traps," Tupuhoe explained to us one day. "It would only mean trouble and quarreling. The stone traps belong to everyone. Suppose we repair them and decide that the catch shall be divided in equal shares on certain days. That's easy enough. But how are we going to prevent people from sneaking off at night and stealing the fish? We can't keep watch all day and all night. In the old days one of the priests used to declare the stone traps taboo, and then no one dared touch the fish. That was a good simple way of doing it. But no one believes in a taboo nowadays."

In pre-European times the Raroians could sometimes effect a slight change of diet by killing whales which were stranded on the outer reef. But they had to give up this exciting sport long ago, when too intensive hunting killed off nearly all the whales in Tuamotuan waters. When lately, for the first time in thirty years, a whale was stranded at the southeastern end of the island, the Raroians were so perplexed that they could not decide what to do till it had both died and decomposed!

The methods of fishing which have been preserved are quite original and interesting. The favorite implement is a harpoon or spear, which is used for fishing both in the lagoon and on the outer reef. I first observed the fish-spearing technique in the lagoon during one of the many fishing expeditions with Maono and Tehei.

As usual, the sun had just risen when my friends came to fetch me. They both had the same equipment: a slender, light spear about ten feet long, with a sharp iron point; a pair of goggles which would closely fit round the eyes; and a loincloth fastened round the waist with a string. That was all.

It had rained during the night, and the coconut-shell bailer was floating in three to four inches of water in the bottom of Maono's canoe. Maono quickly emptied the canoe by drawing it up on the beach and turning it upside down; then we caught hold of the two boughs which connected the hull with the outrigger and hauled it a little way out into the water. The canoe was just large enough to hold the three of us, and the waves splashed in over the rails when we headed it into the wind.

After a half-hour's paddling we reached a large circular shoal a mile or two from the shore. When we were still a long way off, we saw some black spots moving to and fro in the shallow water over the shoal. These were fishes' fins sticking up above the surface, a sign of a good catch. We jumped over onto the shoal, which was as large as a circus arena, and hauled up the canoe. The fish, which had been breakfasting on small creatures and seaweed which lived in the cracks in the coral, had disappeared, but we could see them in the clear water, many feet deeper, beside the shoal.

Tehei and Maono picked up their goggles and spat vigorously on the insides of them (to prevent mist from forming). Then they took their spears and slipped cautiously down into the water. After taking a deep breath, they lay down comfortably on their stomachs in the swell, as if they were arranging themselves on a sofa. They lay quietly for a long time, looking down toward the sea bottom, with their backs and hips above, but their faces under the water. Now and then they pushed their mouths and noses above the surface of the water to catch a breath of air, but as soon as they had filled their lungs they continued the search.

In a little while Maono seemed to have caught sight of a suitable quarry, for he took a firm grip on the butt of his spear and dived. When the eddies of foam had disappeared and the water had become clear again, I saw he was already deep down below the surface. With his spear pointed straight ahead of him he was slowly approaching his quarry, a flounderlike *tarei* about a foot long. Then he checked his forward motion, drew his spear back, and struck.

A few seconds later the spear floated up to the surface with the transfixed fish on the iron point; then Maono's satisfied face appeared. Meanwhile Tehei had dived, and when he came up again, he too had a big *tarei* on the point of his spear. Then they both drew a breath and dived again, still with the fish on the points of their spears. According to the Raroians it is much easier to harpoon a *tarei* if one has another on the spear, for this lulls the new fish into a sense of security, if it does not actually induce it to come nearer. I thought at first that this act was only an ordinary fisherman's superstition, but daily observation has finally convinced me of its merit. Yet, this method works with only certain kinds of fish; some species are scared away.

Maono and Tehei proceeded slowly along the coral shoal, and now they were harpooning one *tarei* after another. They never kept more than one on the spear point at once but threaded each new fish on the strings round their waists as they caught it. It was a good half-hour before they had made the round of the coral shoal, and when at last they got back to the canoe, they had about ten fish hanging like an ornamental wreath about their hips.

When they tossed the catch over to me, I discovered that several of the fish were cut off at the middle, while of others only the heads remained. Curious, I asked how this could have happened.

"Oh," Maono replied, "there must have been small sharks about. You can't always see what's happening behind your back."

"H'm," I said, "but wouldn't it be better to be a bit more careful? Suppose the sharks took you for the fish!"

"Oh, there's no risk of that with these sharks. They're no more dangerous than dogs in this part of the lagoon. Come along, and we'll start again from the beginning!"

I took hold of the paddle, and followed slowly while my comrades made a new round of the shoal. Now and again I stopped and threw overboard a few handfuls of crushed hermit crabs. Tempted by this rare delicacy, the fish forgot all caution and left their safe hiding places in the crevices of the coral shoal and under the large stones at the bottom of the sea. Maono and Tehei were not slow to capitalize on their luck, and when we had returned to our starting point, the bottom of the boat was literally carpeted with a layer of wriggling fish.

I examined them more closely. About half had been holed by the spear in the gills (which most fishermen aim at), some in the head, and the rest in the fleshy parts of the body. This showed a fairly accurate aim, but it was mere bungling compared with what Temorere can do. He harpoons all his fish in the eye, every time!

Even greater sureness and swiftness are required to harpoon fish from the outer reef. This kind of spear-fishing is carried on only in quiet weather and on the lee side of the island, but despite this the difficulties and the risks are great. The reef is full of holes and crannies, which the foaming water obscures; the sea regularly sends in a huge swell, which pours over the reef in rushing rivers, and the seaweed forms a treacherous carpet on which it is hard to get a footing. But this does not trouble the Raroians, who scramble about on the reef, their spears perfectly poised despite the fierce breakers, and manage at the same time both to see where they put their feet and to keep a lookout for suitable quarry.

The reef does not form a smooth level wall; on the contrary, it is jagged and cut into by many deep bays or embankments. When the swell and waves sweep up toward the reef, the water is naturally sucked into these openings with tremendous force, and often fish of all kinds accompany it. At these gaps in the reef barrier the Raroians try to harpoon the fish. They have to watch for the right moment, and the right moment is at the same time the riskiest. It comes just when the water on the reef has reached its maximum height and the treacherous backwash is beginning.

According to the Raroians it is useless to place oneself by a bay in the reef beforehand and wait quietly for the quarry, for this would frighten the fish away. They always stand about ten yards farther in on the reef while the water is rising and hurry to the outer edge of the reef when it begins to run back. It takes about ten seconds for the wave to draw back, and for the first five seconds at least the water is foaming and bubbling too violently for it to be possible to make out the quarry. When the wave has washed completely back, it is, of course, too late to try to use a harpoon. He who would catch a fish has thus about five seconds in which to do it—between the time the water starts to clear and the wave has drawn back, he must get ready, detect the quarry, aim, and throw the spear!

But not even if the harpooner makes his mark is the catch secure. He must grasp the spear before it disappears seaward, and if he hesitates even for a moment, he can be sure that a shark will get there first. The sharks are as a rule unbelievably impudent; several times I have seen one dash up and snap the catch out of the fisherman's hand as he was trying to save it. In spite of the fact that spear-fishing on the reef is hazardous and the fish caught are most often small and insignificant, Raroians persist in employing this method. And their reason is just as valid as that of most Sunday anglers at home: they enjoy the keen sport.

Another amusing and original kind of spear-fishing is practiced on the reef—done with the aid of hunting dogs! The Raroians, as mentioned before, keep numbers of dogs; and dog's flesh is regarded as a great delicacy—which, in fact, it is. Surprisingly enough, these beasts kept for slaughter have an existence which makes them particularly suitable for hunting. Although the Raroians appreciate fat steaks themselves, they find it too much trouble to give their dogs anything to eat. The natural consequence is that the dogs live permanently on the verge of starvation and, in their ravening hunger, often kill fowls and pigs and even one another. One can therefore say without exaggeration that the dogs on the island are actually wolves, always on the hunt for something to eat.

But they are just as much seals as wolves. Even as puppies they are taken on canoe trips or for walks around the reef, and thenceforward they are so continuously and intimately acquainted with the sea that (if they have not been drowned during the period of apprenticeship) they move as easily in the water as on land.

Presumably it is just this circumstance—that the dogs possess the qualities of wolf and seal at the same time—that has given rise to the cunning method of capture which should properly be called fish-hunting. The huge shelf formed by the outer reef—about 50 yards wide on the lee side and about 450 yards wide on the windward side—is covered at high tide by water a foot or so deep, in which fish of different kinds mass. It is useless to try to harpoon them or catch them without the help of dogs, as they always see the danger in time and dart off much quicker than a man can run. But the Raroian dogs are as swift as their prey and pursue the fish tirelessly till they either rush straight toward one of the men who is standing with his harpoon fixed, or find a hiding place under a stone or in some cranny where they are easily caught. In the latter case the huntsman merely reaches down and pulls the fish out.

While spear-fishing of all sorts is carried on all year round, other methods of capture depend more on the season. The most picturesque of these is undoubtedly *rena* fishing. The Raroians had talked a great deal about this kind of fishing and had explained that the season usually began sometime in March, when great shoals of fish found their way into the bay by the village. But it was not till well on in April that we saw the first signs that shoals of fish were at last on their way.

Larger and larger crowds of gulls began to assemble over the lagoon a mile or two from the shore, and they came nearer every day. One clear, still morning, when the lagoon was almost like a mirror, a cry rose from the quay, and everyone immediately took it up. Moments later our faithful friend Tehei summoned us:

"You must come and see. The whole bay's full of *komene* fish!"

We hurried down to the shore, where all our other friends had already assembled. Fifty yards from the land a white cloud of shrieking gulls hung over a big black patch in the water. A gigantic shoal of fish! Despite the savage attacks of the birds the black patch gradually increased in size; in a half-hour's time it was as large as a market place. The time had come to start *rena* fishing, and Teka gave orders to make ready. To our great astonishment the whole crowd dashed off at once, and we were left alone with Teka.

"Where are they going?" I asked Teka curiously. "The fishing nets are here on the beach."

"Wait and see," replied Teka, chuckling.

In a few minutes the villagers began to come back, each one with large bunches of palm leaves under his arm. Everyone carried at least five large palm leaves. The heap grew to imposing dimensions.

"Now, you'll see how we make a *rena*," said Teka, and slit a palm leaf in two along the central nerve. "A *rena* is much better than a net for catching *komene*."

Then he laid one half on top of the other and took a new leaf. All round us Raroians were slitting palm leaves in two in the same way. In a little while the whole beach was covered with neat little piles, each of five half-leaves. The next stage of the work followed immediately. Our friends collected in small groups and began to fasten the bundles together with fibers and palm leaves. Then they joined the bundles lengthwise.

As soon as a length of bundles reached about thirty feet, two men, each catching hold of an end, began to twist it much as one wrings water out of a sheet. This "wringing" caused the lobes of the leaves to point in all directions so that the length looked more like a huge garland, or a tinsel rope on a Christmas tree, than anything else. When all the different groups had done this they began to splice the lengths together to make one single garland—five hundred yards long. At last fishing could begin!

Two of the strongest men took hold of one end of the palm garland, and the rest of the Raroians placed themselves along it at equal intervals. Marie-Thérèse and I hastened to follow their example. With the two men still in the lead, we all waded slowly and cautiously into the shallow water and approached the shoal of fish. Then with even greater care we worked our way around the shoal and back toward the shore. Like a gigantic green snake, the garland encircled the leaping mass of herringlike fish. The air was still full of shrieking, fluttering gulls, which followed us closely as we began to wade back to the beach. Not until we reached foot-deep water and had drawn the circle of leaves together to half its original size did they reluctantly fly off.

A few yards from the beach we stopped. The fish were now packed so tightly that they could no longer move. Nothing remained to be done but to scoop them up. To make this work easier, the women picked up palm leaves which had been left over and in a twinkling plaited together handy baskets; many of the men took off their hats and used them as scoops. A half-hour later a long row of shining silver fish lay on the beach, and the distribution could begin. Everyone collected in a ring, and amid laughter and shouting Teka and Tapakia divided the fish into as many heaps as there were inhabitants of the village. When they had finished, each of us had no fewer than twenty-one fish!

With typical Raroian abandon all our friends ate up every single fish the same afternoon and next day were looking out hungrily for fresh shoals of *komene*. They did not look in vain, for there were plenty of them that day and on the days that followed. For over two months we made at least three *rena* expeditions a week, and each time the catch was between one and three thousand *komene!*

But the fishing we ourselves liked best was night fishing on the reef—the most primitive of all methods of fishing. One midnight we returned to the village with a whole sack full of fish, which was a good catch for only four fishermen —Putake, Tinorua, Marie-Thérèse, and I—and equipment consisting of bush knives and kerosene lamps!

When our friends had come to fetch us immediately after sunset, we could not help smiling a little at their optimism in taking a whole copra sack in which to bring back our catch. But as the evening wore on, we discovered that we had in more than one way underestimated this simple method. Not only is it astonishingly efficient, but the setting is replete with atmosphere.

The stars were shining unusually bright and clear, and only a light breeze was rustling in the palm tops when we set off from the village. Putake walked ahead with the biggest kerosene lamp in the village (the church lamp) which hissed and sang like a coffeepot; next came Marie-Thérèse and I; and Tinorua brought up the rear with the copra sack on his back. Tinorua had taken with him a rusty lamp which refused to function, whatever trick he tried. After several attempts at lighting it he left it behind under a palm and twisted together a torch of dried coconut leaves.

Soon sparks were jumping and flying about our heads like shooting stars, and the contrast between our little circle of light and the surrounding darkness became all the sharper and more obvious. We followed the shore northward at an easy pace. To our left we had the open sea and the encircling reef with its shining white breakers. To our right we had a dark wall of palms. The tide was running out strongly, and here and there on the reef our lights reflected in the red coral stones which stuck out of the water. All nature seemed curiously alive and secretive.

The enchantment of the scene overtook Putake who began philosophizing; he wondered whether Paradise looked like Raroia and if fish or birds were caught from its reef. We replied that we were sure Paradise looked like Raroia, but carefully left the remainder of the question unanswered.

After a good hour's walk we reached the northern end of the island. Here the fishing was to begin, and our intention was to work our way slowly along the reef back to the village. Thus we would be a few steps from our village when the fishing was over. Tinorua waded out into the water and looked round him.

"The water's begun to rise, but it'll be a little while before the fish come in from the sea to sleep," he announced when he came back.

We lit a fire and stretched ourselves out on some palm leaves. Putake again began to speculate as to what the heavenly Paradise looked like, but Tinorua seemed quite satisfied with the earthly paradise we were in at the moment and interrupted him to ask us about something he had been turning over in his thoughts for a long time. He wanted to know how it was that Marie-Thérèse and I had not been able to identify a single one of the many fish that were in the Raroia lagoon. He himself had come to the conclusion that there were no fish in *popaa* country.

Of course, we explained that it was because the fish in cold and in warm water were different, just as in fresh or salt water. That there were colder seas than the South Seas he did not find so very surprising, but that there were lakes as big as the Raroia lagoon full of drinking water both he and Putake refused to believe. And they were even more dumbfounded when we added that there were no sharks in these lakes.

The time passed quickly in profound conversation on these and other equally interesting subjects, and Marie-Thérèse and I began to think our friends had completely forgotten that we were really out fishing. At last, I reminded them of this as discreetly as possible. Unperturbed, they looked up at the sky and Putake answered, smiling, "You see that star there in the south. When that has gone down below the horizon, the fish have gone to sleep. It's no use beginning till then."

The star sank by degrees, and we got ready. Marie-Thérèse and I placed ourselves one on each side of Putake, who had the kerosene lamp in one hand and a large bush knife (not unlike a South American machete) in the other. Tinorua followed ten yards behind us with the sack over his shoulder. We had not got more than a few yards out onto the reef before Putake caught sight of a fish asleep in the shallow water. He approached carefully, aimed with the knife, and struck. The stunned fish floated up to the surface and was washed in by the tide a little way across the reef. Tinorua seized it at once and dropped it into the sack.

It certainly looked easy! I searched out a fish and approached resolutely, with my knife raised. Feeling slightly ashamed of killing a defenseless creature in this mean way, I struck. When the waves had at last subsided and we had all dried the salt water out of our eyes, there was no sign of a fish. Tinorua, choking back his laughter, explained that I must take care not to let my blade enter the water at too narrow an angle, as the water immediately acted as a brake on it.

I understood all this admirably in theory, and hastened to apply my knowledge in practice to the next fish that appeared. Grim-faced, I calculated the angle of attack exactly and then let fly for all I was worth. This time I struck a rock!

Our fishing party continued along the reef. Putake rapidly passed on fish to Tinorua's sack, and I zealously studied his technique. At last I decided to try my luck again and began to look round for a suitable quarry. It was Marie-Thérèse who found it. She suddenly cried, "Come here,

here's a fish for you. It's nearly two feet long. You can't miss."

I hurried over to her and saw a long blue fish, no thicker than my finger, lying quite still just below the surface. Marie-Thérèse was right. It was quite impossible to miss, and with a shout of triumph I struck, cutting the fish in half. Then I turned round and held up the two halves under Putake's nose, that he might duly admire my capture. But instead of owning himself conquered Putake began to laugh, and soon he and Tinorua were laughing till the tears ran down their cheeks. At last he caught his breath sufficiently to say: "But, Penetito, that isn't an edible fish; besides, you've cut it in half. You must strike not with the edge of the blade, but with the back."

We went along the reef, and a half-hour later I succeeded in executing my first fish in proper style. Meanwhile Putake and Tinorua had half-filled the sack. To my astonishment they had let hardly one fish escape, and if they ever happened to miss with the first stroke, they immediately took up the chase. While it was impossible to catch the fish in the daytime without dogs, it was amazingly easy now, in the dark. Those which managed to escape never went farther than ten yards or so; and their pursuers never missed a second time.

When we got back to the place on the reef opposite the village, where we had started on our night walk a few hours earlier, the sack was still not quite full.

"We'll go on a bit farther south," Tinorua said, as he bit off the neck of a fish and began to chew the raw flesh with relish. "The sack must be full, or they'll just laugh at us."

We all agreed with him. For another half-hour of the mild summer night we splashed in the tepid water, and it was not till Tinorua began to walk in his sleep, and we ourselves were so tired that we just cut holes in the water, that we at last were forced to turn homeward.

The Raroians employ many other methods of fishing, but all are considerably less interesting than these I have described. Hooks, for example, are by no means unknown, but in contrast to what we are accustomed to, the Raroians use neither rod, float, nor worm. They hold the line in their hands, and for bait they always use little fish, crabs, or cuttlefish meat. (There are, in fact, no worms on the island.) In most cases they fish from the reef or let the line trail behind a canoe more or less as we use a trolling spoon. But sometimes they simply swim about with the line in their hand, in the ancient Polynesian manner. The boldest go far out to sea without an accompanying boat, or swim about in the lagoon for hours.

The best place for all kinds of fishing with hook and line is the entrance to the lagoon. All the year round huge shoals, containing fish in thousands, pass through the entrance every day, either on their way out of the lagoon or on their way in. The commonest kinds are trigger fishes, jacks, wrasses, and tuna. The Raroians catch huge quantities of these from their canoes, which they anchor in the middle of the entrance or let drift with the stream.

Man cannot live by bread alone, and the Raroians live not only on fish, but also consume great quantities of other sea food. Clams and shells, which used to figure prominently on the menu in old times, are now seldom eaten, but eels and rock lobsters (a kind of lobster which has no claws) are still prized delicacies. Eels are usually harpooned in the same way as other fish, and this method of capture is sometimes used for rock lobsters. As a rule, however, the Raroians are unwilling to use the harpoon for the latter, as it kills them, and they prefer to catch them in a more cunning way. They make the children frighten them out of their hiding places, and simply put a foot on them when they come hurrying along.

Then there are turtles. In old times the turtle was a sacred animal, and every good catch was celebrated with religious ceremonies at the *marae,* or tribal place of sacrifice. When the old was abandoned for the new, it lost its special place as a sacred animal; but its flesh still tastes just as good (something like roast veal) and it is therefore still hunted as keenly. There are many different kinds of turtle, the smaller of which are about the size of a motorcar wheel and the larger about as big as a bicycle wheel. Some live in the lagoon, others only in the sea.

To make clear how these turtles, which often weigh over two hundred pounds, are hunted, I will describe one of the expeditions in which I myself took part. It was at the beginning of June, and one of the first times in the year that any turtles had been sighted. During June and the following months, turtles as a rule collect on the lee side of the Tua-motu atolls for breeding. Throughout this period a boy, or a couple of boys, always sit at the lookout point on the beach or in the palm tops watching for their arrival.

But this time it was two girls who ran up quite breath-less and declared that they had seen a half-a-dozen black spots in the sea west of the village. Immediately all the men pushed their canoes into the sea, and I jumped into my friend Tehei's, as had been agreed, as soon as we had suc-ceeded in making our way through the surf. Sailing canoes are too large and clumsy for turtle-hunting, so the Raroians use their small open canoes which hold at most three men.

Certainly these are nothing to shout about, although they are often compelled to go far out to sea in rough weather. While Tehei and Tara wielded the paddles till they creaked, I had to devote myself to the third man's usual occupation —bailing out the canoe as well as I could with the coconut-shell scoop.

In the bottom of the canoe lay a long supple rope, one end fastened to a large iron hook. This was the entire turtle-hunting equipment! But Tehei would soon demonstrate what this simple implement could do in skillful hands, for we came upon a turtle after only a quarter of an hour's paddling. In most cases one has to stalk a turtle with care and slowly maneuver oneself within range, but this turtle rose suddenly from the depths right under the bow.

It naturally disappeared again as soon as it caught sight of the canoe, but Tehei was as quick as the turtle and dived in with the iron hook in one hand and the rope trailing behind him. For a brief moment we could see two dark shadows vanishing into the depths at furious speed; then they were gone. The only thing we could do was to sit looking at the rope which ran slowly out over the side, fifteen feet, thirty, forty-five, sixty. . . . .

After a minute which seemed an eternity there was a sudden jerk on the rope. This was the signal that Tehei had got the turtle, and Tara and I caught hold of the rope and hauled it in as quickly as we could. Tehei put his head above the surface for a moment to breathe; then he dived again. Slowly but surely we hauled in until we had a turtle as large as a cartwheel thrashing violently beside the canoe, the great hook lodged in the side of his throat.

This performance certainly seems easy to a spectator above water, but for the diver who pursues his quarry under water it is by no means so simple and safe. In the first place, diving swiftly to a great depth strains the lungs and heart, and it has happened more than once that the helpers in the canoe have had to haul in an unconscious comrade instead of a turtle. Secondly, there are plenty of sharks, which on such occasions can easily confuse a turtle with a diver. (Certain sharks are actually capable of biting them both in half.) Lastly, the hook must be placed in the turtle's throat—the only part which is really vulnerable—and at the same time the diver must take good care to keep out of the way of the turtle's jaws. A turtle which has once closed its jaws on a man's hand does not let go till its head—or the man's hand—is cut off.

Even if the diver succeeds in placing the hook in the turtle's throat, all difficulties are not over. The turtle has to be brought up to the surface, and merely hauling on the rope will not accomplish this feat. Most turtles are strong enough to tear the rope out of the helpers' hands or disappear seaward with the whole outfit, if the diver is not adept. Only when he has got a good grip of the turtle's shell, and turned it on its back, keeping it firmly in this position, can the diver prevent the creature from swimming in the opposite direction and manage to steer it to the surface. But this means a wrestling bout requiring both courage and strength, and the turtle wins as often as the diver!

Another but more difficult method of getting the turtle to the surface is to sit astride it, seize hold of its head, and press one's fingers into its eyes. By forcing the turtle's head upward one can compel it to rise to the surface under its own power—provided one has the strength in one's hands to hold on long enough. Many declare that the most skillful turtle hunters in the Tuamotu group, when once they have got their prey up to the surface, can even steer it into the beach and the earth oven that awaits it. But that is a thing I should like to see before I believe it!

An account of fish life on Raroia would, of course, not be complete without mention of sharks. Both the lagoon and the sea teem with sharks, and I have not yet been on a fishing expedition without running across one or more of these brutes. Most of them are small—from three to six feet long—and make off at once if one splashes in the water a bit. But now and then one comes upon big fellows who seem anything but timid.

I soon noticed that the Raroians' demeanor changed with the type of hunting ground. While they dive and swim in the bay by the village without the least fear, they are as a rule not particularly inclined to jump in at other places in the lagoon or into the sea; and if they do they always take care to be armed with a sharp knife. I asked Rauri what caused this difference.

"That's easily explained," he replied. "We bathe and fish so often in the bay by the village that the sharks have been scared away. They've learned that it's dangerous to come in here, and they have got a wholesome respect for men. At other places in the lagoon and in the sea, where people seldom go, they are foolhardy and go for everything that moves in the water. Strangers, more than anyone, ought to be careful. The sharks realize that they haven't our knowledge and skill."

"But why didn't you say so before? I've often swum about and fished like all the rest of you."

"Oh, there's no danger in it for you. You're almost a Raroian."

I asked many other people about the same thing, and always received the same answer. Some even added that one ought never to bathe in the company of sharks if one has quarreled with one's better half. As a melancholy confirmation of the danger they pointed to Titi, who had had one arm bitten off by a shark when, as a young woman, she had gone out fishing immediately after a quarrel with her husband. I quietly observed that with my knowledge of Titi's bad temper I should have been much more surprised if she had *not* quarreled with her husband the day she was bitten by the shark. My friends at last reluctantly admitted that if this was the real reason both Titi and her husband ought to have been bitten by sharks every time they went fishing.

They were able to put up a rather better defense for their conviction that sharks attack foreigners by preference —despite my own experience to the contrary—and produced the Chinese merchant as a witness. He told me that he had been on the island for many years without having ever fished or sailed on the lagoon when one day the villagers persuaded him to go over with his goods to one of the lagoon islands, where they were all staying for the time being. He stowed in a canoe a sack of flour, a carton of canned goods, and a guitar, which one of his customers had ordered, and set off with a couple of young men.

"At first everything seemed to be going well," he continued his story, "but out in the middle of the lagoon the canoe began to shake and tumble in a mysterious way. We leaned over the side and saw a big shark, the biggest I've ever seen, swimming beside the canoe and lashing it with its tail. One of the boys hit it on the nose with an oar, but this only made it more savage and it hurled itself against the canoe, determined to upset it. We tried to get rid of it by changing our course and setting more sail, but it clung to us obstinately and attacked us again. We began to fear it would jump up out of the water and sink its teeth into us, for the canoe was heavily loaded and we were practically sitting at water level.

"After a time I had a good idea. If I poured flour into the water, perhaps the shark would be confused and would lose us. So I opened one of the sacks and, with a heavy heart, began to scatter the contents. When I had finished, the sea round the canoe was as white as milk, and the shark had disappeared. We felt glad and relieved, but before many minutes had passed it turned up again.

"Now it began to snap at my feet. Curiously enough it paid no attention to the others who were on board; it was just me it wanted to get at. Better throw something at it, I thought. Something hard. But there was nothing hard and heavy on board to throw except the cans of food, and at last I decided to sacrifice them. The shark only seemed to enjoy the bombardment, however, for it continued to pursue and even swallowed several of the cans.

"We had now almost reached the island; it was not more than five minutes' sailing at most. The shark seemed to understand this, for it made fresh and still more violent attacks and kept on leaping out of the water. I thought: there's only one thing left to sacrifice, and that's the guitar. I hesitated for a long time, but at last I flung it straight at the shark's muzzle. It stopped and began to nose at the guitar. Just at that moment we reached the island, and while the shark was swimming round the guitar several times, and lashing it to pieces with its tail, I took the chance of getting ashore.

"That is the only time a shark has ever tried to attack

anyone on board a canoe; and there must be some reason why it should have happened just to me. The reason certainly was that I had never fished or sailed in the lagoon like the other men on the island, and that I was therefore a stranger to the sharks."

This could be a fish story; but I am willing to believe it, for compared with the fish stories our friends sometimes tell, the Chinese's narrative is peculiarly modest. As might be expected, the Raroians' fish stories, like the fish themselves, are colossal and fantastic; the most imaginative of our anglers at home have certainly never produced anything equal to theirs. One single example should be convincing.

Tapakia returned from fishing one evening with only half-a-dozen *mu,* a fish so wretched and tasteless that as a rule no one troubles to catch it. All the villagers, of course, collected on the quay and began to poke fun at Tapakia. But he was equal to the situation, and without blinking an eyelid related the following story in a serious voice:

"Just as I got to the Pereva shallows I caught sight of a couple of big *tonu* right down on the bottom. I got a line ready, put a bit of cuttlefish on the hook, and cast it. But it had hardly touched the water before a shoal of *mu* came rushing up and flung themselves on the bait. The only thing to do was to haul in the line again and put on a new bit of cuttlefish.

"Then I tried again, but now still more *mu* had assembled. Before I managed to get out more than a few yards of line, one of them had taken the hook. I tried yet again, but the result was the same. More and more *mu* came from every direction, and at last they were packed so tight that I could hardly see the big *tonu* down on the bottom.

"I put on a bigger sinker, so that the hook might sink

more quickly, but it was no use. The *mu* always managed to swallow the bait before the hook got down to the bottom. I had no more sinkers, but I found a stone in the canoe and put that on as an extra sinker. The result was the same. Then I lost my temper and took the line in one hand and the anchor in the other and jumped in. I sank right to the bottom, and not one *mu* was able even to nose at the hook. While I still had the hook in my hand one of the *tonu* took it, and I made haste to get to the surface again. Luckily I had made the line fast to the canoe, and I had now only to haul in the catch.

"Just as I was stooping down to catch hold of the line the canoe gave a jerk, and I fell head over heels. When I pulled myself together in a little while, I found the canoe was rushing through the water as if it had had an outboard motor. Evidently a shark or some other big fish had swallowed the *tonu*. I thought it would soon get tired or bite off the line and did not worry. But time passed, and the line did not break till after sunset. Of course it was too late then to go on fishing, and that's why the result is so bad."

No one had any objection to make. For indeed what objection would be made to so convincing a story? Didn't Tapakia have the *mu* with him as conclusive proof of its truth?

The Chinese Invasion

Once people were inclined to regard the Chinese as models of wisdom, peaceableness, and humanity. I do not know if the population of China really ever had all these qualities, but it is certain that the Chinese one meets in French Oceania very seldom live up to this ideal.

The first Chinese were introduced into Tahiti in the 1860's to cultivate cotton, and many remained when their contracts lapsed or their employers went bankrupt. They were not slow to send for relatives from China, and during the following decades fresh Chinese immigrants trickled in without interruption. At the turn of the century they already numbered one thousand. Since then the Chinese population, mainly as the result of a phenomenal birth rate, has increased nearly seven times, while the native population has only *doubled* during that time.

The Chinese constitute only an eighth part of the total population of French Oceania, but they have already succeeded in acquiring a great deal of land, and control practically all the retail trade and a large part of the wholesale trade and the schooner traffic. The natives, with their merry and careless nature, shrink from the very idea of shutting themselves up in a shop or an office, and unfortunately offer no resistance whatever to Chinese infiltration.

In this connection it would be interesting to know how many firms and shops in French Oceania are really owned and managed by Polynesians—excluding Chinese undertakings with a Tahitian figurehead. I should not be surprised if they could be counted on the fingers of one hand! Many of the French, other Europeans, and American businessmen naturally offer competition, but most often the struggle is too uneven. Through their solidarity, mutual help, their power over the natives, their endurance (a Chinese shop is open day and night), and their large families which supply free labor, Chinese competition is unfortunately too strong.

A certain amount of legislation has indeed been passed to prevent the Chinese from acquiring more land by trickery and dominating all business, but as long as there are people —Polynesian or white—who are willing to lend their names and act as figureheads, these attempts are naturally futile. The most depressing part of the whole story is that whereas the Chinese formerly once concentrated their activity in Tahiti, they are now spreading all over French Oceania. On many of the Tuamotu Islands the copra trade is already in the hands of unscrupulous Chinese, and a disquietingly large number of the schooners are Chinese owned. Generally speaking, they have a free hand, as the authorities have difficulty in controlling their activities away from Papeete.

The Chinese merchant on Raroia could probably be charged with making himself rich at the natives' expense, as his colleagues on other islands do, but he is not personally unpleasant and many times gave proof of a certain solidarity with the little community to which he belongs. However, one day, when Raroia quite unexpectedly suffered a regular Chinese invasion, we got a taste of what the native population in the rest of French Oceania has to put up with from the Chinese. Unfortunately, similar episodes are quite ordinary in the Tuamotu group.

At the beginning of 1951 several epidemics broke out in quick succession in French Oceania, and as was to be expected with a population which lacks even the most elementary notions of hygiene and nursing and, moreover, is gregarious to the point of promiscuity, the epidemics spread with alarming swiftness and had a devastating effect.

The first sickness to reach the Tuamotu group was influenza, and at least two dozen people died, simply from neglect. We on Raroia did our best to keep the fifty infected persons indoors and in bed (this was the only conceivable method of treatment, as naturally we did not have enough penicillin for all); and with the help of illustrated magazines and more than a little patrolling we succeeded in getting through the epidemic without a single death.

A few months later, just before the diving season was to begin, the next epidemic broke out, and this time it was measles. The French authorities immediately prohibited all transport of divers from island to island and postponed the season indefinitely. As we were not expecting any other schooner at the time, the prohibition was enough to prevent the epidemic from spreading to Raroia, and we felt fairly confident of avoiding the new illness.

We were therefore aghast when one day, a week or two after the prohibition had come into force, we suddenly heard the sound of a motor from the outer reef, in the neighborhood of the village. The boys, who always kept a lookout over the sea to westward as soon as a schooner was expected, had for once abandoned their posts; but they now rushed off in a crowd to see what was happening. Soon a chorus of *"Tero . . . tero . . . tero"* was heard on the outskirts of the village.

Marie-Thérèse and I hurried across to the outer reef. There we saw, under full sail and with her engine at full speed ahead, the schooner *Marara* passing close along the reef, evidently on her way toward the entrance to the lagoon. Her silhouette seemed to us rather curious, and when we shaded our eyes with our hands and looked more closely, we saw that the whole schooner was fully loaded with canoes high up over the cabin roof, and that quantities of parcels, clothes, and blankets were hanging in the rigging. Soon we were able to make out human forms as well—here and there among the canoes, in the ship's boats, on top of the cargo, and even up the mast.

There was no doubt about it. The *Marara* had a full cargo of divers and diving equipment on board! But how could this be? The authorities had long ago prohibited all transport for an indefinite period.

"The schooner may already have left an island when the prohibition came into force, and now she's on her way back," the chief suggested.

"Perhaps," I answered, "but if she was only passing, she wouldn't come so close to the reef. It looks rather as if she is making for the entrance."

And so she was. A half-hour later she glided into the lagoon and steered straight for the quay by the village. The whole population assembled down on the beach and began a heated discussion as to what should be done.

"It's forbidden to transport divers," said one.

"There are sick persons on board, for certain," said another.

"We've just been ill and don't want to be ill again," said a third.

"Measles is worse than influenza," said a fourth.

All those who stood round loudly agreed.

The chief proposed that all should go and hide, but as there was no time for this and, for that matter, no one knew where to hide, I proposed another and simpler solution. The chief should meet the supercargo and the sailors on the quay, while the rest of the population remained at a distance. If the schooner had any goods they were to be left on the wharf and no one was to touch them for a week. The chief himself we could always disinfect with the contents of one of his liquor bottles. The chief was naturally rather unwilling to sacrifice any liquor, but at last he agreed to the proposal.

Soon afterward the schooner dropped anchor in her usual place just off the quay. The tension was at its height. But one thing struck me immediately. All was so strangely quiet on board. Five minutes passed, ten minutes, without anyone showing a sign of wanting to launch a boat. Then we suddenly heard a splash. Then another, louder.

"They're throwing the canoes into the sea," announced one of the villagers who was better placed than we.

The splashing continued, and soon a dozen canoes lay floating on the waves. A few men jumped into the water and began to tow them toward the land. What on earth did this mean? There was no sense in throwing the canoes overboard if the schooner did not intend to stay. But if she did, why did not the supercargo come ashore to talk to the chief as was customary? The whole thing was suspicious, and at last the inhabitants persuaded the chief that it was his duty to go on board and speak to the captain and the supercargo. He went off reluctantly. When he came back he reported as follows:

"The supercargo says that all the passengers and canoes are to be left here on Raroia. They will stay till the diving season begins next month, when the *Marara* will come back to fetch them and take them to Takume. The supercargo says that he has special permission from the authorities to make this trip in spite of the prohibition. They must have got permission by radio."

"But aren't there any sick people on board?" asked an anxious mother.

"Oh, yes, crowds, but as they have permission there's nothing to be done."

This story of a special permit rang untrue. How had they set about asking for it? There was no transmitter on board the *Marara*; only an ordinary receiver. For that matter, how could an exception be made for one schooner in such an important matter as this?

Marie-Thérèse and I explained all this to the chief, and he seemed to pluck up courage. While we were talking, the ship's boat had at last been launched and men, women, and children had scrambled into it.

"Don't let them land," we said to the chief, and at the same time we urgently warned our other friends to keep at a distance. They all agreed with us and promised to do their best. No one would go near the infected passengers— never, never!

Five minutes later, of course, all the passengers in the ship's boat were in the inhabitants' arms, and to demonstrate their joy at the unexpected meetings, they all embraced and kissed one another repeatedly. "You see, they are all Tuamotuans. We should have been ashamed not to greet them properly. Besides, none of them are ill," all our friends declared with one voice when they saw our reproachful looks.

The first boatload of passengers certainly did not look very ill; but the second boatload was a considerably more depressing sight. They all had swollen red faces—and anything redder than a Polynesian with measles it would be hard to find. Many had high fevers and were so weak that they could not walk without help. Like the earlier passengers, they all disappeared in the direction of the water tanks and the merchants as soon as they had thoroughly infected all who came in their way.

The damage was done already, and as we felt sorry for the wretched people, we walked round to see if we could do anything to help them. At the village tank the precious water was running in floods. Of course it was foolish of the sick people to bathe, but we understood them. They had spent two weeks on board the schooner and had only had two pints of water each a day—barely as much as they needed for cooking. Temake's shop was full of people, all wanting to buy condensed milk. Hot milk is regarded as an infallible cure for most sicknesses.

"But is there no milk on board?" I asked in surprise. "The Chinese schooners are usually well supplied."

"Yes," replied a pregnant woman with a skinny child in her arms, "but it's in the hold and the supercargo won't let it be brought up. It's too much trouble for the little it can bring in. The supercargo's a Chinese, you understand. He wouldn't even let the cook give the sick people hot water on the voyage."

A short way off stood a little group of men, who all had a hopeless, crushed appearance. I asked them what was the matter with them.

"We've got no more money," one of them said, dejectedly.

"But what have you done with all the money you earned by diving for mother-of-pearl shells?"

"Oh, we bought food in the Chinese shops on Marutea. It's dear, you know, and when one's diving one's hungry and wants to eat the nicest things—canned peaches, salmon, biscuits, and so on."

I knew very well that this was not the full explanation, and so I pressed them a little further.

"Of course we've bought many useful things, too," one of them said proudly. "I've got five silk antimacassars and an iron bed which they say comes all the way from Peretane [England], and that man's got a gilded pendulum clock. It doesn't go very well, but it's pretty to look at."

Still not satisfied and almost positive of the real reason for their financial embarrassment, I quizzed them until they admitted that they had gambled with the Chinese on the island and, of course, lost. A hasty computation showed that the result of the recently concluded diving season on Marutea was about 300 tons of mother-of-pearl shells. At a price of 30 francs per kilo, this represented earnings of no less than 9,000,000 francs ($144,000) for the divers.

If all the divers had been as thoughtless as these poor wretches—and there was no reason to think they had not—the diving must have been very good business indeed for the Chinese, especially as the Papeete price was 50 francs per kilo. And, knowing what the Chinese were like in money matters, there could be little doubt that the greater part of the natives' wages had gone into Chinese pockets.

I gradually succeeded in also finding out the reason for the sudden invasion of Raroia. About a fortnight earlier the *Marara* had arrived at Marutea to fetch "her" divers and their families, who had been waiting for a long time to be taken home. These divers had all, as is the rule, a contract with the owner of the *Marara* assuring them free transport home as soon as the diving season on Marutea was over.

For reasons best known to the *Marara*'s Chinese owner, several months passed before the schooner appeared to fetch them. Almost all the divers were tired or ill and wanted to return home at once, but as most of them had run through their money, the *Marara*'s owner managed to persuade a large number of them to go on diving for him on another island. The remainder, however, he faithfully promised to put ashore on their respective islands.

Just as the *Marara* left Marutea the ship's radio received a message from Papeete saying that an epidemic had broken out and that all transport of divers was prohibited. As a further confirmation of this news measles broke out on board among passengers who had come aboard at Papeete.

Instead of returning to Marutea or steering for Tahiti, where there was a possibility of looking after the sick persons, the *Marara*'s owner naturally preferred to go on to his original destination. He understood quite well that by so doing he would spread the disease, but why lose money and time out of consideration for natives? The authorities were a long way off, and as soon as the divers were well again they would, with their usual thoughtlessness, forget the whole business. He was an experienced fox and knew their mentality well. So the *Marara* steered for the nearest mother-of-pearl island, Hikueru.

Here, however, the Chinese met with a disappointment.

The chief had sufficient authority and support from the population to be able to prevent the *Marara*'s passengers from landing. The prohibition of the transport of divers before the season began was clear and had been repeated several times by radio, and the chief emphatically declared that if anyone tried to disobey it, he would report the infraction to the authorities at once.

The supercargo profited by this lesson and made a new plan. There was clearly no point in trying to disembark the passengers on one of the mother-of-pearl islands, where diving took place regularly. On these islands, the chief and inhabitants would certainly be as experienced and energetic as on Hikueru. But on one of the many other islands a coup ought to be successful—especially if an island was chosen where the chief was a man of less energy. He steered for Raroia.

The chief of Raroia, who also had listened to the passengers' stories and complaints, now at last began to understand that he had been tricked, and called a council to discuss what ought to be done. To our great delight it was decided to act resolutely and demand that the owner should go to Papeete at once with all his passengers.

Therefore, when the owner of the *Marara* finally came ashore, he was met on the quay by a resolute committee.

"How can you disembark sick passengers in this way despite the prohibition?" the chief began. "It will certainly be a long time before the diving season begins, and the passengers may have to stay here for several months. There's no room for them, and what are they to eat and drink? The water tank only just provides for us, and there's only food for a few weeks ahead in the shops."

The Chinese listened attentively, and nodded agreement

once or twice. "If you have any difficulties over food supplies, I might be able to help you," he proposed. "I haven't much on board myself, but in this case of course I—"

"It isn't a case of food supplies," a keen-witted person interrupted him, clearly realizing that the conversation had got off the track. "It is forbidden to transport divers from one island to another before the season begins, and no one knows when that will be."

"But my dear people, I have a special permit," the Chinese replied, pretending astonishment as his eyes swept from one face to another.

"How did you manage to get it?" I asked impatiently.

The Chinese jumped when he saw a *popaa,* and this time he had no need to feign astonishment.

"Why, you understand, by radio, permission by radio. Don't you know there's a receiving station on Marutea?"

"Yes," I said, "but you had already left Marutea when the prohibition was issued. How could you be so farsighted as to ask for an exemption long before it came into force?"

"H'm, I don't know. I don't know anything about radios. The captain does. You'd better ask him."

We asked the captain, who put the responsibility onto the supercargo, who in turn referred us to a third person who could not be found. Our friends recovered their courage, and some of them even accused the Chinese of lying, which, curiously enough, he very much resented.

The battle seemed to be won, however, for after a prolonged discussion and incoherent talk with the captain and supercargo the latter told us that they must have "misunderstood" the radio message and that the *Marara* would proceed to Papeete at once. (In other words, the Chinese intended to attempt the same coup on another island, where there were no white people and the chief was even more credulous than on Raroia.) We breathed sighs of relief and began to distribute aspirin for the coming journey to all who wanted it.

We wanted to be present at the embarkation of the sick passengers and the *Marara*'s actual sailing, but just at that moment we were called to Kataha's house. Ihi, a girl of twenty, was, we were told, seriously ill. One look was enough to tell us that something was really seriously wrong. She had a high temperature, was thin and hollow-eyed, and breathed heavily with a wheezing noise.

We supposed, of course, that it was pneumonia and in reply to our persistent questions she told us that she had lately returned from the other side of the island, where she had spent a week in a tumble-down hut. As if to confirm our theory she added that she had a pain in her side which pricked like pins. We gave her an injection of penicillin and told her to stay in bed and wrap herself up well.

When we returned we saw, to our astonishment, that Temake's kitchen was full of Chinese! They were busy cooking and evidently felt completely at home. Two of them were rummaging among the pots and saucepans, while some others were lighting the fire, and a third group were opening canned goods. Temake's wife had been sent by them to fetch water.

Temake's living room swarmed with Chinese women, presumably the businessmen's wives, and they were making themselves as much at home as the men, to say the least. Some were performing their toilettes in front of a mirror, while others had found an iron and were pressing their clothes. In Temake's fine bed, which no one ever dared touch, lay a stout matron with three children.

"What in the world are all these Chinese doing in your house?" I asked Temake. "The schooner was to leave at once and take all the passengers with her."

"Well, you see," said Temake, wriggling, "the motor's broken down. So they must all stay till it's repaired. The Chinese here are merchants who've had business on Marutea, and as they offered their services, I thought it was a good idea to let them cook the food. There's nothing so good as Chinese dishes, as you know."

"Oh, I see, but who's paying for all the canned goods?"

"Well, I am, but, you see, they're cooking the food for nothing."

Anyone who has spent a few weeks on board a schooner will certainly want some other food than canned goods and soon the Chinese were all over the village in search of fowls, geese, pigs, and fruit. The rest of the villagers at least tried to be a little warier than Temake and asked high prices for everything. A goose, which in ordinary circumstances was sold for 150 francs, shot up to 400, a fowl commanded 200 francs, and so on. But the Chinese did not seem to attach any importance to prices; they only laughed, pulled fat bundles of notes from their pockets, and paid.

In regard to breadfruit and papaya they encountered for the first time some slight resistance. No one, understandably enough, was willing to part with such rare delicacies (the only fruits to be found on the island, by the way). But this time again, the Chinese hit on a cunning method of gaining their object. They distributed chewing gum liberally to all the children, and promised a few more packets to each child if they would bring them fruit. The Raroians could certainly have withstood a Chinese attack, but they were naturally powerless against plundering by their own children, and soon the Chinese's sacks were full of breadfruit and papaya.

"They did us out of the fruit, but at any rate they had to pay dear for the fowls and geese," said Taipuhia, trying to console himself.

But I had seen something of Chinese methods before, and was not quite convinced that the Raroians had triumphed finally, even in the case of the poultry.

On our return to our house we found an uninvited visitor. A young Chinese was walking about brazenly in our bedroom.

"Nice house this," he said on catching sight of us. "I think I'll rent it."

"You may think so," I said stiffly. "But we live here, and anyway it might be best to ask the owner first before you decide to rent a house."

He changed his tone at once and humbly begged my pardon and then sat down on a chair without asking permission. But nevertheless he clearly found it difficult to give up his first idea, for his eyes continued to wander searchingly round the walls. They rested on a large map of the Tuamotu group.

"Fine," he said, taking a notebook from his pocket. "I'll take the opportunity and make a sketch of Hao. I've got some land there."

"How can you have land there?" I asked. "Why, no Chinese or any other foreigners can own land."

"Oh, the deeds are in the name of a native. Haven't you any land here yourself?"

"No, I'm an honest foreigner." By this time my tone was decidedly cool.

"H'm, but then what do you do here? Do you do business?"

"No, I don't do any business."

But this was beyond his comprehension, and he smiled incredulously. Then he looked round again and had a fresh try at it.

"What rent do you pay?" he asked.

"It's no business of yours," I replied, "but if you want to know, we pay nothing."

He stared at me round-eyed.

"You see, we are not here to exploit the people on the island," I tried to explain, vaguely hoping to make him understand a philosophy of life a little different from his own. "We're here because our friends invited us to come and see them. The owner of this house lends it to us because he is our friend. In return we do him services and now and then give him presents. That's a good Polynesian custom. When one comes to a country one must follow its customs."

He listened attentively and at last evidently thought he had understood, for he suddenly burst out:

"Yes, that's right. The natives here are stupid. It's easy enough to trick them into giving things for nothing. But you ought to do business; there are great possibilities here in the Tuamotu group."

Again without asking permission, he pulled a book out of my bookshelf. It was an anthropometric book in English with long tables giving the head and body measurements of different Polynesian racial groups.

"Aha," he said, "a price list. Let me see, I understand English. It's much more important to know that than French."

He studied the book, but, of course, could not make out what kinds of merchandise it dealt with. At last he gave up and resumed the conversation, this time in English.

"France no good. America very good. In America you make business. No difficulty. Here many papers. Ah, America—but you can't go to America."

His face grew sad, and he began to take out books at random and turn over the pages backward and forward with his dirty fingers. That was more than I could stand.

"That'll do," I said. "Clear out."

He smiled propitiatingly and began to move toward the door. He stopped on the threshold.

"Look, haven't you any old magazines to give me? With pictures of women in them. . . ."

If I had had any magazines, I would have flung them at his head.

The evening came and still the *Marara* had not left. Ihi was worse, and when we went to give her the next injection she was delirious. Perplexed by her cold, wet clothes, we asked those present for explanations. After much coaxing the truth came out at last. As she had pain in her chest, they had made cold-water compresses to ease the pains.

"She's put cold compresses on her chest for several weeks, but it doesn't seem to do any good," one of her friends told us naïvely.

"Several weeks? Has she had pain in her chest as long as that?"

By degrees we learned the whole story. About a month before Ihi had been at a party, at which denatured alcohol mixed with hair tonic had been drunk, and since then she had continually had pain in her chest. It need hardly be added that it was a Chinese supercargo on board another schooner who had sold denatured alcohol, although he, of course, understood quite well what it was to be used for. It has happened more than once that unscrupulous supercargoes—

not always Chinese, it must be admitted—have sold more than the permitted quantities of denatured alcohol, and that natives have died as a result of similar drinking bouts.

We did the only thing possible: we gave Ihi a fresh injection and recommended absolute rest. This was unfortunately a quite futile recommendation, for the inhabitants had already started a huge carouse, and bawling and singing filled the air. It was, of course, the doing of the Chinese, who had begun to sell smuggled liquor as usual at 600 francs a bottle. I could not help thinking of Taipuhia and other villagers, who had so proudly declared when selling the fowls that this time it was the Chinese who had been cheated. Moreover, several of the Chinese had already begun playing cards, which naturally did not stop till the Raroians had lost their last centime.

Next day most of the Raroians began to have second thoughts, and as they grew more sober they became, to our great delight, really savage. They demonstrated so violently against the *Marara's* owner and supercargo that the "breakdown" was suddenly and miraculously repaired and the schooner suddenly ready for sailing. All the passengers were assembled down on the quay, and when at last all the Chinese businessmen came along in a party, both we and the Raroians began to draw sighs of relief. Without a goodby to anyone, or a word of excuse, the whole gang of Chinese got into the ship's boat, which left the quay loaded to the gunwales.

We saw them reach the schooner and clamber on board. Then suddenly the motor began to spit, and before we could quite understand what they were doing, the anchor was up and the schooner on her way out of the lagoon, leaving behind all the divers and their families.

But these poor people were not all the *Marara* had left behind. A huge heap of corrugated iron lay in Temake's yard, and various other goods were spread about there.

"You understand," our merchant friend explained, "this is iron which they're going to reload when the *Marara* comes back. The supercargo is afraid of a new world war beginning. When the last world war broke out the authorities confiscated all goods, rationed them, and fixed the price. So he daren't take the iron back to Papeete, but would rather leave it in safety here, like the gasoline and a lot of other things."

I understood perfectly. But why on earth had the supercargo left behind a kerosene iron, a piece of silk cloth, a photograph frame, a hat, a soup tureen, and a lot of other rubbish? Temake's explanation was illuminating:

"Those are things I bought on board."

"How much did you pay?"

"I don't know, the accounts are so complicated."

"Didn't you buy any more useful things?"

"Oh, yes—flour, canned goods, cigarettes, and wooden shoes."

"Wooden shoes! Who's going to buy wooden shoes here on Raroia? Everyone goes barefoot on weekdays, and for Sundays they want smart leather shoes."

"The supercargo wouldn't give me any flour unless I took the wooden shoes as well. There are only two dozen pairs."

"H'm, and you don't know how much you've paid?"

"No, but really I haven't paid anything. They took my copra and it worked out all square. I'm quite satisfied."

The divers and their families who had been left behind were considerably less satisfied. Most of them had been away from home more than five months and longed to get

256

Spear-fishing is a popular sport and the fishermen sometimes keep the first fish on the spear while harpooning others (*above*). Although Marie-Thérèse had seen many strange fish at Raroia, she could not help being amused when she picked up this "nosefish."

Harpooning fish on the outer reef requires sharp sight and great agility (*above*). The natives also fish-hunt with dogs (*below, left*). Catching turtle is another sport (*below, right*).

A *rena,* a garland of palm leaves, is used to encircle a shoal of fish and slowly pull it inshore (*above*). On the beach, after the catch has been brought in, everyone takes his share (*below*).

The Chinese, who control most of the retail trade, are slowly spreading over the Tuamotu atolls (*above*). (*Below*) natives with the measles lie on the Chinese schooner's deck.

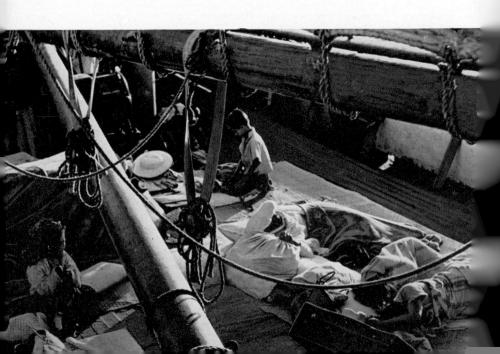

back. They were now forced to stay on Raroia for an indefinite time until the *Marara* was pleased to come back and take them home in accordance with the contract. Of course they could take another schooner at their own expense—if one appeared, contrary to all expectation—but they had no more money.

Even worse, they had nowhere to live on Raroia. Only in a few cases would the Raroians receive them into their houses, and the schoolmistress, as can well be understood, firmly refused to let them occupy the schoolhouse. The consequence was that they had to settle down as best they could in provisional houses made of galvanized iron and palm leaves on the outskirts of the village. It need not be said that such accommodations did not help to accelerate the recovery of the invalids.

For the Raroians, too, this unexpected increase in the population presented serious problems. The canned goods available were roughly sufficient, but the drinking water situation was not so good, and it would now have to be rationed. Another serious problem was that of coconuts. With the prevailing copra prices it meant a heavy loss if fifty people each took a few nuts from the trees every day. The Raroians, therefore, would not give them free, and the divers neither would nor could pay for them, and began to steal on the quiet. Consequently the Raroians remained in the village to guard their trees instead of going off into the interior of the island to make copra, as they had planned to do. They not only lost money and time but also began to be irritated at continually coming across strangers stealing nuts. Several fights took place.

But the real catastrophe did not occur until a few weeks later, when the measles epidemic began to rage in earnest.

Incapable of understanding that a disease could be contracted simply by contact, when no immediate result was seen, the islanders had recklessly associated with all the sick persons whom the *Marara* had left behind.

We knew from experience that it was useless to try to isolate the sick people, and we therefore did the only possible thing: we tried to organize patrols to go round the village and see that the patients stayed indoors, wrapped themselves in blankets, and drank something hot. Despite this we daily met sick people on the beach in the strongest wind, and their regular explanation was this:

"We tried to stay indoors as you told us to, but that's a bad method. We felt as if we were being suffocated. We feel much better out here in the wind. We can breathe here."

At last what we long feared happened: Ihi caught the measles. Her condition, already very critical, became rapidly worse, and it was apparent to all that she would not recover. Her friends' reaction when they realized this was most unusual.

"She can't stay here any longer," they declared with one voice. "If she dies here, everyone will think it's our fault."

"Nonsense," I protested. "Everyone knows that you've done your best to look after her."

"That won't be any good. Everyone will certainly think it's our fault. Perhaps we'll be punished too. She'd better go."

"But she can't even raise herself up, and she's absolutely nowhere to go."

"That may be, but in any case we won't have her here with us any longer."

We tried to find someone who was willing to take her in, but we found no one. Unlike most of the other islanders Ihi was Tahitian and had no relations. She had been adopted when she was little by a woman from Raroia; but this woman had married a man from another island and gone away. Ihi stayed behind on Raroia with her "husband," but since this cohabitation and several later ones had ended in separation, she had led a nomad existence, living now in one household and now in another—which shows one of the few disadvantages of the illegal system of adoption so widely practiced.

The only solution to the problem we could find was that all the Raroians in turn should come and help to look after Ihi, in which case they would all, according to their own ideas, be equally responsible. After a little persuasion they agreed to this. It need hardly be added that this was only a theoretical solution to quiet their consciences. In reality no one bothered about her at all. Everyone still had plenty of smuggled liquor, and it was all they could do to look after themselves. But the most important result had been achieved: Ihi's friends let her stay with them.

We did our best, but neither care nor medicine could help Ihi any longer; she died a few days later in terrible suffering. Whether the principal cause was the internal trouble caused by the denatured alcohol, the cold compresses, or the measles, we could not decide. But one thing is certain—that it was a quite unnecessary and senseless death, like so many others in the Tuamotu group at the same time!

Of course Ihi had not left a centime, and naturally no one offered to pay for a coffin for her. But the chief hit upon an unusually shrewd and just solution. He decreed that all the men who had lived with her should contribute a sum of money and the result was that Ihi got the most beautiful coffin which had been seen on Raroia for a long time.

The wake took place on the following night, as is customary on Raroia. Ihi lay in her fine coffin in the middle of the mortuary under a canopy of gaily colored pieces of cloth, and behind her head a few bright-colored blankets were spread on the wall. The whole population, including all the strangers, had gathered round, and with one of the catechists leading the singers, hymns followed one another in rapid succession.

Nevertheless, everything was not as usual. Ordinarily at wakes people came and went freely and formed small groups here and there inside and outside the mortuary to exchange ideas and discuss the funeral arrangements. But everyone here sat staring apathetically straight in front; and even more curious, many did not even take part in the singing. Nor were any coffee or other refreshments served, as is always done at funerals.

This difference in atmosphere was, of course, due to the fact that nearly all those attending the funeral were ill. Many had high fevers, others coughed and groaned unceasingly, and several lay absolutely silent and motionless, as if they had fallen into a trance. The measles had spread in a terrifying manner, and this would certainly not be the last burial. I do not know whether the mourners were fearfully asking themselves whose turn it would be next, or if they simply had not the strength left to trouble themselves about the outside world, but in any case I have seldom taken part in such a painfully depressing assembly.

When at last dawn came, all were so exhausted and weak that we had the greatest difficulty in scraping together half-a-dozen men capable of acting as gravediggers and bearers.

This quiet continued to prevail for a long time—broken only by a few similar funerals—and but for the tragic aspect of it we should have found it refreshing after the noise, carousing, and fighting of the past weeks. By degrees—but very, very slowly—the patients began to regain health, but many weeks after the *Marara*'s disgraceful visit there were still plenty of convalescents.

The end of the story? Of course everything went exactly as the Chinese had intended. When at last the *Marara* returned several months later and the postponed diving season finally started, most of the divers were so penniless and so weary of Raroia that all of them, even those who earlier had been most homesick, hastened to sign a fresh contract with the *Marara*'s owner.

Some of them asked to be repatriated in accordance with the terms of the contract, but the Chinese declared that he "unfortunately" had no opportunity of sending any of the people home; so they had no choice but to start diving again.

The most distressing part of all this is not that Raroia was once unlucky enough to suffer a Chinese invasion, but that the worthy islanders are so forgetful that they certainly will not remember this lesson. The Chinese, therefore, will return and perhaps in the end dominate them in the same manner as they now dominate so many other islands in French Oceania.

Money in the Sea

In the copious, romantic, and sentimental South Sea literature the Tuamotu atolls are called the "pearl islands." This name undeniably had a certain justification a hundred years ago, but nowadays it is a misnomer. The time when a diver was dissatisfied if he did not find at least one or two pearls as large as peas for every dozen mussels he opened is long past, and in our day it is the exception to find a more or less fully developed pearl.

The cause is quite simple: mussels are now collected for their own sake and consequently are never left in peace long enough for a decent pearl to be formed. While the mother-of-pearl trade has increased tremendously in the last few years, Tuamotu pearls have almost disappeared from the market.

Not even the rather more modest—but for South Sea romantics almost as satisfying—name of "mother-of-pearl islands" is particularly appropriate. On most of the seventy-eight Tuamotu Islands there are few mussels or none; and only on half-a-dozen of the islands are there sufficient quantities to make regular diving worth while. The reason is that mother-of-pearl mussels are highly sensitive organisms, which only develop and thrive under ideal conditions not found everywhere in the Tuamotus.

In contrast to the oyster, the mother-of-pearl embryo is not developed in the mother mussel, but instead floats about in the water. The embryos, one twenty-fifth of an inch long, are at first quite unprotected, which, of course, makes them an easy prey for fish and greatly reduces their number. The first condition for an increase of mussels in a lagoon is therefore that the lagoon shall be comparatively poor in fish.

But even more fatal than the ravages of fish are the tidal currents, which often carry the floating organisms far out to sea, where naturally they are destroyed or vanish into the depths. Thus a good result can only be hoped for on atolls which have a complete, or almost complete, coral ring, and it is significant that all the richest mother-of-pearl islands have no gaps in the reef. (A further advantage for the divers is, of course, that on these islands there are no sharks in the lagoons.)

If the young mussel remains and continues to develop in the lagoon, it gradually forms a shell and sinks to the bottom. If it lands on a hard coral shoal it attaches itself firmly and grows quickly. If, on the other hand, it lands on a sand or clay bottom, it is lost and soon dies. Thus a further large number of atolls are eliminated as suitable breeding places for the mussels.

Even a completely enclosed island with a coral bottom, however, is not always rich in mussels. These sensitive organisms also require a frequent circulation of water and a certain depth. Many islands which form an unbroken ring of coral are too high for the waves to be able to wash into the lagoon even at high tide. The mother-of-pearl mussels cannot thrive under such conditions.

As Raroia has not only a lagoon abounding in fish and an entrance with a strong current, but also a sandy bottom in the lagoon, it does not satisfy any of the three most important conditions and thus is poor in mother-of-pearl mussels. On the neighboring island of Takume, on the other hand, the conditions are quite ideal and the Raroians regularly emigrate to Takume in crowds during the diving season, which is usually several months in the year.

When the season was approaching once more, all the villagers were seized by a sudden desire to travel, and left all their occupations. Of course Marie-Thérèse and I, true to our determination to see and experience everything that our friends did, decided to accompany them as usual.

The shortest distance between Raroia and Takume is only three or four miles, but the sailing distance from the pass on Raroia to Takume village is considerably longer, about twelve miles. As the Raroians have no other vessels but the small light lagoon canoes—15 to 25 feet long and 3 feet broad—a trip to Takume is a quite daring enterprise, and they only go out to sea when the weather is particularly calm and favorable. Thus we, too, had to wait for more than a week before the wind went round into the southeast and dropped sufficiently for our flotilla to risk the journey.

As on many other canoe expeditions, we again preferred to make the trip with our faithful friend Tehei, and when the little squadron left the village we were sitting in our usual place on the outrigger of his blue-and-yellow canoe *Araimoana,* while he himself hung over the tiller aft and his wife lay on her stomach in the bow, keeping a lookout for coral shoals. Small waves splashed playfully against the bow, and the canoe floated safe and steady on the faintly rippled water of the lagoon.

But hardly had we been swept out through the entrance, close behind the leading boat—Tepuka's fast sailer *Turia*—when our canoe began to jump and dance like a thing possessed. We had been caught by the powerful eddies outside the reef, and for a long time the canoe spun round like a runaway merry-go-round, till at last, with the aid of the paddles, we worked our way out of the danger zone.

Although we were now flying along the reef at a safe distance from all breakers and currents, the voyage was a good deal less quiet and safe than we had expected. The wind was still moderate, as we were under the shelter of the land, but the water was very much rougher than the lagoon inside, and heavy swells came rolling across the sea at regular intervals.

The canoe was tossed about violently, and now and then there was an ominous cracking noise from the outrigger boom. The waves often washed over the deck, and suddenly one of the hatch covers broke loose! Before we could put it on again, a gallon or two of sea water had splashed down into the hold. Tehei only laughed and declared that it was nothing to worry about. He added, presumably to reassure us, that these misadventures were mere trifles compared with the difficulties we should encounter when we came out into the open sea.

Unfortunately he proved to be right, for we had hardly entered the wide strait which separates the two islands when the canoe began to lurch so violently that we had the greatest difficulty in keeping ourselves on board. The waves were as high as the canoe and washed over us every other minute.

I began to feel a trifle uneasy. Nor did I feel any better when I got a chance to look round a little—between two drenchings of salt water—and discovered that Tehei was steering northeast right out toward the open sea.

"Where are you going?" I bellowed at him. "Don't you see that Takume is much farther north?"

"Yes, I do," he yelled back. "But there's a strong westerly current here between the islands which we must look out for."

I meditated on this fact for a long time in silence and tried to calculate where we should end up if we missed Takume. As I did not carry the whole map of the Tuamotus neatly printed in my head, I gave it up and asked Tehei, in another interval between two seas, what would happen to us in such a case.

"It's best not to miss Takume," he replied. "Tara and Kainui were rather careless once, and their canoe was caught by the current. Before they could stop it, they were far out to sea, and soon both Raroia and Takume had disappeared below the horizon. A squall broke the mast off, and they began to drift helplessly before the sea. They drifted for two days before they sighted an island. As it looked as if the canoe would drift past, they left it and swam to land. It took them half a day to reach the island."

Tehei was certainly right. If we did not want to drift about for two days and swim for half a day, it was best not to miss Takume! We clung to the outrigger boom so tightly that our knuckles grew white, and let Tehei steer on out toward the empty horizon. Two hours passed and during all that time we bumped and soaked and shook as if we were in a washing machine. At last he managed to steer the canoe into the shelter of the Takume reef. Three of the other canoes from Raroia had already arrived, and the rest were not far behind. They all bore evidence of a good shaking-up but no one was in the least upset.

"Oh, it was nothing this time," said Tehei, as, safe and sound, we continued our sail along the reef. "I remember once going from Takume to Raroia in a storm. I had the whole family with me, and everyone on Takume said we should come to grief. However, I started. The wind was so strong that we had to lie down on the deck, and the seas so heavy that the whole lot of us were nearly washed overboard.

"At last I made my wife and the children crawl down into the hold, and I jumped overboard and held on tight to the rudder. As luck had it, the wind was blowing straight for Raroia and we were carried up high onto the reef. When I opened the hatch, my wife and the children had fainted. That may have been because there was no air left, for after they lay on the shore a little while, they came to."

"Our Lord is the protector of all fools," I attempted to say in my best Tuamotuan, but Tehei did not understand me. I therefore contented myself with asking why in the world he had started on such an idiotic voyage. His reply was typically Polynesian:

"Well, you see, a friend of mine on Raroia was having a birthday party, and of course I didn't want to miss a chance of a party like that."

Tehei found a narrow gap in the reef, and we rode in through it on the crest of a huge wave. The moment the canoe bumped against the coral bottom, we jumped out and took a firm grip of it to prevent it from following out with the backwash. Then we waded slowly to land and pulled the canoe up onto the beach.

Pahoa, a relative of our good friend Temake, was waiting for us a little way along the beach in the shade of some bushes. Although we had never seen him before, he greeted us as long-lost friends and immediately accompanied us to the village to help us settle. The changes since our last visit were astounding. On the lightning visit paid with the *Teretai,* when on our way to Raroia, we had found a tumbledown village with about fifty sleepy Polynesians. Now, on the contrary, the village streets were teeming with people, and we saw shops and bars everywhere through the palms.

In an open place a party of gaily dressed men and women were dancing to music from a phonograph; in one corner a Chinese had set up a wheel of fortune; and we heard the rumbling and grating of radio sets from many temporary tents and palm-leaf houses. Bicycles lay in heaps under the palm trees, and down on the shore of the lagoon a hundred canoes and four motorboats rocked on the water.

The most original sight, however, was a newly built wooden house with a large, open veranda furnished in the best style of the 1880's, with bright-red, plush-covered furniture, ornamental cupboards, carved tables, and sofas with crocheted antimacassars. An ingenious businessman had found a new and quick method of enriching himself at the expense of the Tuamotu natives; according to his own account the demand was so great that he had made a trip to Paris to buy up old furniture at auction.

"They're a pretty strange collection, as you see," said Pahoa smiling. We had completed our tour of inspection and now sat round a "restaurant table" consisting of an inverted wooden box. "But they're certainly not all here yet, for the diving season only started two weeks ago. At present I should think there are only about three hundred divers on the island, and we usually have about five hundred. Most of them are not professional divers, but adventurous Tuamotuans and Tahitians who dream of earning a fortune quickly. They earn a lot of money all right, but as a rule they spend every centime on drink or dissipate it in some other way, and go home again as poor as when they came.

"Of course crowds of other people come besides the divers —relations, assistants, shopkeepers, prostitutes, recruiters, buyers, and boatowners—all of whom have the same dream of getting rich quickly and sometimes make it a reality. Only some of these secondary figures are Polynesians. For example, we now have many shops on the island owned by Chinese. All the bakers are Chinese too.

"Then we have the recruiters. They are most often Europeans, former sailors and adventurers who go round to all the Tuamotu Islands months before the season begins and persuade the natives to go with them to Takume and other mother-of-pearl islands and dive for them. They generally pay for the journey there and back, and in return the natives promise not to sell their mother-of-pearl shells to any other person. Last come the buyers, who rank highest; they are French or Chinese, and as many of them also own schooners, they dominate the trade entirely.

"The market has always been unsteady," Pahoa continued, "as mother-of-pearl shell is a luxury article and one dependent on fashion. In the years after the First World War the demand was tremendous, but right through the thirties it was impossible to find any buyers even long after the depression was over. During the last war someone had the idea of making mother-of-pearl souvenirs, which were sold in masses to the American troops in the Pacific, and this created a new interest which still holds its ground.

"At present the demand for mother-of-pearl is even greater than the supply. The buyers fight for every day's take, and they've every reason to. They pay 30 francs [48 cents] a kilo here and sell for 50 francs [80 cents] on the world market. Diving's over for today, but wait till tomorrow, and you'll see a good row when the canoes come back fully loaded."

However, we also wanted to see how the diving itself was done, and therefore decided to go with some of the Raroians next morning. It had hardly begun to grow light when we heard a fierce hooting of sirens from the bay by the village. We bolted a little food and hurried down to the shore of the lagoon, where our friends Tehei and Tinorua were already waiting for us. Tehei had left a paddle canoe of his on Takume the season before; we found and launched it. Although a trifle leaky, it floated—and that was the main thing.

Numbers of canoes had already collected round the four motorboats, and laughing Polynesians were busy stringing them together. We paddled over to the nearest boat, and one of the Raroians threw the end of a rope over to us. A quarter of an hour later the captain gave the signal for departure, and at last we moved off in a long procession. I counted the canoes and found that our flotilla consisted of no less than sixteen.

"How much do you pay for the towing?" I asked Tehei.

"Thirty mother-of-pearl mussels a day."

"Thirty mussels! But if you want to pay in money, how much does it cost?"

"The boatowner doesn't want any money, he wants mother-of-pearl mussels."

This hardly surprised me. Thirty mussels weighed at

least 15 kilos (about 33 pounds) and were worth 450 Tahitian francs ($7.20). With sixteen canoes in tow the boatowner earned 7,200 francs (over $115) a day. This was undeniably good pay.

After a half-hour's towing we reached some large shoals in the southern part of the lagoon. Here the motorboat left us and returned to the village. The canoes spread out quickly, every diver seeking his favorite place. We ourselves paddled over to the nearest coral shoal, where we made our canoe fast to a large rock.

"It's best to be a bit careful at first," said Tehei. "A lot of people start deep diving at once, but that's just stupid. They grow tired too quickly and risk getting cramps. I always begin by diving for the mussels which are on the sides of the shoal. It's an easy and pleasant way of warming oneself up."

As he spoke he put on his goggles, tied a net bag tightly to his belt, and drew a canvas glove over his right hand. Then he slid down into the water and vanished beneath the surface. After a time his head came up again.

"There are plenty of mussels here," he announced with satisfaction. "Jump in, all of you, it's not more than twenty-five or thirty feet deep."

We followed his advice and jumped in. We sank slowly toward the bottom. Tehei and Tinorua moved about in the water with perfect ease, but I myself was hopelessly clumsy and slow, and when they began to pick the first mussels I had got hardly more than halfway. Although the pressure round my head did not feel any worse than that of an army steel helmet, my ears were singing. I therefore decided to stay where I was, for after all I had nothing to lose by doing so.

The water was clear and transparent, and I could clearly see my companions and all that they were doing. They had a firm hold of the coral wall with their left hands and with their gloved right hands they were breaking large, bearded mussels loose and dropping them into the bags on their belts. It looked simple.

I caught sight of a huge mussel just under my nose and immediately decided to follow their example. I remembered warnings not to stick fingers into the opening and took a firm grip on the lower part of the shell. Then I tried to bend it sideways as I had seen my friends do. But the result was far from what I expected. The mussel did not budge an inch, but I myself involuntarily floated back from it. I took hold of it again, braced myself and flung myself at it. Same result. I tried several more times, but naturally, the harder I went at it, the farther away and higher up I floated. I might as well have tried to knock over a tenpin with a rubber balloon.

I studied Tehei's and Tinorua's technique for some seconds and discovered that they always took hold of the coral wall with the left hand a little way *below* the mussel. This was clearly the trick. I did as they did and actually succeeded in making the mussel budge a little. My breath was giving out, but I had resolved not to return to the surface empty-handed and stubbornly launched a fresh attack. To apply greater force I put my feet into a crevice lower down in the coral shoal and caught hold of the mussel with both hands. Then I pulled. At last it gave way and came loose.

I floated up to the surface, blue in the face and struggling for breath, with my trophy in my hands. A few seconds later Tehei and Tinorua came up. They had each collected about a dozen mussels. Chagrined, I decided in the future to de-

In outrigger canoes such as these (*above*) we sailed from Raroia to Takume. (*Below*) the eternal trade wind gently sways the palms.

Maono brings up from the depths of the Takume lagoon a pearl mussel. Mother-of-pearl, the hard internal layer of these mussel shells, is a profitable source of income in French Oceania.

After I gave up trying to dive and collect mussels as the natives do, Tehei showed us how to open a pearl mussel.

The longer we stayed on the island, the more Polynesian we became in our ways. More and more we found ourselves sitting and simply doing nothing. Here Marie-Thérèse leisurely strokes our cat . . . .

. . . . but sometimes I summoned enough energy to do a little exploring on the island, and this time I found a whale vertebra.

The Raroians are indeed carefree! A youngster is given a ride on a palm-leaf sled (*above*), little girls munch pandanus nuts (*left*), and a boy engages in his favorite pastime, playing with a spin made from a palm frond (*below*).

vote myself to *cleaning* mussels, and to watching the divers.

After one or two more immersions my friends thought the time had come to dive in the deeper water, where the mussels were larger and more numerous. We paddled about fifty yards from the shoal and dropped anchor which did not reach bottom till we had let out nearly a hundred feet of rope. Unperturbed, Tehei and Tinorua quietly produced a couple of sinkers to which thin lines were attached, and put on their goggles.

"It's no good swimming down a hundred feet," Tehei explained. "It would take too long. So we always use sinkers to carry us down to great depths. And to be able to move more easily we don't bring the mussels up with us each time, but we use small baskets like these; we leave them at the bottom and only hoist them up when they are full."

He showed us a net basket furnished with lead sinkers. Then he fastened a line to it and flung it overboard. Meanwhile Tinorua got ready and jumped into the water. Tehei gave him one of the sinkers, and without having made any apparent effort to fill his lungs with air, he vanished into the depths. I looked at my watch. It took fourteen seconds for the line to run out. I continued to follow the second hand. Half a minute. One minute. One minute, fifteen seconds—suddenly the water began to bubble, and a few seconds later Tinorua came shooting up like a rocket. One minute, twenty-three seconds. Not bad. Tinorua exhaled with a whistling noise, heaved himself up onto the edge of the canoe and rested. He sat for a long time silent, relaxed, and huddled up. Then, as it were, he returned to life again and began to talk and laugh.

Meanwhile Tehei had hauled up Tinorua's sinker and got his own ready, and in a few minutes they both jumped in. After that they glided up and down through the water as regularly as if they had been using an elevator, and Marie-Thérèse and I were kept busy cleaning.

In one of his rest periods Tinorua told us that many divers stayed under water a good deal longer than they did, but that these record-makers also had to rest longer between their dips. He himself considered a minute and a half under water and three minutes above to be the ideal times. A minute and a half was just the time he and Tehei spent under water, but on the other hand, they often rested for more than three minutes. I counted the number of dives, and they varied between ten and twelve an hour.

A hundred similar canoes were bobbing up and down all round us, and shining, brown divers were slowly filling them with mussels. Most of the divers were strong Tarzan-like men who would have done credit to any South Sea film. But more surprising, we discovered a few parties of women who seemed to be diving as energetically as the men. I asked Tehei what he thought of the women divers, and he replied at once:

"Most of them are better than the men because they're fatter. A fat person doesn't get so cold as a thin one down in deep water and also comes up to the surface more quickly. But the result is seldom any better, for the women waste at least half the time in gossiping."

While the divers were generally men and women in the prime of life, most of the mussel-cleaners were old people and children. The authorities have forbidden all mussel-cleaning in the village on hygienic grounds, and therefore it is always done in the canoes at the same time as the diving.

Even a practiced cleaner can sometimes have difficulty in keeping up with the divers, and, of course, it was even harder for Marie-Thérèse and me. However swiftly we picked the contents out of the mussels, the heap in front of us grew without interruption. Like most novices we found the work intensely exciting to begin with and hoped at any moment to find a large gleaming pearl, but the humdrum monotony gradually dampened our spirits, and at the end we dreamed no longer of pearls but of refreshing green coconuts.

The sun and the smell, too, became more unbearable every minute, and when at about eleven o'clock the motor-boat appeared, we were already so tired of the dismal business that we would gladly have exchanged the work even for copra-cutting. Tinorua and Tehei seemed, however, completely unaffected by their considerably more tiring work and joked and chatted merrily with the other divers in the flotilla, which was beginning to reassemble.

While we were being towed back to the village, we counted the mussels. The result was anything but bad: 211 mussels, many of which were as large as a plate and certainly weighed about five pounds. We cleaned up the most unsightly and cut off a number of excrescences here and there, so that we could sell them as soon as we arrived at the village. This proved to be a good idea.

We had hardly landed when the mother-of-pearl merchants swarmed about us. They had cunningly displayed masses of bicycles, phonographs, bathing suits, and other attractive things, and our friends, like most of the other divers, quickly fell for the tempting wares and gave the merchants all their mother-of-pearl in exchange for the rubbish.

After a few hours' rest we went off on another and shorter trip, which yielded about half as much mother-of-pearl as the morning expedition—94 mussels. We again accompanied our friends when they sold their take and found that it weighed as much as 67 kilos (about 147 pounds). Earlier they had weighed in 142 kilos (about 312 pounds) so that the total result was 209 kilos (about 460 pounds). As the price was 30 francs per kilo, that meant that their day's earnings were 3,135 francs each (about $50), which must be considered good pay!

This may seem easily earned money, but in reality it is blood money. No one can long resist the severe pressure down in the depths and endure the too violent ascents and descents. Their health is ruined sooner or later, and every season one or two divers inevitably lose their lives, generally beginners, who get cramps or are attacked by giddiness while on the sea bottom. Others fall victim to a hemorrhage of the lungs or meet the most insidious danger of all—giant mussels. Here and there, in crevices in the coral shoals and on the sea bottom, huge tridacna mussels lie hidden, and a man who happens to tread on one of them has no chance of escape. The mussel shuts on his foot like a trap, and all attempts to loosen it are in vain.

During our short stay on Takume—a little more than three weeks—we, significantly enough, witnessed three fairly slight accidents and one death. The latter took place one morning when we chanced to be in the village. Diving is always stopped immediately when a serious accident happens. Therefore, as soon as we saw the whole flotilla of canoes on its way home, we knew what had happened. All the inhabitants of the village collected down on the beach, silent and anxious.

Suddenly a woman began to weep, and soon all joined in her lamentation. Before long there was not a woman who was not convinced that it was her husband or her son to whom the accident had happened, for they were all calling out the names of their relations and sobbing as if their hearts would break. When the flotilla came nearer one or two boys climbed up into a coconut palm and in a little while one of them announced shrilly:

"It's Paiva, it's Paiva. He's dead."

We too, one after another, saw the fatal signal. One of the canoes carried a red *pareu* (loincloth) at half-mast, and bystanders assured us that there was no doubt of its being Paiva's canoe.

As soon as everyone had ascertained who the victim was, tears and lamentations ceased as by magic, and the whole crowd disappeared toward the village in small groups. Soon we were alone on the beach. Clearly Paiva had neither family nor friends on Takume. In a little while we heard a cracked record strike up an American popular song, and a few minutes later the village once more sounded with shouting and laughter.

We waited till the flotilla arrived and poor Paiva was carried ashore. He had been seized with cramps and drowned before anyone could come to his help. There was, of course, the usual rush by the whole gang of buyers and mother-of-pearl merchants, but they did not so much as cast a glance in the direction where Paiva's body lay, and disappeared as soon as they had weighed in the mother-of-pearl.

The divers seemed just as unconcerned, and most of them hurried up to the village at once to eat and amuse themselves. Only a few men from one of the motorboats and we ourselves accompanied the dead man to the churchyard, where he was left without ceremony until the burial on the following day. A little later the bearers, too, were dancing to their heart's content on the festival ground of the village.

We understood. The universal distress and weeping were due only to the uncertainty of waiting and the fear that disaster had overtaken some relative or friend. That a death had occurred was, in itself, not a thing which could have much effect on hardened mother-of-pearl divers. It was only an occupational risk which had to be taken into account.

Another danger which lies in wait for the divers is the so-called *taravana*. One day when we returned from the mother-of-pearl waters I saw a man ceaselessly bailing out his canoe with a force and speed which I had never before seen any Polynesian show. I decided to keep my eye on him. In a little while I discovered that he was bailing pure air. There was not a drop in the scoop when he "emptied" it over the railing.

"What's the matter with that man?" I asked Tehei curiously.

"Oh, that's Tepava," he said. "He's got the *taravana*."

"*Taravana?*"

"Yes, he's done so much diving that he's become queer in the head. That happens to a lot of divers. My father got the *taravana* here last year. He did everything the wrong way round. If, for example, I asked him to come out fishing with me, he put on his Sunday clothes and got out his hymnbook. If I told him to dress for church, he put on his working clothes and went and cut up copra. But the most absurd thing was that when we ate he tried to pour coffee onto the fish and stuff the meat into a tumbler!"

"How dreadful!" said Marie-Thérèse with true feminine sympathy.

"Why?" Tehei replied. "We thought it was great fun and were almost sorry when he got well again. I know two Takume men who've never got well. One of them, as soon as he gets hold of a pillow, pulls out the feathers and tries to make them into soup. The other rings the church bell for days on end. For a long time they tried to make him verger and get him just to ring for morning and evening service, but it didn't work. So what they do now is to stop his ringing for a short time in the morning and a short time in the evening. When the church bell isn't going everyone knows it's time for the service."

"Can nothing be done to cure the sickness?" I asked.

"The only thing is to drink a lot of rum. Sometimes that does good, sometimes it doesn't."

I turned to my favorite subject and made one more attempt to convince Tehei of the advantages of wearing diving dress. He was as skeptical as usual and declared that it was much more dangerous to dive with diving dress than without. He stated, by way of proof, that several merchants in Tahiti had imported complete diving equipment, but that all who had used it had died while in the water. I took an opportunity later of asking Pahoa what the facts of the case were.

"It's true enough that many people who've tried diving dress have had accidents," he said. "But that's the fault of the divers, not the equipment. We made an experiment once here on Takume, but it was the same as on all the other mother-of-pearl islands. We gave the divers proper instructions as to what to do, but they did everything wrong; some even started a competition to see who could stay under water longest.

"The assistants were hardly any better. They fooled and ragged all the time, and forgot about the air pumps or broke them. But that wasn't the worst part. A diver ought not to bend quickly and must never have his head lower than his diaphragm, but of course none of them paid any attention to that, and the result was that many of them had hemorrhages, sometimes so serious that they died."

"But why not use European divers?" I asked.

"Several merchants have tried it, but the natives have always stopped such experiments for fear of competition. So we've gradually gone back to the old diving methods, and at present there isn't one island in French Oceania where modern equipment is used. It isn't particularly sensible, but it's obviously the only solution, unless one cultivates mussels."

"Cultivate mussels? I've read about it. How's it done?"

"Come home with me and have a drink, and I'll tell you something interesting," Pahoa replied mysteriously.

Of course I did not wait to be asked twice, but accompanied him to the lee side of the island, where he lived in distinguished isolation. Pahoa took two crystal glasses out of his fine antique cupboard and sent one of the maids to fetch two bottles of champagne. He was clearly a man who knew not only all about mother-of-pearl and diving, but also how to profit by his knowledge. I listened, therefore, with peculiar interest when he sat down comfortably in an armchair and began to narrate:

"My father came here as far back as some time in the sixties, when a white man's life was hardly safe in the Tuamotu group. But somehow or other he succeeded in getting on with the leading men on the island, and after a time he married the *tahunga's* daughter. He began to dive for mussels as soon as the first trading schooners appeared, and gradually induced the rest of the islanders to follow his example. This was certainly worth while, for at that time there were still plenty of pearls. Soon Takume was one of the best-known pearl and mother-of-pearl islands, and my father was one of the richest men in all French Oceania.

"By degrees, however, the pearls became rarer and rarer, and at last there were none left in the lagoon. A few years later the number of mussels also began to fall off, and toward the end of the eighties it was hardly worth the trouble to go diving for them. The cause was the same old one. The bottom was covered with a thick layer of sand and mud, and the mussels could no longer take hold.

"Then came the great cyclones of 1903 and 1906. They drowned Takume like so many islands. When they had swept past nothing was left of Father's house and wealth. The house was built of mahogany and full of antique furniture which Father had bought in Paris. What was still worse was that several boxes of silver coins and pearls which he kept in his study had disappeared too.

"Father built a house of pandanus leaves and began to make copra like everyone else. Several years passed. Then one day, when he was out fishing, he suddenly saw some big mother-of-pearl mussels on the bottom. He dived down and found that the bottom was covered with stones and broken-off palm trees, on which thousands of mussels were growing and thriving. Soon, of course, Takume was prosperous again. But my father had had an idea.

"The coconut palms and stones which the cyclones had hurled into the lagoons had given the mussels a hard foundation again, which they could take hold of. Thus all was well for the time, but how long would it be before the palms rotted and the stones were covered with mud again? When this happened there would be an end to Takume's second era of prosperity.

"No one knew, or troubled to think, how long it would

last, but my father decided at once to study the mussels and the bottom of the lagoon methodically to find an answer to the question. Father died just before the Second World War, but I continued his investigations. Would you like to know the result? Everything looks bright at present, but believe me, in twenty or thirty years there will be no more mother-of-pearl mussels in the Takume lagoon.

"However, I have found a solution. There is no possibility of sweeping the bottom clean of the mud and sand which are now being deposited. But why not do as Mother Nature herself does? The cyclones strewed palm trunks and stones over the whole lagoon and so formed a bottom. Assuming that everyone would co-operate, it would not be difficult to form a new bottom again by flinging in coral blocks. If, for example, all the divers took one or two blocks each time they were towed out to the mother-of-pearl grounds, it would be possible to complete the work in a few seasons."

"That's certainly an excellent idea," I interrupted him. "But were you not speaking of cultivating mussels?"

"Wait a bit," said Pahoa, smiling. "Just when I had got so far in my reflections that I had decided to try to make the divers think of the future, I had a new idea. As the floating mother-of-pearl embryos suck themselves onto stones and tree trunks on the bottom, perhaps they would just as well be able to fasten themselves to objects hanging loose in the water. I made a buoy and tied a coral block firmly to it with a rope.

"Then I adjusted the length of the rope so that the coral block hung fifteen or twenty feet above the sea bottom, and anchored the buoy. In a month's time I paddled out and examined the coral block. It was quite smooth, with nothing on it. I did not give up, but waited another two months and then took up the buoy again. This time the coral block was covered with countless small mother-of-pearl embryos which seemed to be thriving.

"I tried to move half the embryos to another stone which I hung out in the same way, but they died in a few days. But I found out by degrees that if I waited till the mussels were eight months old it was all right to move them. The next link in my experiment was to fasten stones all along the rope from the surface to the bottom, at intervals of about two feet. In this way I found out the least favorable depth at which the mother-of-pearl embryos would thrive.

"Having got so far, I came to think that perhaps some other material would do as well as stone, and began to try everything between heaven and earth. At last I found that the best material was a fine-meshed, steel-wire netting. It was easy to handle, and a buoy which would only hold a stone as big as a saucer could bear a great many feet of steel-wire netting.

"After many years of experimenting I was able to harvest the first cultivated mussels. They were naturally just as large and fine as the other mussels in the lagoon and were not different from them in any way. So far I have only done a little experimental cultivation, but I am convinced that it would be possible to cultivate about one hundred thousand mussels per acre of sea bottom, and that they would be able to reach their full size in four years.

"The most difficult part remains, however—to make pearls! The only person who has succeeded so far is the Japanese Mikimoto, but I have read everything that has been written about artificial pearls and have already made a number of experiments which promise well. Wait, and I'll show you."

Pahoa disappeared into the next room and reappeared with a cloth bag in his hand. He opened it carefully over a large round table of dark *tou* wood. Half-a-dozen pearls rolled out and were scattered over the polished surface. They were no bigger than grains of sago, but well shaped and gleaming white. They seemed to have a light of their own, for they shone and glittered magically, although the sun had already begun to set and the room was dark. Pahoa and I looked at them in silence.

My host seemed to have fallen into a trance. I myself was struggling with a question, the answer to which I had long been seeking in vain: Why was he telling me all this? As far as I could see, Pahoa had no reason whatever for disclosing his secrets to a stranger. The contrary seemed to be true. At last I broke the silence and asked him:

"But if you already know how to cultivate mussels, why don't you get on with it? You could make a fortune in a few years, and at the same time you would have an opportunity of experimenting in pearl cultivation."

"I understand your being surprised," Pahoa said, blinking. "But unfortunately it isn't all so easy as you think. I'm old and have no children. I might be able to continue the work for a year or two longer, but even that isn't certain. I have wanted for a long time to engage some workmen and a white foreman. But, to tell the truth, there are no workmen to be had in the Tuamotu group. All the natives detest regular work, and I can understand. Why should they work for anyone else when they have land of their own, can dive for mother-of-pearl when they like, and have more money than they want?"

Pahoa fell silent. Then he moved his chair nearer mine and continued in a low voice:

"When I saw you, I thought, 'Here's the man for me.' Perhaps you would like to stay here and help me? If you have any friends who are interested, perhaps you could bring them here too, for there's work for more than one man. I think I could rely on you. We would divide the earnings equally. What do you think of the proposal?"

Of course it was quite impossible to accept his offer, so I refused as delicately as possible. Nor, for that matter, was I quite convinced that the whole of Pahoa's story was absolutely true. Pahoa had the reputation of being a shrewd man of business and who knows? Perhaps he had exaggerated his successes somewhat to induce me to join him? During the rest of our stay on Takume hardly a day passed by without Pahoa trying to win me over or giving me sly winks when I met him in the village; but I was firm.

While I was talking mother-of-pearl with Pahoa or strolling about the village with Marie-Thérèse, studying the native life, our Raroian friends went on diving. But as we had foreseen, their early zeal soon disappeared, and most of them gave up after only two weeks. Tehei and Tinorua had then earned over 30,000 francs ($480) and considered that they well deserved a little rest and diversion. I do not know exactly how they managed to get rid of practically every centime in the following wild week of merrymaking, but I suspect that most of the money went in drink or gambling.

The only person who tried to follow our advice to buy something useful (we knew it was useless to advise anyone to save money) was Tehei. He came to us one day radiant and announced that he had bought something which would be of use to the whole family for many years. When he unfolded the dirty bundle of newspapers he carried under his arm, we saw that it was samples of a complete table service for twelve persons, with soup tureen, meat dish, and four different kinds of plates. It was in fact not a bad idea, and we praised Tehei warmly till we heard the price. He had paid 10,000 francs ($160) for the service.

Before we had sailed from Raroia, our friends had talked of staying on Takume for the whole diving season (three months). But when the week of merrymaking was finished —and their money, too—they all thought they had had enough; and although a number of Chinese dealers and speculators tried to entice them with toys, razors, flowered cloths, and even rocking chairs, they refused to begin diving again. Of course, they would have had no objection to continuing the festivities for a little while, but as this was impossible without money, they at last agreed to Tinorua's sensible proposal to return to Raroia, have a good rest for a time, and then come to Takume again for another spell of work. We ourselves, more than tired of the noise and drunkenness and longing to return to Raroia, welcomed the thought.

Our journey home was unforgettable for several—and not altogther pleasant—reasons. Just when we were beginning to stow away our possessions on board and get the canoes ready, a schooner appeared whose captain declared that he intended to return at once to Papeete via Raroia and several other interjacent islands. This was naturally too attractive for our friends to resist, and they immediately decided to take the schooner.

"But you haven't any money left," was my astonished objection.

"Oh, that doesn't matter," Tepuka answered. "We've a little copra on Raroia we can give the captain, and if that's not enough any of the merchants will gladly lend us money."

"H'm, but what shall we do with the canoes?"

"We'll take them with us, of course."

I looked skeptically at the schooner. About ten canoes, lashed fast, lay on the deck, and homeward-bound divers were waiting on the beach with at least as many. The schooner's captain, however, acted on the generous principle that nobody must be disappointed, and, roaring with laughter, took on board not only all the canoes and divers, but also a hundred tons of mother-of-pearl and several boatloads of copra. No one seemed ever to have heard of Mr. Plimsoll, for I searched for his ingenious load lines and could not find any. But, of course, that might have been because they were far below the water line already.

From our place on an inverted canoe in the afterdeck we had a good view over the chaos. The company was mixed to say the least, for besides the yelling crowd of divers, adventurers, dealers, and prostitutes from Takume, there was a large party of white-clad Mormons, on the way home from the consecration of a church on an island farther west.

I counted the passengers and found that there were 143 of us; undeniably a bit too many for a schooner of 200 tons, which usually took not more than 25 persons. The canoes totaled 31, and there were also innumerable cases and boxes in every corner of the deck. As a result of this we were immoderately crowded; indeed we sat so tightly packed that we had difficulty in stretching our legs. But others were still worse off than we were, for they sat huddled up in the ratlines and had to hold on tight not to tumble overboard. Naturally there was no lavatory, and as for food, everyone had to fend for himself as best as he could.

No one complained; on the contrary, all seemed to enjoy

this intimate social life and laughed, yelled, and chattered without end. The sound of hymn-singing and string music came without interruption from the party of Mormons. They had been the first passengers on board and had been clever enough to take with them two large tables, under which they lay comfortably extended in the shade.

A party of card-playing divers had seated themselves on the top of one of the tables and seemed to enjoy the company they were in, for they sometimes joined in the hymn-singing. Elsewhere on the deck the few who still had any money left played games of chance, while old people told stories of days long past and mothers suckled their children. Now and then the captain looked out of his cabin, blew a whistle, and waved his arms at the steersman as a sign that he was to alter course.

All the crowd and noise would have been bearable if only the boat had not begun to toss. But we had hardly got out into the strait between Takume and Raroia when the schooner began to roll and put her prow into the seas. We were lucky enough to be sitting near one of the ship's boats and had something to hold onto, but the poor souls who were sitting in the middle of the deck were quite helpless and began to roll to and fro like peas.

Boxes and cases, too, began to slide, and suddenly the tables on the afterdeck rushed off at such a pace that the card players tumbled down among the psalm-singing Mormons and silenced several of the voices for a time. This gave everyone a good laugh, but when a little later the sea grew rougher hardly anyone laughed any more.

Contrary to what one would expect, by no means all natives can stand the rolling, and many of the passengers soon became green in the face and hurried to hang themselves, doubled up, over the rail. As the confusion and disorder had scarcely become less, but rather greater, everyone did not always get to the rail in time; and in a little while we preferred, for reasons that are obvious, to climb up into the rigging, where we remained until, a few hours later, the schooner glided into smooth water.

After the noise, greed, and sham of Takume, it was refreshing to experience anew Raroia's peace and quiet and see again the kindly idyllic life of Ngarumaoa Village. We looked at the shores as they slid past us and felt deeply thankful that so unspoiled a paradise still existed on earth. We had been just as moved that day long ago when we arrived on board the *Teretai,* but there was one important difference. Then we were still uncertain and wondering how we should be received. Now, on the other hand, we were happy and safe and felt as if we had at last arrived home after long years of wandering.

We Look Back

THE village has just waked up. Windows and doors are opened a little and sleepy faces look out. Some cheerful shouts and laughter break the silence, and soon the first yawning Raroians are seen through the palms. Most of them have, as usual, slept with their clothes on under a blanket or pandanus mat and therefore start the day by undressing to perform their daily grooming. More and more brown forms in red and blue *pareu* begin to appear in the back yards.

Two little girls run by on their way to the village tank to fetch a few bottles of the precious water. They give us a wave of recognition. Others cry *ia ora na* when they catch sight of us or stop for a moment to shake hands with us. Everyone is cheerful and unreserved; no one now thinks of us as strange incomprehensible *popaa*. We have long been accepted into the community and are regarded by all as genuine Raroians.

In a little while Temarama and Terava come along with

a few bunches of coconuts, cool from the night, picked just outside the village. They leave two on our veranda and hurry on. We cut holes in them with practiced hands and empty them with pleasure. We are quite satisfied with this simple breakfast, but most of our friends want, as usual, to start the day with a considerably more solid meal and are already busy preparing it.

Across the village street Hamani is squatting on the front steps making the morning coffee. First she fills a little cloth bag with the green unshelled beans. Then she lays the bag on the stone step and beats it smartly with a stick. In a little while the shells come loose; she opens the bag and carefully removes them. A fire of coconut husk is already burning in the garden. She lays the coffee beans in a large frying pan and puts the pan on the fire. Soon the beans are roasted, and she disappears behind the house to grind them.

I suddenly catch sight of Terai down on the beach. He first looks round carefully and then steals cautiously out on to the quay with a large spear in his hand. He knows from long experience that many fish come into shallow water during the night and that there is a good chance that the firstcomer will take them by surprise.

A light easterly breeze ripples the water, but Terai has eyes like a gull; it is not long before he sights a suitable quarry. His spear darts on its errand like lightning, and immediately behind it, he dives headfirst into the water. He sends clouds of foam flying as he wrestles with his invisible opponent, but at last he succeeds in throwing him up onto the beach. It is a big *kito*. The whole family comes running down at once to help him carry the welcome breakfast fish home. When he approaches our house he shouts as usual:

"How much do you want? Come and choose a piece!"

This time we decline his offer with thanks, as we have already more fish than we can eat. Terai mutters discontentedly for a few moments, as if he has made a bad bargain, but at last gives up the attempt to persuade us and goes on.

A few hundred yards out in the water Maono stands on a large coral block, net in hand. He has been standing practically motionless for the last half-hour and seems, as usual where fishing is concerned, to have unlimited patience. The morning sun gilds him, and he shines like a copper statue.

A little farther down the bay several outrigger canoes are rocking on the waves. A couple of boys are hoisting sails. We can see no pandanus mats, boxes, or water bottles on board. So it is evidently just a pleasure trip. Quite right: when we look in their direction a little later they are racing their canoes in the lagoon. The wind has freshened a little, and now and then the outriggers rise out of the water.

On such a day we ourselves are sitting on our veranda in the shade of a huge *tiare* tree, trying to draw up a "balance sheet" after our year and a half on Raroia. Our diary gives us an abundance of material, and more, and we turn the pages to and fro as we talk and argue. Our intention, when we decided to visit Raroia, was quite simply to live the everyday life of a coral atoll long enough to discover in what respects it was better or worse than civilized everyday life. Of course this is a very subjective and personal question, and the only thing we can do is to give our own answers and let others judge for themselves as best they can on the basis of our account.

Marie-Thérèse and I are indeed in complete agreement as to our answer but are a trifle dubious as to how to express it so that it will be easily understood. Perhaps the clearest and simplest way of putting it is just to say that we found Raroia the ideal place for people weary of civilization who want for a time to live a pleasant open-air life among cheerful, open-minded friends.

Of course, this should not be taken to signify that all the South Sea romantics are always right when they praise "the simple natural life" and condemn the curses of civilization. In truth, everything worked in a particularly fortunate way to make our stay a success. The island is an exception in a group of islands which as a whole is also an exception. I first made the Raroians' acquaintance under especially happy and favorable circumstances, and therefore we did not come as strangers. Few other white people had previously undermined the Raroians' trust or abused their friendship. We have, moreover, been completely independent and lived only as casual visitors or tourists, which naturally has prevented any of the conflicts or difficulties that continually arise with the settlers, officials, missionaries, and businessmen.

Last, but not least, we fortunately have been able in some degree to repay our friends' generosity and hospitality by caring for those who were ill and by helping them in their intercourse with the queer *popaa* world, represented by Papeete and the French authorities. This mutual nature of our relations has, of course, increased their cordiality.

But let us analyze this exceptional island Raroia a little more closely to find out exactly what are the principal things of value that life here has to offer. First of all, like all "civilized people" who have had similar experiences, we would name the vast, unbroken peace. There are no street noises, no noise of machinery, the nearest telephone is 470 miles away, newspapers are unknown, and no one uses a clock except as an ornament.

But, of course, there is not complete silence. Complete silence is notoriously oppressive and trying. Just occasionally absolute quiet prevails all over the island, but as a rule the trade wind rustles through the palm tops by night and day with varying strength. This harmonious song of the wind, instead of disturbing the island peace, only enhances it. Of course there are quarrels and sometimes even fights in the village, but in general the people, too, bear the stamp of this peace.

The Raroian peace stems from the fact that the people have no material anxieties and no other object in life than just to live. When we first came to the island, we were often astonished at men being able to sit for hours on end waiting for fish and turtles; but now the Polynesian peace has penetrated us too, and we do the same.

Another refreshing experience in life on Raroia is its independence. We have no hours to keep, no duties that call us, no etiquette, no fashions to follow, and no other relations with our fellow men than those which friendship dictates.

A further advantage of Raroian life is that one practically never need have any money dealings. We regularly order most of our goods in Papeete, so we have only to get out our *tou*-wood cashbox when a schooner calls, which only happens every fourth or fifth week. We pay Temake and the Chinese merchant at the same time, if we happen to owe them anything. There is no other way of spending money on Raroia— apart from Mass on Sundays, when we, like the rest of the

Raroians, put 10 francs each into the community's pandanus collection basket. Even if the concentration of expenditure in this way does not make the cost of living less, it is a relief not to have to fiddle about with money continually.

But what about the cost of living on Raroia? The following short summary of our monthly budget may be of interest:

Food	2,500	Tahiti francs	$40.00
Kerosene	200	Tahiti francs	3.20
Medicine	300	Tahiti francs	4.80
Transportation	0		
Rent	0		
Water	0		
Amusements	0		
Total	3,000	Tahiti francs	$48.00

To this can be added expenditure on clothes, which would amount to a few hundred francs a month, if we were compelled to buy the few necessary articles of clothing from stock on board the schooners. It should be pointed out that apart from medicine (for all the inhabitants of the village) none of this expenditure is *absolutely* necessary, and can therefore be reduced at will. Canned goods and imported sweet potatoes can be replaced by fish, turtle, and various coconut dishes; and instead of using kerosene one can cook over a fire of coconut fiber. However, on account of the trouble and the monotony of such a diet we have never been tempted to reduce our budget, and we should not care to advise anyone else to try such an experiment.

There are two sides to everything, and naturally there are certain inconveniences and disadvantages. For example, during the summer months—from October to April—there are several heat waves, in which the temperature often rises to 100°. At these times it is so scorchingly hot and oppressively sultry that even the least movement and the simplest work are an effort. It sometimes happens that we spend several days in succession on our bed in a state of unbroken inertia. But there are not more than twenty-five or thirty of these stifling days in a year, and they are, as I have said, spread over a period of about six months.

The geographical isolation of Raroia is the principal reason for its undisturbed quiet and peace; but naturally this same isolation has other and more unfortunate consequences. As the schooner traffic is scanty and unreliable, it is only a stroke of luck if a boat turns up when it is most needed—for instance, in the case of serious illness. A dramatic experience of our own is a good illustration of this.

We were awakened one night by a little girl who, in reply to our sleepy questions, told us that Tehetu had suddenly been taken ill. We hurried out into the pitch-darkness and managed somehow to find our way to her palm-leaf house, all the time dodging coconuts that were falling like hail. Tehetu was sitting huddled up on the floor with a pillow in her lap, moaning loudly. We examined her. She was fearfully tender on the right-hand side and had a high temperature—obviously appendicitis!

We obtained a bottle of iced water from Temake's refrigerator and laid it on the tender place. It was all we could do, but it was not much good. The only thing which could save her was a speedy operation, but we understood that it would be at least two weeks before a schooner appeared on her homeward voyage to Tahiti.

Next day Tehetu was worse, and we changed the water

bottles with the courage of desperation and hoped quite unreasonably that a schooner would come at once, in spite of the unlikelihood. After two days, however, we began to lose hope, both for the patient and the schooner, and Tehetu declared resignedly that she knew she was doomed and that it was useless to try to do anything for her. The morning of the third day dawned without any change in the situation. On the fourth day Tehetu was groaning loudly and flinging herself backward and forward on her bed of palm leaves. Still, of course, no schooner was to be seen.

The same night, however, quite unexpectedly, there was a sudden change. Tehetu sat up, put her hands on her stomach, and said:

"The pain's moved over to the left-hand side."

In a little while it had disappeared altogether.

When, according to schedule, the schooner came two weeks later, she went with it to Tahiti. After a time she returned fit and well with the good news that she had only had some temporary trouble with her ovaries, and that the doctors had succeeded in curing her without an operation.

But it is not every case of illness that ends so fortunately, and in the last few years more than one has had a fatal result.

Another result of Raroia's isolation and the lack of regular communications with Papeete is the random delivery of supplies. To begin with we buy our groceries, like everyone else, from Temake or the Chinese merchant. They are pretty well stocked and this method is simple and practical for us. But one day when we went to buy a little flour, Temake shook his head and told us there was no more flour. We went across to the Chinese merchant and received the same answer. A few days later there was no more rice and sugar, and a few days after that there were no more canned goods. No one knew when the next schooner would come.

"How does it happen that the stock runs out so suddenly?" I asked Temake. "There were enough groceries on board the last schooner to fill all the shops several times over."

"Yes, that's true enough," he replied, "but how am I to know how much I need? I'm not very good at reckoning."

"H'm, does it often happen that everything runs out like this?"

"Oh yes, several times a year," Temake answered, with an unjustifiably satisfied air.

Of course we ran no risk of starvation, for there were always fish and coconuts, but after a few days we were undeniably weary of this monotonous diet. We therefore asked our neighbor Manumea what he was eating, in the hope that he knew of some food with which we were not acquainted. This was clearly a good idea, for he replied at once:

"When there's no flour, of course we eat starch. There are plenty of *pia* plants and my wife has just made a couple of pails of fresh starch."

"Starch? Do you mean that you make *poe* pudding?"

"No, fruit's needed for that. We mix the starch with coconut water and boil the mixture till it stiffens. Come with me, and you'll see how it's done."

We trudged across to Manumea's house, where his wife had just filled a large wooden bowl with coconut water. Manumea produced a three-gallon pail, full of starch, and poured the contents straight into the bowl. Then, with his wife's help, he collected a large heap of coconut fiber and set light to it.

We wondered for a moment if they meant to put the wooden bowl on the fire, but soon realized that they were using an ancient Polynesian method of heating which is now seldom seen. They put two or three large coral stones into the fire, and when these were red-hot, they took them out carefully with the aid of a couple of sticks and threw them into the starch bowl. In a little while the white soup congealed and assumed a grayish-green color. The dish was ready.

Manumea gave us a large piece of the shapeless dough, and we went home pleased with the unexpected addition to our midday meal. We sat down at our table, laid more festally than usual for the occasion, and I put a spoon to the lump of starch. Before I had properly established contact it slipped away in a cowardly manner and teasingly installed itself a little way farther off on the table. I pursued it in vain for a good half-hour (I'm sure it was that long), but gave up at last in sheer exhaustion.

"You're too badly armed for starch-hunting," Marie-Thérèse said, and fetched a large kitchen fork.

With a triumphant expression she stuck the fork into the lump of starch, spun it round several times and lifted it. The result was crushing. Only a few thin threads came up with the fork. That was all. Clearly quite new tactics were needed if we were to have any prospect of success.

I remembered that in a candy factory I had once seen a man cutting a mass of sugar in pieces with a large pair of scissors. We immediately tried this method, and it proved excellent. We each cut off a piece of starch and bit into it. Five minutes later, after desperate efforts, we at last succeeded in opening our mouths again, at any rate enough to be able to mumble a few words. Manumea's original concoction was stickier than paste and tougher than a bicycle tire. It took us a good hour to finish the lump of starch, and it was the most silent meal at which I have ever been present.

The lump of starch, however, took its revenge for its inglorious defeat. A few hours later it began to swell and ferment in our stomachs, and soon it was raging and tearing at our poor intestines till we writhed like worms. We gave Manumea a good talking-to the next time we met him and asked him if the starch dish was really prepared in the right manner.

"Oh, yes, indeed," he replied, roaring with laughter, "but perhaps I forgot to say that starch always gives one a stomach-ache. Everyone in the village has had stomach-ache for several weeks."

After this experience, we kept to coconuts and fish, and when we wanted a change we ate fish and coconuts. In a few weeks' time a schooner came, and we wisely laid in a stock sufficient to stand a siege. But, as sometimes even the schooners do not have certain articles, we have taken to ordering all our groceries in Papeete, which moreover reduces the cost to about one-half. Despite our example everyone else on the island clings to the old system, and sure enough they have had to eat starch at least five times in the past year!

A further consequence of Raroia's isolation is that one has to rely solely on one's own powers and knowledge. A Raroian is architect, boatbuilder, hairdresser, undertaker, tailor, and artisan all in one—indeed a jack-of-all-trades! In many cases, of course, a little reflection is all that is needed to know what should be done; but now and then one finds that he unfortunately lacks the simple but necessary knowledge to solve a problem or execute a piece of work, just simply because he has never been faced with similar difficulties in our more specialized society.

For example, how should one set about making a spare part for a benzine lamp? How does a clock work? In what soil do potatoes do best? Why do fowls die suddenly? How is putty made? Can one cut glass in any other way except with a diamond? How are the springs fastened into a mattress so that it will be level? These and similar questions are continually cropping up, and however many handbooks one has, there remain many queries to which one can find no answer. Of course one can do as we have done on several occasions: write to some acquaintance and ask. In this case, however, one must not be in a hurry, for it takes as a rule two or three months before an answer to a letter reaches Raroia.

These disadvantages—the great distance from a hospital and a drugstore, the occasional heat waves, the capricious shipping connections, and the limited resources on the island—are, however, many times outweighed by the advantages. The timeless quiet, the freedom from worry, and the independence are beneficial; and for a long time we have felt completely at home in our idyllic existence. This fact has more than once raised the question, whether we should remain in Raroia forever.

That afternoon on our veranda, Marie-Thérèse and I came to the conclusion that despite the advantages, permanent residence on Raroia would be impossible: we could not give up our former life completely for the simple reason that there is in it far too much which ties us and interests us. Only an exceptional person, we were sure, could suddenly abandon everything and completely change his way of life, without developing a split personality. Besides, we had new tasks and duties waiting for us on the other side of the globe. We had already stayed too long on Raroia, and it was without a question time to leave.

We had hardly returned to so-called civilization before we started to long for Raroia and the South Seas again. In this longing we are, of course, not alone. But what really surprises us is to meet such a large number of people who seem to cherish serious plans of settling permanently on a South Sea island, definitely making their home and living there. Let us, therefore, examine the possibilities of carrying out such a plan on Raroia. The following letter—one of several dozen I have received—seems to me to represent quite well the motives and hopes of this group of South Sea lovers:

I am a young clerk who has become tired of the monotonous grind. I can no longer endure sitting in front of a typewriter all day, being squashed in an overcrowded bus morning and evening, continually having to hurry in order not to be too late and miss my opportunity (which for that matter I have already done only too often). Also I have a touch of rheumatism for which the northern cold is not good.

I have read a great deal about the South Seas and have begun to wonder if that is not the right place for me. I am no starry-eyed optimist who sees everything in rose color, and do not think that the South Sea islands are incarnations of paradise on earth. But the climate and the people must be better there, and there cannot be so little real happiness as here at home. I have not thought that one can live on nothing and am therefore ready for a "settler's life."

I am young (twenty-eight) and not afraid to put my shoulder to the wheel.

My plan would be to settle on some out-of-the-way island, where there are no white men as yet, buy a bit of land, clear it, and cultivate it myself. I have a little capital, and to make that last longer I have thought of living to begin with in the same simple way as the natives. I am not married, but perhaps it would not be impossible to find a a native woman who would be willing to share my life. For a companion in life one must have.

I am writing to you because my knowledge of the geography of the South Seas is very small indeed, and therefore I thought you could advise me as to which might be the most suitable island or group of islands to settle on. From every point of view, of course, previous knowledge of the actual conditions is important, and that is what I lack. It does not matter what the island is like, so long as it is not too hot and there are no tropical diseases . . . . .

The answer to this and similar letters is ever so simple. This optimistic South Sea dream is one that cannot possibly be realized—at least on Raroia. No foreigner would ever get permission to settle on the island, and even if he succeeded in getting the permission from the authorities, he would not find anyone who was willing to sell him land. To try, as a last resource, to live without either land or income is, of course, unthinkable for a foreigner, who lacks the Polynesians' dearly acquired knowledge of atoll life.

If anyone finds this answer dream-shattering, I should only like to point out that the existence of such idyllic islands as Raroia is the direct result of the ban on foreign settlement. If the gates of paradise were opened to all those who had no other qualifications but that they liked the place, it would naturally soon cease to be a paradise.

No one who wishes the best for the Raroians and Polynesians can help finding this policy of protection laudable and wise. But perhaps someone will ask, "Will it do any good in the long run?" and to this question—the last and the most important—the only possible answer must unfortunately be in the negative.

Just how many years it will be before Raroia loses its exceptional character, despite all precautionary measures, it is, of course, hard to prophesy. But this at all events is true: that those who are now children will have a more difficult, harder, rougher, and sadder life than their parents. The influence of Tahiti is already great; and with the improved communications which have been promised, it will become even more noticeable.

New but unwholesome foodstuffs will induce the Raroians to abandon the last of the old native dishes which still exist. More and more will be ruined by drink. Diseases and epidemics will take their toll. The Chinese will gradually get them into their power altogether, if their present exploitation is not stopped. The simple, idyllic conditions of life will gradually disappear. Tahitians and advanced Tuamotuans will teach the new generation contempt for the old values, and with every old person who dies more and more of the Polynesian friendliness and magnanimity will be replaced by more modern and profitable virtues.

However long we wrestle with the problem, the conclusion is always the same: Even if at some future time chance should enable us to return to Raroia, we shall never again find the same happy island.

PRINTED IN U.S.A.